W9-CJW-730

Criminal Justice
Recent Scholarship

Edited by
Marilyn McShane and Frank P. Williams III

A Series from LFB Scholarly

Civil Commitment of Sexual Predators

A Study in Policy Implementation

Andrew J. Harris

LFB Scholarly Publishing LLC
New York 2005

Library of Congress Cataloging-in-Publication Data

Harris, Andrew J., 1961-
Civil commitment of sexual predators : a study in policy implementation / Andrew J. Harris.
p. cm. -- (Criminal justice)
Includes bibliographical references and index.
ISBN 1-59332-095-7 (alk. paper)
1. Sex offenders--Government policy--United States. 2. Civil commitment of sex offenders--United States. I. Title. II. Series: Criminal justice (LFB Scholarly Publishing LLC)
HV6592.H38 2005
364.15'3--dc22

2005012791

ISBN 1-59332-095-7

Printed on acid-free 250-year-life paper.

Manufactured in the United States of America.

Table of Contents

List of Figures

List of Tables

Acknowledgements

Throughout this project, dozens of people have extended their ideas, assistance, and support in both large and small ways. To all of these people, I am tremendously grateful.

During the course of my research, I received phenomenal input, guidance, cooperation, and information from dozens of content experts, program managers, prosecutors, defense attorneys, and budget and program analysts in the states included in this study, far too numerous to list here. I would like, however, to extend special thanks to a select few who helped me during the formative stages of this research -- Roxanne Lieb, Eric Janus, John LaFond, Janice Marques, Larry Fitch, and Anita Schlank – each of whom graciously took considerable time to provide much needed perspective.

I must also thank a very special group of people without whom this project simply never would have come to fruition -- Dennis Smith, for keeping me honest, focused, and on course; John Billings, for his many years of valuable and good-humored guidance and cajoling; Bill Fisher, for his wisdom, perspective, and unwavering encouragement; Ken Appelbaum and Ira Packer, for their friendship and always penetrating insight; and June Binney, who first planted the seed for this project, and to whose friendship and support has immeasurably enriched my professional life.

Preface

This book investigates a series of state laws and policies providing for the involuntary civil commitment to state custody of individuals defined as "sexually violent predators" (SVP's).[1] Typically applied following completion of a criminal sentence, SVP civil commitment laws permit the state to retain custody of individuals found by a judge or jury to present a risk of future harmful sexual conduct by virtue of a mental abnormality or personality disorder. Following commitment, states generally remand individuals to the custody of mental health authorities, which provide treatment for the condition that makes the individual likely to engage in acts of sexual violence and retain custody until the individual is determined to no longer pose a threat to society.

Since the state of Washington passed the nation's first contemporary SVP civil commitment law in 1990, seventeen states have adopted such laws, and over two dozen others have considered their passage.[2] In the intervening period, the laws and policies have generated significant attention and controversy, especially within the legal and mental health professional communities.

The attention that the policies have attracted within the mental health professions is particularly notable, since SVP civil commitment

---

[1] Many of the states adopting the laws investigated in this study have adopted alternative nomenclature to refer to their target populations, including "sexually dangerous persons", "sexual psychopathic personalities", or simply "sexual predators." For the sake of simplicity, the term "SVP" will be used as a generic reference to the policies and their target groups.

[2] States with SVP civil commitment laws include Arizona, California, Florida, Illinois, Iowa, Kansas, Massachusetts, Minnesota, Missouri, New Jersey, North Dakota, Pennsylvania, South Carolina, Texas, Virginia, Washington, and Wisconsin. Fitch and Hamen (2001) indicate that SVP civil commitment legislation has been introduced and debated in a total of 41 states. For a detailed review of statutes in effect as of 1998, see Lieb and Matson (1998).

policies rely on psychiatry and psychology for both legal validation and technical expertise. Criticism of the laws from within the mental health community has focused on a range of issues, including the perceived "co-opting" of the mental health system for decidedly non-clinical purposes (Appelbaum, 1997; Wettstein, 1992; Zonana, 1997); the need for caution in applying currently available actuarial and clinical tools in legal proceedings (Campbell, 2000; Grisso, March 6, 2000; Petrila & Otto, 2001); the equivocal nature of the evidence concerning likely treatment success, given the profile of the SVP population and the timing of the intervention (Schwartz, 1999; Wettstein, 1992); and concerns from mental health policy leaders and advocates that the significant costs of SVP programs risk diverting much-needed resources away from programs for the "truly mentally ill", and that placing sex offenders under the care and custody of mental health agencies adds to societal stigma of mental illness (National Association of State Mental Health Program Directors, 1997; National Mental Health Association, 1998). The concerns over resource allocation have gained particular resonance in light of growing attention to mounting program costs associated with carrying out SVP civil commitment policies (La Fond, 1998, 2003).

In the legal realm, critiques of the policies have evolved over time, amidst the emergence of a growing body of case law and associated legal analysis. Early challenges arguing that the laws, while nominally civil in nature, were in fact extensions of the criminal justice system and therefore violated constitutional prohibitions against double jeopardy and ex post facto lawmaking, were effectively put to rest by the U.S. Supreme Court's landmark decision in *Kansas v. Hendricks* (1997), and the Court's subsequent ruling in *Seling v. Young* (2000). The laws, however, remain subject to continued debate and challenge, as state and federal courts have focused their attention on issues such as the validity of and standards applied in "expert" risk prediction (Janus & Meehl, 1997; Petrila & Otto, 2001), legal requirements surrounding volitional and/or emotional impairment ("Kansas v. Crane," 2002) and conditions of confinement, including right to treatment and provision of "less restrictive alternatives" (LRA's) to total confinement ("Turay v. Weston," 1994). These cases and dozens of others concerning SVP civil commitment have produced a steady stream of legal analyses and commentaries, and a legal landscape that remains in a state of evolution.

Considering the issues just described, how have states with SVP civil commitment policies responded to such issues as the equivocal role of mental health systems, uncertainty over key technical issues, the shifting legal landscape, and mounting program costs? In a best-case scenario, these issues might be viewed as contextually limiting factors that will guide the evolution of an ultimately effective policy strategy. Alternatively, the issues may emerge as bellwethers for the eventual demise of a misguided policy experiment.

These issues provide general context for the present study, which examines the manner in which states have deployed and implemented their SVP civil commitment policies and, more importantly, the implications of these implementation experiences on the policies' future viability. **The primary question addressed in this study is fundamentally a prospective one – what are the prospects for SVP civil commitment, and what are the conditions under which they will succeed or fail?**

While the limited state of prior structured inquiry in this area renders the analysis exploratory in many respects, the study aims to generate a series of observations that may form the basis for further investigation. Drawing both on existing studies and on specific state experiences with SVP civil commitment policies, this book presents a prospective evaluation of SVP civil commitment policies. The book consists of seven chapters:

- Chapter one presents the current state of applicable knowledge regarding SVP civil commitment program implementation, drawing upon general theory and historical inquiry regarding sex offender management policies and upon recent efforts to describe and analyze SVP civil commitment policies across states;

- Chapter two describes models and theories of policy implementation, and explores how those models relate to the issues presented in this study;
- Chapter three delineates the study's methodological approach, including descriptions of the analytic framework and of the sampling and data collection methodologies;
- Chapter four presents the policies' conceptual and operational models, providing the benchmarks against which the policies' implementation will be assessed;
- Chapter five presents a conceptual analysis, drawing both from existing literature and from a series of case studies undertaken for the purposes of the current analysis;
- Chapter six presents an operational analysis, again combining the findings of prior research and original data compiled for this study; and
- Chapter seven presents conclusions regarding the prospects for SVP civil commitment, summarizing the findings of the conceptual and operational reviews, examining interactions between the two, and describing directions for future research.

Supplemental data, including case study narratives and summaries of key policy provisions across the states examined in this study, are appended as supporting documentation.

CHAPTER 1

State of Current Knowledge

As referenced in the introduction, SVP civil commitment policies have received considerable attention within certain circles, notably among constitutional scholars, forensic mental health experts, and authorities on the treatment of sexual abusers. While the literature in these areas certainly has a critical bearing on the current scope of inquiry, it also contains many intricacies that risk diverting attention from the study's broader issues. Accordingly, this initial chapter focuses on two key areas – the placement of SVP civil commitment policies into a relevant historical and social context, and an assessment of literature related directly to the policies' implementation and structural characteristics. The "inside baseball" connected to critical areas of the law and mental health practice will be presented and applied as needed in the ensuing conceptual and operational analyses.

HISTORICAL AND CONCEPTUAL FOUNDATIONS OF SVP CIVIL COMMITMENT POLICIES

Historical and sociological assessments of sex offender management policies in the United States have cited a series of critical shifts during the past 75 years. Brakel and Cavanaugh (2000), describing the "pendulum effect" that has characterized societal approaches to sex offenders in the 20th century, cite four primary stages:

1. The period before 1930 characterized by undifferentiated treatment between sex offenders and other criminals;
2. 1930 to 1970, coinciding with the growing influence of psychiatry and the therapeutic ideal, and the corresponding rise of "sexual psychopath" laws that separated sex offenders

from the general criminal population with the belief that their behavior should and could be treated;
3. 1970 to 1990, during which time sexual psychopath laws were repealed in the face of both waning support from the psychiatric field (Group for Advancement of Psychiatry, 1977), and a series of legal challenges ("Allen v. Illinois,," 1986; "Specht v Patterson," 1967); and
4. 1990 to the present, a period which has marked a return to the idea that managing sex offenders requires special policy provisions above and beyond those provided through the general criminal justice system, including community notification laws and civil commitment of sexually violent predators.

Several reviewers and researchers have explored the social and political forces behind these shifts, citing such factors as social attitudes towards sexuality and gender roles (Denno, 1998), changing perspectives within psychiatry and the mental health establishment (Group for the Advancement of Psychiatry, 1977), and public outrage over certain high-profile acts of sexual violence (Sutherland, 1950). The general lesson drawn from many of these reviews is that the policy in this area may be more closely linked to prevailing social and intellectual standards and practice than to the problem's actual magnitude (Blacher, 1995).

A pivotal variable in the equation has been the position and influence of the mental health establishment, especially the influence of psychiatry. Sutherland''s (1950) analysis cites the confluence of generalized public anxiety and the "solution" presented by psychiatry and its therapeutic ideal as central to the diffusion of sexual psychopath laws throughout the 1940's and 50's. Similarly, it was the waning support of psychiatry, linked to a growing body of evidence concerning the limited efficacy of sex offender treatment that led states to gradually abandon these laws beginning in the 1970's (Group for the Advancement of Psychiatry, 1977).

As we fast-forward to the 1990's, there are strong indications that these two sets of forces – societal demands driven by key events and the roles and positions of the mental health establishment – have been central to the emergence of SVP civil commitment. The birth of Washington's 1990 Community Protection Act has been linked by several sources to a series of high-profile crimes and resulting community mobilization, and the strategy is implicitly dependent on mental health professionals and agencies for its implementation and legal validation.

Yet in contrast with the synergy between social demands and the psychiatric agenda observed by Sutherland in 1950, the development of SVP civil commitment has occurred amidst strong dissent from organized psychiatry (see, for example, American Psychiatric Association, 1996). Additionally, the field of forensic psychology, a professional group that has emerged as the principal source of "technical experts" for purposes of case identification and commitment, has experienced strong dissent from many within its ranks, who caution against the potential misapplication of psychological measures (Campbell, 2000; Petrila & Otto, 2001). In fact, the principal drafter of the Washington statute explicitly differentiates the circumstances described by Sutherland from those surrounding the birth of the Washington law, noting a more pronounced role of citizen's groups and a diminished role of the psychiatric establishment (Boerner, 1992).

SVP POLICY IMPLEMENTATION EXPERIENCE

With this contextual backdrop, we now turn to SVP civil commitment policies themselves. While the legal complexities and technical practice of SVP civil commitment policies have received considerable attention from legal scholars and mental health experts, their implementation has received relatively scant attention in the literature (Janus & Walbek, 2000). Examinations of the policies' implementation has effectively taken three forms – **descriptive surveys** of statutes, legislative activity, and program practices (Fitch, 2001; Lieb & Matson, 1998; Lieb & Nelson, 2001); **population reviews**, describing characteristics of individuals committed under the policies (Janus & Walbek, 2000; Lieb, 1996); and **cost reviews** describing the resources utilized by states in the implementation of their SVP civil commitment policies (La Fond, 1998).

Descriptive Surveys of Policy Characteristics

The most comprehensive descriptive survey of SVP civil commitment policies, produced in 1998 by the Washington State Institute for Public Policy, describes the basic mechanics and elements of SVP civil commitment programs (Lieb and Matson 1998). The survey notes several areas of variation across states, including eligibility standards, case identification procedures, the standard of proof required for commitment, and commitment program settings. The survey also presents a series of cost data related to custody, treatment, and legal proceedings, indicating a range in annual costs-per-commitment from $70,000 in Washington to $110,000 in Minnesota.[3]

Fitch and Hammen (2001) present additional survey data in their review conducted on behalf of the Forensic Division of the National Association of Mental Health Program Directors. While the survey in certain respects covers similar ground as the WSIPP review, it is distinguished by its focus on legislative activity surrounding SVP civil commitment laws, with particular attention paid to states that have considered and rejected such measures. They note that, while SVP programs at first glance may appear to be political "no brainers", the majority of states have yet to adopt such legislation, despite the fact that it has been considered in at least 41 states. Additionally, one state that adopted SVP legislation twice delayed its implementation pending resolution of certain programmatic and fiscal issues.[4] The Fitch and

---

[3] The cost data presented in the WSIPP survey were based on telephone conversations with facility managers, and in many cases is incomplete and not directly comparable from state to state.

[4] See Virginia General Assembly, Act to Amend Chapters 946 and 985 of the Acts of Assembly of 1999 (Approved April 19, 2000) and Act to Amend and reenact Ch. 18.2-370 of the Code of Virginia and Chapters 946 and 985 of the Acts of Assembly of 1999 (approved March 26, 2001).

Hammen review cited multiple factors, including fiscal considerations, the position of the state mental health agency, positions of professional or advocacy organizations, and the introduction of alternative criminal sentencing provisions, as contributing to the withdrawal or legislative failure of SVP legislation (Fitch and Hammen, 2001).

An additional recent review by Lieb and Nelson focuses on the mechanics of treatment programming for committed SVP's (Lieb & Nelson, 2001). This review, citing data from an earlier survey conducted by Hennessey (1999), notes variation across states in areas such as program settings, staffing ratios, treatment program components, and provisions for less restrictive alternatives. While many of the survey's findings pertain to treatment program details beyond the scope of the present analysis, it is notable that the authors conclude that treatment programs designed to manage the committed SVP population "remain in their infancy."

Population Reviews

A second area of inquiry connected to the implementation of SVP civil commitment policies addresses a fundamental question – who are the individuals that end up being committed? Attempts to answer this question have been somewhat incomplete. Hennessey (1999), in a survey of six states with SVP civil commitment laws, presents aggregate information pertaining to psychiatric diagnosis and offense profiles. Among the six states surveyed, diagnoses ranged from 67 percent with personality disorder, 53 percent with pedophilia, and 48 percent with other paraphilias. The analysis also identifies 38 percent of committed SVP's as rapists and 53 percent as child molesters, with the remaining 9 percent crossing both categories. The analysis, however, does not present state-level data, and does not account for overlap between diagnostic categories. Moreover, as noted by Lieb and Nelson (2001), the results are likely skewed considerably by the fact that California represented approximately 50 percent of the sample.

Two additional reviews (Janus & Walbek, 2000; Lieb, 1996), present state-specific data for the committed populations of Minnesota and Washington. The Janus and Walbek study involves some perspective and analysis of the data, while the Lieb release simply presents the raw case-level data on the approximately 40 individuals held in Washington's civil commitment program as of 1995. Both sets of data appear to support the general contention that SVP civil commitments represent a diverse spectrum of individuals, representing a range of offender types, diagnostic categories, demographic characteristics, and criminal histories – a diversity that represents a critical factor in analyzing general program requirements and the viability of program designs.

Cost Reviews

The third and final series of defining issues involves SVP program costs. While cost estimates available in the literature are constrained by certain methodological issues that will be explored throughout this book, current figures range from $60,000 to $103,000 per commitment (Lieb & Matson, 1998) for annual housing and treatment, and approximately $100,000 per case for legal processing (LaFond, 1998). Caseload growth, coupled with litigation-driven program reforms and capital construction costs, stand to make cost an increasingly critical issue for SVP programs.

La Fond (2003) puts forth a range of recommendations for dealing with issues of rising costs associated with SVP civil commitment programs, including tightening of commitment criteria, investing more "up front" resources in evaluations prior to probable cause hearings, "de-politicizing" the release process by placing conditional release decisions in the hands of treatment staff, and broadened legislative focus and investment in less-restrictive alternative (LRA) programs. These recommendations, along with their practical viability and their attendant implications will be explored further throughout this study's conceptual and operational analyses.

LIMITATIONS OF EXISTING REVIEWS

While the aforementioned studies and surveys provide a useful foundation for assessing the implementation of SVP civil commitment policies, they are constrained in three important respects.

First, surveys of program practices have employed "snapshot" approaches, focusing on the state of the policies at the time of the survey, with only minimal emphasis on the policies' evolution, including shifts in program practices and utilization patterns over time. This approach proves useful in conveying the state of the policies at a particular point in time, but is less effective in explaining how the policies have reached that point and, in turn, where they are likely heading.

Second, comparisons of SVP civil commitment practices across states have concentrated predominantly on statutory provisions and less on implementer-driven program practices. While such a perspective may permit a broad-based comparison of state provisions, the approach is limited in its capacity to inform critical assessment of state policy implementation practices.

Third, research to date has been somewhat compartmentalized, focusing on structural elements, conceptual issues, legal or technical questions, cost factors, or population characteristics, but rarely on the interactions between these disparate elements. In contrast, the current investigation is predicated on the belief that such interactions and roles are significant elements in understanding the path that SVP civil commitment policies have taken and, in turn, the path that they are likely to take in the future.

CHAPTER 2

SVP Civil Commitment Policies in an Implementation Framework

While the present analysis addresses SVP civil commitment policies' underlying design, it is primarily concentrated on their **implementation** -- that is, the web of relationships and organizational processes following policy design and adoption that are responsible for translating general policy directives into concrete program outputs.

Consistent with this focus, we turn our attention in this chapter to existing policy implementation models, exploring both their theoretical foundations and the manner in which they may be applied to a prospective assessment of SVP civil commitment policies.

The chapter consists of three sections. The first section provides some general theoretical background, reviewing the evolution of policy implementation theory and research; the second explores a series of five themes contained in the policy implementation literature, and applies these themes to the issues under investigation in this study; and the third focuses on one particular model of policy implementation, that is particularly salient to the project at hand.

GENERAL BACKGROUND ON POLICY IMPLEMENTATION THEORY

The structured study of policy implementation is often traced to Pressman and Wildavsky's 1973 examination of a federal jobs program on Oakland, California (Pressman & Wildavsky, 1973). This study, carried out amidst a general focus of policy scholars on Great Society programs that had failed to meet their expectations, challenged classical notions of rational bureaucratic organization, and called upon policy scholars to pay closer attention to implementation processes.

In the decade following Pressman and Wildavsky's study, the field of implementation theory and research began to gather steam, with Hargrove (1975)citing implementation as the "missing link" in the study of public policy, and theorists emerging with a range of explanatory models that drew attention to a range of organizational and psychological factors and to the relationships and respective roles of policy formulators and implementers (Bardach, 1977; Mazmanian & Sabatier, 1983; Nakamura & Smallwood, 1980; Rein & Rabinovitz, 1978; Van Meter & Van Horn, 1975).

Through the mid-1980's, studies on policy implementation proliferated, with some setting forth new models and taxonomies, and others applying and testing existing frameworks.[5] By 1985, however, some within the field had begun to question the direction that scholarship in this area was taking. O'Toole (1986), concluding a review of the implementation literature up to that time, commented:

> "The field is complex, without much cumulation or convergence. Few well-developed recommendations have been put forth by researchers, and a number of the proposals are contradictory. Two reasons for the lack of development may be analyzed: normative disagreements and the state of the field's empirical theory. Yet there remain numerous possibilities for increasing the quality of the latter. Efforts in this direction are a necessary condition of further practical advance."

As a reflection of this sentiment, the focus of policy implementation research has shifted considerably in the past 15 years. While no new models of policy implementation *per se* have emerged

---

[5] For a review of the literature through 1986, see O'Toole (1986). Also, in a post-script to their 1989 edition, Mazmanian and Sabatier list 25 studies between 1983 and 1987 applying their model to specific policy initiatives (Mazmanian and Sabatier, 1989).

since Goggin's 1990 call for a "third generation" of policy implementation research (Goggin, 1990), applications of existing models have continued to appear in the literature (see, for example,Sarbaugh-Thompson & Zald, 1995). Moreover, some have recently suggested that the apparent diminution of analytic interest in policy implementation may simply reflect that fact that the inquiry has shifted its focus and terminology (O'Toole Jr, 2000). To this point, Mazmanian and Sabatier suggested as early as 1989 that the field was shifting its focus away from a focus on the short-term dynamics of implementation, and towards the longer-range emphasis on policy learning and other factors associated with policy change over time (Mazmanian & Sabatier, 1989).

IMPLEMENTATION THEORY & SVP CIVIL COMMITMENT

As noted above, models of policy implementation emerged in part from policy scholars' quest to explain the roots of policy failure. Accordingly, it is not at all surprising that policy implementation models have generally been applied by researchers in a retrospective context, in attempts to dissect the events, actors, and processes that have led to particular policy outcomes.

The current investigation, in contrast, is fundamentally prospective in its focus. While states' experiences with the SVP civil commitment policies to date certainly represent critical pieces of information, the primary questions before us – whether the policies will prove to be viable in the long-term – has yet to be answered.

The methodological framework set forth in the next chapter consists of two levels of analysis – a conceptual analysis focused on the definition of the policy problem and the ' underlying soundness of the policies' causal model, and an operational analysis, focused on the policies' operational viability, specifically in terms of organization and resources. In each of these areas, theories and models of policy implementation have set forth a range of germane variables and classification schema. Equally important, the models have articulated the relationships among these variables, and have set forth conditions and parameters for implementation success.

Hence, while much of the policy implementation literature has involved retrospective inquiry, the literature's constructs, variables, and relationships may be readily applied to prospective questions such as those put forth in this study. The following section identifies series of themes and constructs that have been validated through prior implementation studies, that may be embedded within a prospective framework, and that may inform the design of the conceptual and operational analyses.

AN EXAMINATION OF FIVE THEMES

The key questions concerning SVP policy implementation may be divided into five areas:

1. **Concept**: What are the antecedent events, deliberative processes, conceptual underpinnings, and assumptions associated with SVP legislation? How explicitly does the legislation define policy goals and criteria for success?
2. **Structure:** How are policies crafted with regard to locus of program authority, decision rules, and the level of delegation from policy makers to policy implementers?
3. **Investment**: How do policy makers assess and address the programs' immediate and future resource requirements? How do they respond when resource requirements increase or are not otherwise consistent with expectations?
4. **Evaluation**: What type of evaluation feedback emerges during the SVP policy implementation process, and from what sources?
5. **Change**: How do SVP civil commitment policies and practices evolve over time, and what are the catalysts for such change?

The five areas cited above represent a relatively well-developed series of themes explored in the policy implementation literature. Hence, briefly addressing these issues in the context of implementation theory may conceivably provide critical insights into SVP policies' future viability.

Concept

What are the antecedent events, deliberative processes, conceptual underpinnings, and assumptions associated with SVP legislation? How explicitly does the legislation define policy goals and criteria for success?

While theories of the implementation process differ considerably in their emphasis and orientation, most acknowledge that implementation success depends at least partially on the policy's underlying conceptual soundness, the establishment of clear and workable policy objectives, and policy makers' clear communication of those objectives (Bardach 1977; Nakamura and Smallwood 1980; Mazmanian and Sabatier 1983; Goggin 1990). Several critical variables come into play, notably the consistency between implicit and explicit policy goals, the limitations of available technical means for achieving those goals, and the clarity of expectations and standards for success.

Mazmanian and Sabatier, whose model is explored in greater detail towards this chapter's conclusion, cite conceptual complexity as a potential threat to policy clarity and to the implementation process:

> "....when the statement of the problem is ambiguous, implementers must guess at how the means selected relate to the problem being solved. This, of course, raises a problem for policy implementers, who must devise solutions for unclear problems, and for evaluators, who must gauge the adequacy of those solutions." (Mazmanian and Sabatier 1989)

This quote may be aptly applied to two critical elements of SVP civil commitment policies. First, regarding the problem statement, legal observers have noted the lingering ambiguity associated with the true goals and focus of SVP policies. Although the policies have been upheld by the courts as civil processes grounded in treatment (*Kansas v. Hendricks*, 1997; *Seling v. Young*, 2000), the genesis of these laws has been documented as being fundamentally driven by a perceived failure in the criminal justice system (Boerner, 1992).

Second, concerning the relationship between the "means selected" relating to the problem, it is essential to note that SVP policies, by legal necessity, have adopted the therapeutic orientation of the mental health system over the incapacitative/punitive model of the criminal justice system. While treatment goals and public safety goals may not be entirely incompatible, they should, at a minimum, be viewed as potential sources of implementation confusion. Moreover, as described in the background section of this proposal, the two predominant "technical means" associated with SVP civil commitment policies - assessment of risk for the purposes of commitment and treatment of committed individuals - remain subjects of considerable debate within both relevant professional communities and as matters of law.

Structure

How are policies crafted with regard to locus of program authority, decision rules, and the level of delegation from policy makers to policy implementers?

A second theme germane to SVP civil commitment policies, and often cited within the policy implementation literature, involves structural parameters. Structure may encompass organizational factors such as allocation of responsibilities and accountability mechanisms, as well as process factors such as decision rules and communication.

Regarding organizational structure, Goggin and colleagues have set forth the hypothesis that "the greater the number of organizational units involved in the implementation process, the greater the likelihood of delay and modification during implementation" (Goggin 1990). On a more qualitative level, Goggin also cites compatibility of goals across implementing agencies as a critical criterion for successful implementation.

Each of these phenomena may be readily related to the study of SVP civil commitment policies. Regarding the former, SVP policies typically involve a range of agencies and organizations, and often require collaboration between criminal justice agencies such as Departments of Correction and human service agencies, primarily those dealing with mental health (Lieb and Matson, 1998). For example:

- Initial referrals may emanate from Departments of Correction, although some states refer more loosely to "agencies with jurisdiction" - a term that may refer to juvenile justice agencies, parole or probation departments, and in some cases mental health agencies;
- Pre-prosecution screening processes may involve multiple agencies from within the mental health and/or criminal justice system, in many instances requiring review by multi-disciplinary review boards comprised of attorneys, mental health professionals, and corrections officials;
- Legal commitment process may similarly involve more than one agency, in many places involving multi-jurisdiction prosecutors review panels and in others granting case filing authority to the attorney general and county prosecutors in multiple jurisdictions;
- Programmatic jurisdiction for managing the committed population often requires collaboration between mental health agencies, which typically maintain statutory custody and programmatic responsibility, and corrections agencies, which in many cases provide facility management services. Some states have also opted to use contracted providers to perform duties ranging from facility operations, security, and treatment programming;
- Processes for case review, re-commitment, and release, by definition, require interaction between those charged with custody and treatment and the legal system.

Beyond the fundamental matter of the number of agencies involved, the nature of those agencies, their orientations, and their core missions may be incongruent in many respects. Thus, in accordance with Goggin's hypothesis, it should be clear that a critical review of organizational roles and interactions is warranted.

Nakamura and Smallwood (1980) present a second critical dimension of implementation structure that is germane to an examination of SVP policies, specifically the linkage between formulators of policy (generally legislatures) and policy implementers (generally executive agencies) regarding their relative roles in implementation. The Nakamura and Smallwood typology presents five levels of delegation, ranging from "classical technocracy," in which the policy-making body dictates all but the most technical aspects of a given policy's implementation (a traditional "top down" model), to "bureaucratic entrepeneurship," in which all but the most fundamental goals are delegated to the implementing entity. The implicit theory here is that the probability of breakdown between "legislative intent" and implementation reality is directly related to the degree to which authority is ceded to implementing entities. Further, the model states that the appropriateness of a given delegation approach is dependent on a variety of factors, notably the technical complexity of the problem, control of information, and relative allocation of resources between formulators and implementers.

In the context of SVP policies, the degree of delegation figures prominently in the analysis for two main reasons. The first pertains to the policy's organizational complexity and the potential for conflicts among implementers. As noted, SVP civil commitment programs may involve coordinated activities among Departments of Correction, Departments of Mental Health, independent officials such as local prosecutors and state attorneys general, and the judiciary. Given this multitude of players with their varied missions, organizational cultures, and levels of accountability, a strong case may be made that the enabling legislation should play a strong mediating role in establishing implementation structure and rules.

The second rationale for assessing the means of delegation involves the policy's technical complexity, and the related application of technology as part of the implementation process. Nakamura and

Smallwood note that one reason for legislative delegation of authority is that policy makers often lack the level of knowledge required to clearly define implementation processes. This circumstance, in turn, may lead to potential technical breakdowns in which the policy formulation process does not fully reflect programmatic resource demands or limitations of available technology. Given that SVP civil commitment programs rely heavily on psychological risk assessment and that they target a population for whom evidence of treatment success is equivocal at best, it is important to critically evaluate the technical implementation assumptions built into legislation.

Investment

How do policy makers assess and address the programs' immediate and future resource requirements? How do they respond when resource requirements are not consistent with expectations?

Information regarding SVP program costs for selected states has been presented in several sources (Lieb & Matson, 1998; Janus & Walbeck, 2000), often in the context of a general critique of the laws themselves (see, for example, LaFond, 1998). Reported costs per case for housing and treatment vary, ranging from $70,000 in Washington to $103,000 in California (Lieb & Matson, 1998). Washington reports legal costs of approximately $60,000 per case, while research in Minnesota has indicated the costs of prosecution at closer to $100,000 (LaFond, 1998).

Several factors may explain this substantial variation, such as the allocation on non-direct program costs (e.g. costs of prosecution or litigation), capital construction cost accounting, and the relative distribution of fixed vs. incremental costs. Additionally, data sources from these review range from telephone surveys with facility directors to reviews of legislative appropriations, neither of which is necessarily inclusive of the full range of costs. As we have seen, SVP programs may involve multiple agencies and administrative entities.

Hence, although there is general consensus that costs are both increasing and of growing concern in SVP civil commitment programs, the cost data that has been reported is generally not comparable across states, nor has it been systematically presented in a manner that permits detailed analysis. Considering the incremental projected growth connected to high rates of admissions and low rates of discharge, and potential for increased treatment or physical plant requirements due to legal mandates, it can be reasonably assured that program costs will grow in coming years.

In the context of implementation theory, the question of resources may be explored on multiple levels. In the most rudimentary form, some theorists have asked the simple question of whether policy makers provide sufficient resources for implementers to achieve the stated policy goals (Mazmanian and Sabatier, 1989). On this level, one might hypothesize that resource deficiencies lead to a "technical failure of means" in which implementers simply are not provided the resources they need to get the job done. A 1999 survey of SVP program directors (Hennessy, 1999) indeed revealed a general concern among those charged with providing SVP treatment that the true resource requirements for working with this population were not being met.

An alternative view of the role of resources in SVP policies, however, is to examine the matter in terms of cost-effectiveness. Given the wide variation in spending across states, and considering the uncertainties regarding treatment technologies, it is appropriate to critically examine what the "appropriate" level of funding is for such an initiative. More specifically, one might ask whether there are either programmatic (greater treatment success) or ancillary (for example, greater insulation from legal challenges) benefits to spending more on an SVP program.

Viewed in this context, the resource question may be construed as much a political matter as a technical one. That is, one might hypothesize that spending too little on an SVP program may result in either technical failure or costly legal action, and spending too much may ultimately erode the program's political viability, especially during times of fiscal retrenchment.SVP civil commitment policies:role of resources in

Evaluation

What type of evaluation feedback emerges during the SVP policy implementation process, and from what sources?

Several states have conducted critical reviews and evaluations as part of the policy deliberation and implementation process (California Legislative Analysts Office 1997; Minnesota Dept. of Corrections 1999; Virginia State Crime Commission 1999; Florida Office of Program Policy Analysis and Governmental Accountability 2000). Moreover, as previously described, Courts at both the federal and state levels have reviewed and legally analyzed SVP policies from multiple dimensions. The role of evaluation in the SVP policy process, however, has not been systematically analyzed - to date, there has been no multi-state assessment of the manner in which evaluation feedback contributes to the process of changes in policy and practice.

Despite this lack of analytic attention, there is a strong theoretical argument for such an analysis. Nakamura and Smallwood (1980) view evaluation as one of three policy environments related to the politics of implementation (the other two environments being formulation and implementation). They posit that evaluation serves notably different functions for policy makers and policy implementers. For policy makers, the primary function is conceptualized as "monitoring feedback," referring to the role that evaluation plays in legislators' ability to respond to constituents' attitudes about a particular policy. For policy implementers, Nakamura and Smallwood designate the primary function of evaluation as "mobilizing support" - that is, using the evaluation process as a means of institutionalizing programs and competing for resources.

While these two functions - monitoring feedback and mobilizing support - are indeed potential applications of evaluation, they are also decidedly political in nature. It would be misleading - not to mention overly cynical - to suggest that evaluation cannot play a genuinely constructive role in improving the implementation process. Applied to SVP civil commitment policies, the fundamental question before us pertains to the roles that program evaluation, as conducted by legislatures, implementing agencies, the courts, and social scientists, have had both on the political dynamics of implementation and in ongoing efforts towards policy refinement.

Change

How do SVP civil commitment policies and practices evolve over time, and what are the catalysts for such change?

The final set of questions associated with the current analysis involves the change of SVP programs over time. While the literature regarding this aspect of SVP programs is virtually non-existent, there is evidence to suggest that the policies and their related programs are indeed in an evolutionary process. The Washington program in particular has undergone significant change during the past seven years, as evidenced by court documents (see Special Master Reports #1-17, filed with U.S. District Court, Western District in case of *Turay v Weston*), and by two major revisions in the statute since its original adoption.

From a theoretical framework, the examination of change is central to the study of policy implementation. Mazmanian and Sabatier (1989) contend that implementation cannot possibly be viewed in a static context, noting that policies may follow a range of possible evolutionary trajectories. Their model posits that "effective implementation" typically involves an initial learning process, followed by a gradual stabilizing of program outputs that can withstand such factors as changes in program personnel, shifts in socio-economic conditions, and advances in technology. Alternatively, implementation may follow a "cumulative incrementalism" pattern in which policies are modified over an extended period of time prior to achieving a state of equilibrium; a "gradual erosion" pattern, in which initial learning follows a relatively normal pattern, but implementation processes and policies fail to adapt to changing circumstances ultimately leading to policy failure; and a "rejuvenation scenario" in which policies that had been either dormant or in a state of decline re-emerge due to policy reform and/or changing circumstances within the political or economic environment.

Beyond the path that change takes, implementation theory also considers the drivers of change - specifically, change may be driven from within the policy itself or from external factors. Regarding the former, we may conceive of policy change as a response to policy feedback provided by a range of formal and informal evaluators, including implementing or legislative agencies, social scientists, the courts, the media, the public, or other involved constituencies (Nakamura and Smallwood, 1980). These influences were discussed earlier in our assessment of the evaluation environment.

As for the latter, policy modifications may also result from contextual factors such as changing economic circumstances or advances in technology (Mazmanian and Sabatier, 1989). These factors may be readily applied to SVP policies, in which political support for programs may be challenged when mounting program costs collide with declining state revenues, and in which program scope and practice may be easily altered by technical factors such as empirical validation or repudiation of screening tools or treatment techniques.

ONE MODEL'S PERSPECTIVE

From a taxonomic viewpoint, one of the more comprehensive models of the policy implementation process is set forth by Mazmanian and Sabatier, in their book *Implementation and Public Policy* (1989). The key variables associated with this model are summarized in Figure 1.

The model views policy implementation as a manifestation of three types of variables – those pertaining to the inherent *tractability of the problem* being addressed, those related to the policy's *statutory parameters*, and those connected to *"non-statutory" elements* including public attitudes, the activities and attitudes of implementers, and socioeconomic conditions. The effects of these variables on the implementation process itself are expressed in terms of a series of "dependent variables" beginning with policy outputs and leading to statutory modification.

Figure 1: Mazmanian and Sabatier (1989) Implementation Variables

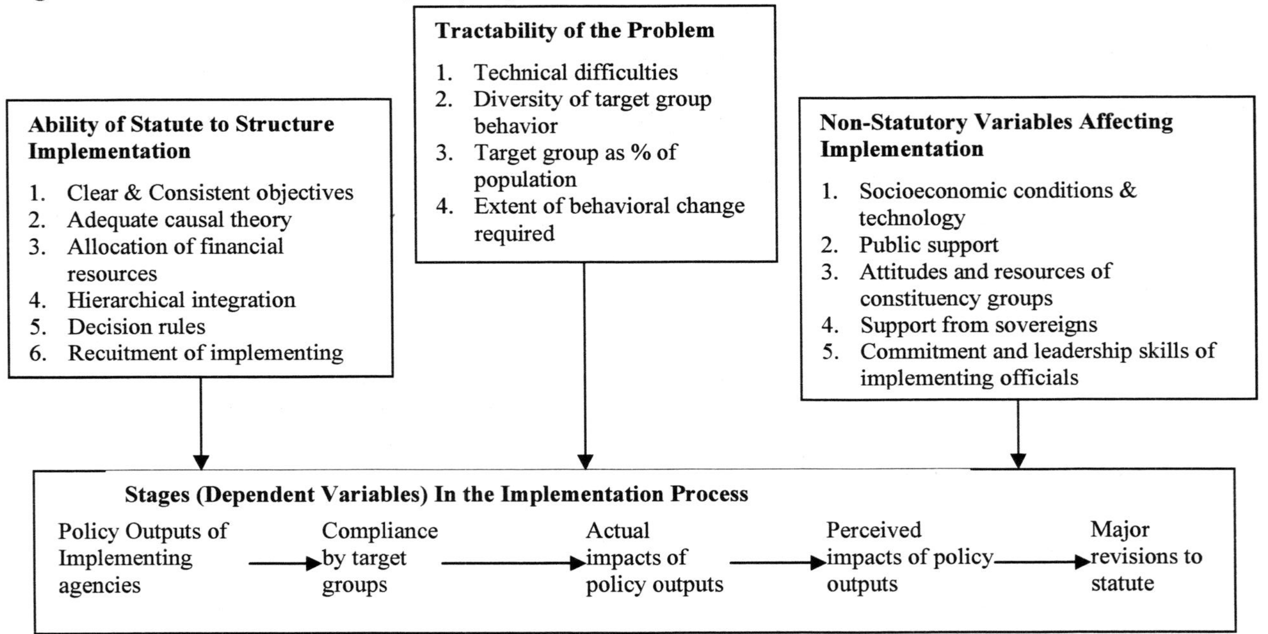

As an extension of this model, Mazmanian and Sabatier set forth six sets of conditions for effective implementation. These conditions are set forth below, along with a series of questions directly related to SVP civil commitment policies. These questions, which will be addressed at various points in the ensuing analysis, may in part form the basis for analyzing the future viability of the policies under investigation. The six conditions will be revisited in our concluding chapter.

Enabling legislation or other legal directive mandates policy objectives which are clear and consistent or at least provides substantive criteria for resolving goal conflicts.

- How effectively does the initial enabling legislation mandate clear and consistent policy objectives?
- Does the legislation account for potential goal conflicts between criminal justice and mental health implementing agencies?
- How have major court rulings connected to SVP laws served to further clarify or obscure legislative policy objectives?

Enabling legislation incorporates a sound theory identifying the principle factors and causal linkages affecting policy objectives and gives implementing officials sufficient jurisdiction over target groups and other points of leverage to attain, at least potentially, the desired goals.

- Does the initial legislation successfully account for the range of factors affecting the efficacy of SVP civil commitment in meeting fundamental public safety and treatment goals?
- Is the legislation framed crafted in a manner that firmly establishes the parameters of civil jurisdiction over SVP's, as affirmed by the courts?

Enabling legislation structures the implementation process so as to maximize the probability that implementing officials and target groups will perform as desired. This involves assignment to sympathetic agencies with adequate hierarchical integration, supportive decision rules, sufficient financial resources, and adequate access to supporters.

- Is legislation framed in a manner that acknowledges the broader missions, mandates, service delivery structures, and operating practices of relevant criminal justice and mental health agencies?
- Is legislation accompanied by a realistic set of assumptions regarding program costs, and are those costs accurately captured in subsequent appropriations processes?

The leaders of the implementing agency possess substantial managerial and political skill and are committed to statutory goals.

- What are the attitudes and philosophical approaches within the various agencies charged with carrying out SVP programs, and how do they align with legislatively mandated policy goals?

The program is actively supported by organized constituency groups and by a few key legislators (or a chief executive) throughout the implementation process, with the courts being neutral or supportive.

- Does post-statute legislative activity (for example, during the annual appropriations process or special legislative hearings) reflect an ongoing commitment to SVP civil commitment programs?
- What positions have state and federal courts taken with regard to SVP civil commitment processes and programs?

The relative priority of statutory objectives is not undermined over time by the emergence of conflicting public policies or by changes in relevant socioeconomic conditions which weaken the statute's causal theory or political support.

- How have legislative and public/media opinions regarding SVP civil commitment responded to growth in the size of the committed population and corresponding increases in program costs?

CHAPTER 3

Methodological Approach

Applying the constructs of policy implementation, this study investigates SVP civil commitment policies through a forward-looking framework, combining the findings of prior research with supplemental data gathered through a series of in-depth case studies. This chapter presents an overview of the chosen analytic approach and its applicability to the problem under investigation, and describes the sampling and data collection processes associated with the case studies that provide much of the study's key operational data.

ANALYTIC FRAMEWORK

The study's analytic framework is adapted from the Prospective Evaluation Synthesis (PES), a methodology developed by the U.S. General Accounting Office as a means of assessing the conceptual and operational viability of proposed policy strategies (General Accounting Office, 1989).

Two particular characteristics of the PES methodology make the approach particularly suited to the present investigation. First, the PES contains a significant measure of flexibility, providing a means of integrating the wide array of technical, legal, clinical, fiscal, and operational issues associated with the SVP civil commitment policy. Second, while the PES applies the knowledge gathered from historical observations and from prior empirical analyses, it remains fundamentally future-oriented, consistent with our current focus on the prospects for SVP civil commitment policies. In accordance with the PES approach, the analysis consists of three main steps:

1. The specification of the conceptual and operational models guiding SVP civil commitment policies (Chapter 4);
2. The testing of these models and their implicit assumptions, based on available evidence and observations (Chapters 5 and 6); and
3. The generation of preliminary conclusions regarding the conditions and prospects for the policies' success (Chapter 7).

Central to the analysis is the specification and testing of the policy's conceptual and operational models. The conceptual model focuses on how the policy is designed to work as a matter of general principle, focusing on the policy's underlying logic and the strength of its presumed causal linkages. The operational model focuses on matters of policy practice, examining the extent to which systems can be organizationally structured and funded in a manner that ensures effective policy implementation and outcomes.

Consistent with the prospective focus of this study, the conceptual and operational analyses are focused, first and foremost, on the long-range viability of SVP civil commitment policies. This viability may be assessed examining the models' implicit assumptions in four main areas:

- **Technological viability**, or the extent to which the policy aligns with the capacities and limitations of applicable technology;
- **Legal viability**, or the manner in which the policy is supported or impeded by constitutional factors as interpreted by the courts;
- **Organizational viability**, specifically pertaining to dynamics within and relationships between implementing agencies and to structural incentives that may affect implementation activity; and
- **Resource viability**, as reflected both in costs of adopting the policy as a long-range strategy and in the willingness

of legislatures and others to provide resources that align with those costs.

The conceptual analysis focuses primarily on technological and legal viability, while the operational analysis is predominantly concerned with matters of organization and resources.[6] Taken together, these two levels of review aim to generate a series of conclusions concerning the likely prospects for SVP civil commitment policies, based on the broad range of technical, legal, organizational, and resource issues associated with the policies' design and implementation, and upon the interactions between these issues.

Table 1: Conceptual and Operational Analyses Areas of Focus

	CONCEPTUAL	OPERATIONAL
General Focus of Analysis	General logic behind policy	Practical viability of policy
Key Questions	**Problem**: Is problem clearly defined? **Strategy**: Do policy's strategic assumptions align with available evidence and constitutional parameters? **Solution:** Do the strategy's outputs effectively align with expected policy outcomes?	Is policy structured, and are resources appropriately deployed, to ensure consistent performance, production of assumed outputs, and achievement of policy objectives?

[6] Certainly, this is not to imply that technological and legal factors are irrelevant in the operational realm. To the contrary, they provide critical context for operational practice. For current purposes, however, the question of whether the policies are technologically and legally feasible is viewed fundamentally as a matter of theoretical significance that precedes any discussion of operational practice.

STATE CASE STUDIES

As referenced earlier, SVP civil commitment policies have attracted considerable attention among mental health and legal scholars, providing a fairly strong basis for assessing the empirical and legal foundations of the policy's conceptual model. The operational aspects of the policies' implementation, however, have remained largely uncharted, with the exception of the surveys of statutory provisions and program practices described in Chapter 1.

Recognizing these limitations, this study supplements existing published studies and data sources with a series of six case studies developed from a combination of sources, including official records, media accounts, and informal interviews with program principles and stakeholders. These examinations of state experiences are intended to provide additional data and context to support and inform the analyses of the policies' conceptual and operational models.

Six states were selected for review, based on a series of four main considerations. First, the variation in certain key state policy provisions demonstrated by prior surveys (Lieb & Matson, 1998), required a sample that encompassed a reasonably broad range of state experiences and permitted inter-state comparisons. Second, on the opposite side of the coin, practical considerations required a sample small enough to permit in-depth examination. Third, the prospective focus of the study, and the associated need to understand changes in the policies over time, required a focus on states that have been operating their SVP programs for several years, and therefore have established a sufficient baseline of program utilization. Fourth and finally, recognizing that the range and structure of available data varies considerably from state to state, the sample selection process necessarily involved consideration of both general data availability, and the comparability of that data across states.

Hence, the fundamental challenge involved selecting a sample of states that:

1. Is limited enough to permit in-depth analysis;

2. Reflects a range of organizational approaches to SVP programs;
3. Have established a historical track record that provides a basis for investigating program change; and
4. Have disseminated or otherwise made available relevant data and information that may be applied to the models under analysis.

The six focus states – California, Minnesota, Wisconsin, Florida, Washington, and Kansas – were selected primarily based on the criteria defined above. They represent a range of structural permutations and patterns of resource investment, and each have been operating their SVP programs for at least five years.

DATA COLLECTION PROCESS AND SOURCES

Variability in the sources and structure of program data across states presented particular challenges in the data collection process. To address these challenges, the data collection process was approached from a hierarchical perspective, beginning with primary data sources and working down to informal interviews with key individuals.

Much of the data collected for purposes of this study was gathered through a combination of legislative research and direct outreach to a range of organizations and individuals involved in the design and implementation of SVP civil commitment policies. Specific sources of data included:

1. Primary data sources including annotated statutes, legislative histories, administrative directives, and program policies and procedures;
2. Program reports, utilization data, and budget information provided by implementing agencies, executive budget bureaus, and legislative committee staff;
3. Published surveys of existing SVP programs or their populations;
4. Legislative and implementing agency reports, analyses, or disseminated data;

5. Court documents including legal rulings, court-ordered reports, briefs, and documentation of legal proceedings;
6. Relevant scholarly literature;
7. Media coverage of SVP laws and their implementation;
8. Constituency perspectives, as expressed by official statements, internet message board postings, or supplemental interviews;

Quantitative information, notably budget and workload information, was corroborated across multiple sources wherever possible. Inconsistencies across sources were addressed through clarifying communication with the providers of that information. In some cases, it became necessary to combine information or extrapolate from multiple data sources for purposes of data presentation and analysis. These cases are noted in the presentation of the data.

Finally, several discussions and informal interviews were conducted with individuals involved in implementation, monitoring, and evaluation of SVP programs to corroborate data and interpret findings as needed. In most cases, these interviews were conducted "off the record" and are therefore not cited.

CHAPTER 4

Conceptual and Operational Models

This chapter sets forth conceptual and operational models that specify the causal and structural logic of SVP civil commitment policies. The conceptual model describes the policies' theoretical foundations, addressing the manner in which SVP civil commitment is assumed to produce a set of desired policy outcomes. The operational model focuses on the organizational provisions and resources connected with the policies' implementation, addressing how the policy is designed to work as a matter of practice.

This chapter presents each model, including a diagram depicting the model's key elements and a narrative describing how those elements will relate to the ensuing analyses. These two models lay the foundation for the analyses presented in Chapters 5 and 6, and in turn for the conclusions presented in Chapter 7.

CONCEPTUAL MODEL

The conceptual model underlying SVP civil commitment policies is outlined in Figure 2. The model's logical chain begins with the primary "input" of the potential target population – the universe of sex offenders who have been released or are pending release from custody.7 This group, in turn, is gradually refined through a series of

[7] The target population universe is presented generically in the model for purposes of illustration. It should be noted, however, that the precise scope of this population varies across states, which in addition to adult correctional populations, also selectively include groups such as juveniles, psychiatric patients, and previous offenders currently living in the community.

Figure 2: Conceptual Model for SVP Civil Commitment

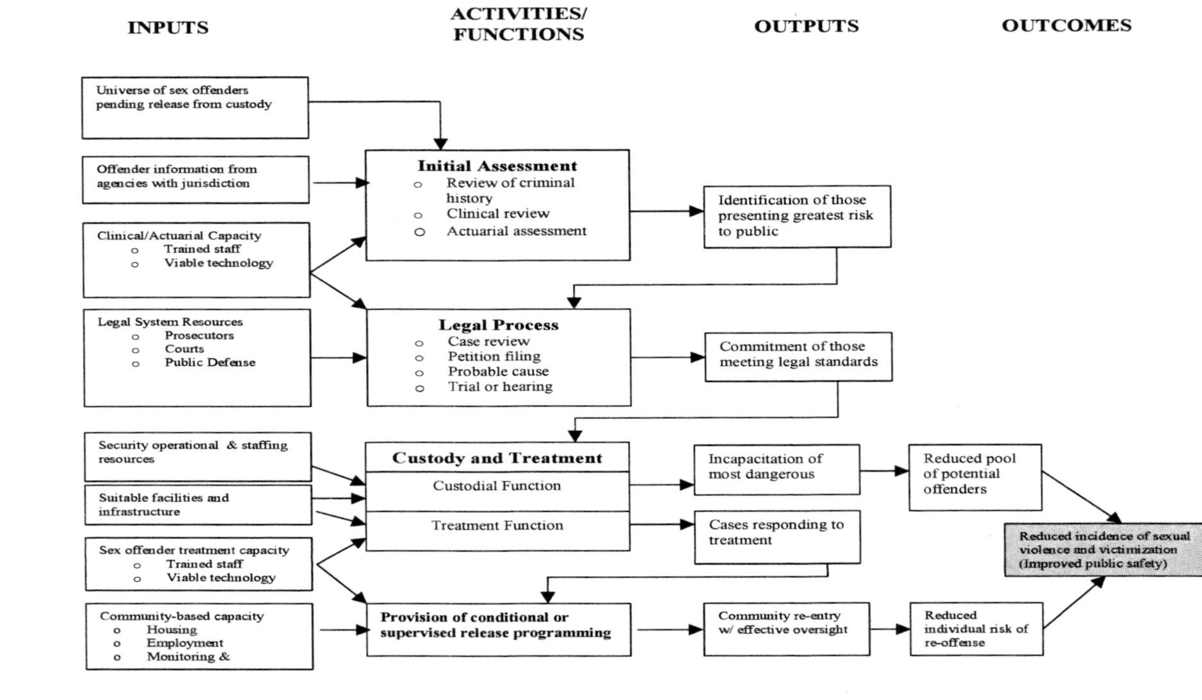

activities – case screening, legal commitment, custody, treatment, and release programming -- each of which entail their own set of inputs required for that activity's successful execution. This combination of inputs and activities provides a series of outputs associated with various types of case dispositions. Some of these outputs, notably those at the earlier stages, feed back into the activity chain, while others lead to preliminary outcomes that are proximal to the principle policy outcomes, namely reduced incidence of sexual violence and associated improvements in public safety.

The conceptual analysis presented in the next chapter consists of three levels -- problem, the strategy, and the solution. The first, the **examination of the problem**, establishes the general assumptions made by policy makers regarding both the population at which the intervention is targeted, and the type of system failure that SVP civil commitment is intended to address. The second level of analysis focuses on the **strategic assumptions** of SVP civil commitment, examining the conditions under which the inputs and activities specified in the model may or may not produce the desired outputs. Focusing on the activity-output linkages specified in the conceptual model, the strategic analysis will examine relevant empirical data and legal precedents to ascertain both the theoretical capacity to produce the required outputs and, equally as critical, the shape that those outputs are likely to take. The third level of the conceptual analysis focuses on **the solution** emanating from the assumed strategy, specifically examining the two alternative pathways (incapacitation and successful treatment) to the desired policy outcome. This final segment will critically examine the policy's overall conceptual consistency, as manifested in the interactions between the problem conception, the strategy, and criteria for success.

OPERATIONAL MODEL

As with the conceptual model, the operational model is specified as a means of establishing a baseline against which SVP civil commitment policies' viability may be assessed. The two models also each share as their focal points the policy's key processes and activities. Yet where the conceptual model focuses on how the policy should work in principle, the operational model focuses on how it should work in practice. Can resources be provided and structured adequately to meet policy objectives? Are clear decision rules in place? Are assigned agencies and individuals sufficiently situated, committed to policy objectives, and in possession of requisite skills? While these factors may be "assumed away" in the conceptual analysis, they represent the "meat and bones" of the operational assessment, which must gauge the policy's core practical viability.

The operational model for SVP civil commitment programs is presented as Figure 3 on the following page. The model's key components are:

- **Processes**, closely linked to the activity areas presented in the conceptual model, which serve as focal points for the operational analysis;
- **Operational parameters**, denoted in general by the shaded boxes, and representing the analysis' key organizational and resource variables; and
- **Operational indicators** associated with each process, noted at the end of the shaded arrows, which provide the analysis with dependent measures against which to gauge implementation practices.

The model's upper tier denotes a series of **critical actors**, who along with implementing authorities, contribute to the shape of the operational policy. State legislatures delineate the policy's basic structural parameters (both in terms of processes and general decision rules), delegate implementation authority, and allocate resources; county or local authorities are typically called upon to fund and carry out functions related to the civil commitment process; and state and federal courts are assumed to play a prominent role in validating, clarifying, or in some cases modifying the rules and standards under which the policies operate.

Figure 3: Operational Model for SVP Civil Commitment Policies

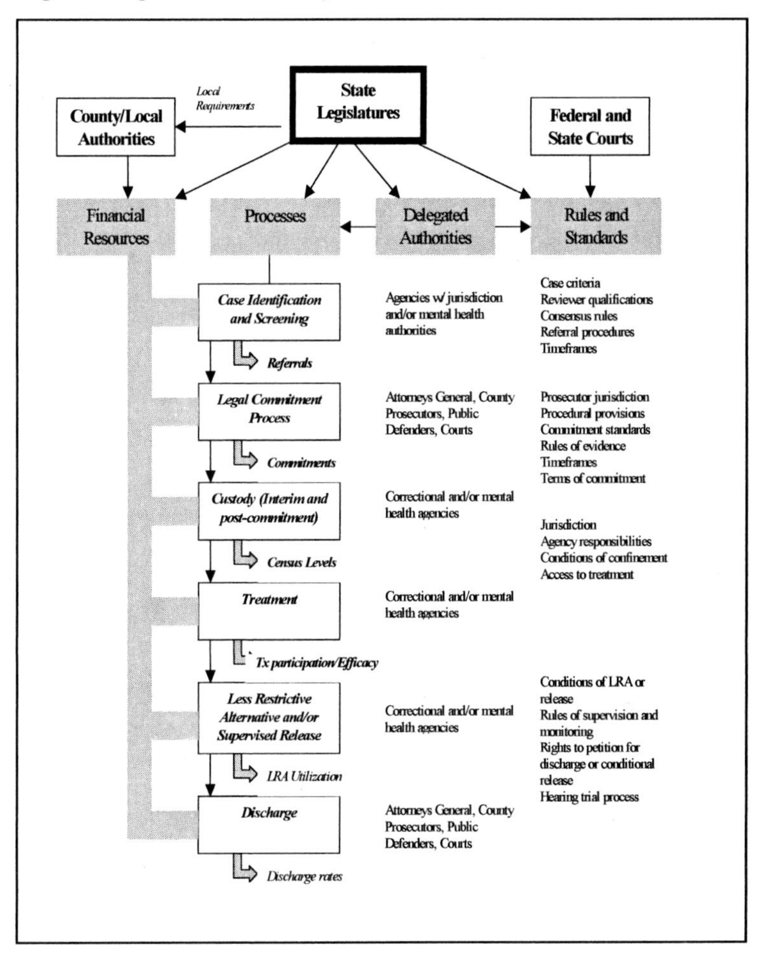

The focal point of the analysis is the sequence of processes associated with the SVP civil commitment. The operational analysis will be built around a critical review of these processes, which for purposes of analysis will be divided into three broad categories – **case**

selection, encompassing both case screening and legal commitment; **custody and treatment**; and **transition and release**, including provision of "Less Restrictive Alternative" (LRA) programming, legal discharge provisions, and systems of case review associated with these activities.

Within each process area, the operational analysis will consist of three main elements:

1. A review of **operational indicators**, noting critical trends and patterns that may reflect policy practice;
2. An **organizational assessment**, focusing on *rule, standards,* and *organizational authority*, specifically as they relate to the policies' underlying organizational viability; and
3. A **resource assessment**, focusing both on the resources assigned to carry out the policies' key processes, key drivers of resource demand, the budgetary incentives of policy implementers, and the likely future sufficiency of resources.

CHAPTER 5

Conceptual Analysis

This chapter analyzes SVP civil commitment policies in the context of the conceptual model presented in Chapter 3. Consistent with the study's general goals, the conceptual analysis aims to test SVP civil commitment policies' underlying logic and strategic assumptions, identifying factors that might present challenges to policy viability. Further, its particular focus on matters of technological and legal feasibility provides critical context for the operational challenges to be analyzed in Chapter 5.

The analysis consists of three main sections. The first focuses on the **problem**, as defined and understood by policy makers and their constituents, drawing primarily from the six case studies performed for the purposes of this study. The second section, comprising the majority of the chapter's detail, examines the **strategy** of SVP civil commitment, testing the causal assumptions implied in the conceptual model against both empirical evidence and legal parameters. The third section focuses on the **solution**, exploring in detail the "back-end" of the conceptual model and analyzing the model's alternative pathways from its policy outputs to its desired outcomes.

EXAMINING THE PROBLEM

> "....when the statement of the problem is ambiguous, implementers must guess at how the means selected relate to the problem being solved. This, of course, raises a problem for policy implementers, who must devise solutions for unclear problems, and for evaluators, who must gauge the adequacy of those solutions." (Mazmanian & Sabatier, 1983)

Before analyzing the conceptual model's strategic foundations, we turn first to the nature of the problem that the SVP civil commitment policy is intended to solve. As referenced in the quotation above, the manner in which the problem is framed by policymakers and understood in the context of both public discourse and program implementation, provides both the rationale for the selection of inputs, activities, and outputs, and the parameters for defining criteria for program success.

A Generic Problem Statement

The problem statement associated with SVP civil commitment policies may be based on a pair of fundamental questions:

1. At whom is the policy is targeted? and
2. What is the perceived nature of the system failure that requires special policy provisions for this group?

Viewed in tandem, these two questions might be framed in terms of a generic problem statement -- "Our ability to deal with target population 'x' is constrained by system limitations 'y'. The following section examines the implicit assumptions concerning the values of *x* and *y* as made by states considering SVP civil commitment policies.

An Assessment of Seminal Events

This portion of the analysis examines the policies' implicit problem definition through a critical review of the factors, dynamics, and assumptions associated with the legislative adoption of SVP civil commitment policies. While the case narratives set forth in Appendix A indicate variation across states concerning the policy adoption process, we may identify a crucial common thread. Namely, every one of the six state case studies involved in this analysis involves one or more high-profile cases that led the states to consider the adoption of SVP civil commitment legislation.

There is academic precedent for examining the role of the "seminal event" in explaining the diffusion of public policies concerning sex offenders (Sutherland, 1950). The ubiquitous presence of such events across all states examined in this study, coupled with the proximal nature of those events to a typically rapid progression of legislative activity, presents strong support for a close examination of the "catalyst cases" and their implicit assumptions. While such cases may not reflect the full range of factors feeding into policy makers' perception of the problem, neither can they be ignored as vital drivers of the problems' initial definition.[8]

In the case of Washington, generally regarded as the precursor to laws in other states, we have the benefit of the fairly detailed history of the policy's genesis provided by David Boerner, the statute's principal architect. Boerner's account opens by describing the spring 1989 abduction, rape, and mutilation of a 7-year-old boy in Tacoma by a mentally retarded man named Earl Shriner, who had been released from prison two years earlier, following a 10-year sentence for sexually assaulting two teenage girls. The account also describes a chain of inter-system failures associated with Shriner's case, involving repeated official attempts to have Shriner institutionally committed, in the period between his release from custody and the Tacoma attack (Boerner, 1992).

Explaining the standards applied during the deliberations of Washington's 1989 Community Protection Task Force, which ultimately produced the draft civil commitment legislation, Boerner writes:

---

[8] Throughout this analysis, reference will be made to several specific events and circumstances associated with the development and implementation of state SVP civil commitment laws. For the sake of brevity, the analysis presents abridged references to these events. For greater detail on the events and circumstances described here, the reader is referred to the appended case study narratives.

> "From the beginning, we knew that any reform proposals would be tested against one fundamental question. If the reform had been in effect in 1987, would it have given the state the power to act to prevent Earl Shriner from committing future violent acts?"

Later in the account, Boerner continues:

> "The core of this problem was not the exercise of governmental power but the absence of that power."

Viewing the generic problem statement cited earlier through the lens of Boerner's account, the problem might be stated as, "our ability to deal with people like Earl Shriner is constrained by the lack of available laws that permit us to keep such individuals under state custody." We might also further qualify this statement by noting that Shriner was widely viewed as having "fallen through the cracks" between the criminal justice and mental health systems. Hence, Earl Shriner and the inter-system gap that precluded his confinement, became the benchmarks and underlying rationale for the development of Washington's civil commitment law.

Viewed in this limited context, one might fairly conclude that the general conceptual basis for civil commitment of "people like Shriner" is sound and defensible. Here we have an individual with a history of involvement in both the criminal justice and mental health systems, and a set of legal obstacles that precluded his continued custody despite authorities' best efforts.

In the realm of politics and public opinion, however, the rather circumscribed problem statement articulated by Boerner becomes significantly less refined. While Shriner was held up as the "poster boy" for Washington's burgeoning reform movement, there are indications that the state's lawmakers and general public were focused on a broader range of cases, including that of Gene Kane, a work release inmate who raped and killed a Seattle woman in the fall of

1988, and Gary Minnix, another released rapist who committed a brutal attack in December of that year.

In Kane's case, for example, the situation was not one of a developmentally disabled individual and a history of official attempts at engagement in the mental health system, but rather a calculating anti-social rapist who was actually under criminal justice supervision at the time of the attack. While Shriner's case may have had much to do with the "grey area" between the correctional and mental health systems, Kane's case illustrated a more explicit failure of the state's broader criminal justice policy. In Boerner's terms, the problem in Kane's case might have been more readily attributed to the "execution of power" than the "absence of power."

Yet the public outcry in Washington during 1989, and in the other states and times described in this study, was framed less by the pragmatism characterized in Boerner's approach, and more by a broader sense of societal vulnerability to random acts of sexual violence. The target population, reframed in this political context, may be broadened to encompass a wider array of "bad people" who are likely to do "bad things" if not confined. Similarly, the definition of "system failure" becomes significantly less refined, resulting in less of a call for discriminating approaches, and a greater emphasis on radical change.

Indeed, it appears that other states following in Washington's path have pursued passage of SVP civil commitment based on a wider set of circumstances than that considered in Boerner's account. In many cases, the "catalyst cases" more closely resemble Gene Kane's than Earl Shriner's. In the Kansas case of Don Gideon, one might have focused primary attention on the conditions of his prison release; in California, the pending releases of two individuals named Melvin Carter and Reginald Muldrew had provoked high-profile attention to the state's parole system for convicted rapists; in Wisconsin, rapist Gerald Turner's pending return to society was linked primarily to fundamental inadequacies in the state's system of calculating prison release, and resulting political heat placed upon Governor Tommy Thompson.[9]

Paradoxically, David Boerner's cogent and compelling rationale for Washington's civil commitment policy may be partially responsible for the laws' first major conceptual hurdle. By building his case on the extreme example of Earl Shriner, Boerner creates a divergence between the policy's intellectual justification and its political foundations. We therefore emerge with two potential perspectives on the problem – an expansive perspective, as developed in the political arena and applied as a remedy to a range of system failures, and a selective perspective focused on a handful of exceptional cases.

Political Risks and Consequences

These divergent perspectives have a direct bearing on the likely actions of policy implementers. Under an expansive orientation, those charged with implementing the policies may be expected to cast a relatively broad net to fulfill the policies' fundamental public safety mandate. This approach brings a greater likelihood of "false positive" or "Type II" errors, in which individuals who might fact never re-offend will be designated as SVP's and committed to state custody, perhaps indefinitely.

Alternatively, if one adopts the selective perspective, implementing agents would be charged with minimizing the number of false positives and selecting only those cases that fit a circumscribed profile. Under these circumstances, the policies would operate under the specter of potential "Type I" errors, in which the system fails to identify a particular individual who proceeds to re-offend – a circumstance closely reflecting the types of events that gave rise to the laws in the first place.

Placed in a socio-political context, the selective approach carries with it potentially significant political and organizational consequences, while the expansive orientation presents a much more subtle form of

---

[9] Specific details on these cases are included in Appendix A.

risk. In a Type I error, an innocent citizen may be victimized, bringing the threat of recriminations associated with perceived policy failure. Under a Type II error, the "victim" would be a previously convicted sexual offender held in state custody under erroneous pretenses – a circumstance that may easily fall under the political radar. Assuming that innocent victims of crime represent more potent players in the political arena than perpetrators of sexual violence, it is reasonable to establish that SVP civil commitment policies, from the outset, are oriented towards an expansive view of the target population.

Problem Tractability – A First Cut

The alternative perspectives on the target population also have a direct bearing on the standards against which SVP civil commitment policies' implementation success or failure will be gauged. If adopting the expansive approach, the policy will be assessed on its capacity to protect the public from a relatively large and diverse target population. Alternatively, the selective approach permits deployment of a more focused set of program provisions, but ultimately requires technology to meaningfully narrow the population.

In their model of policy implementation, Mazmanian and Sabatier (1989) cite the construct of "problem tractability" as a critical determinant of policy success or failure. They present four criteria for assessing problem tractability: the size of the target population, the diversity of the target population, technical difficulties, and the extent of behavioral change required. While the latter two criteria will be examined during the remainder of this chapter and revisited at its conclusion, we may make an initial assessment of problem tractability based on the range and magnitude of the target population.

In Table 2, the "expansive" perspective reflects the broader political view of the target population, while the "selective" perspective reflects the more circumscribed approach discussed in Boerner's rationale for the law. Each of these criteria – the size of the target population and the diversity of that group – may be viewed as inversely related to problem tractability. That is, the broader the population, the more strategically difficult and resource-intensive it will generally be to effect change in outcomes related to that group. In both cases – the size of the target population and the diversity of the group – the expansive scenario ranks higher, implying a problem that is likely significantly less tractable.

Table 2: Problem Tractability Assessment: Part 1

Tractability Variable	"Expansive" Perspective	"Selective" Perspective
Target Population as % of total population	High	Low
Diversity of Target population	High	Low

As we move on to our analysis of strategy, then, it is reasonable to state that **the policies' viability has much to do with how effectively strategic parameters and operational practices are capable of narrowing the scope of the target population**.

EXAMINING THE STRATEGY

Consistent with the challenge noted above, the processes delineated in the conceptual model may be viewed as a sequence of selection and attrition, aimed at identifying the "right" group for commitment, providing an intervention, and ultimately selecting those among the group who may be safely returned to society following that intervention. For purposes of analysis, this sequence will be assessed in terms of three systems of activity – systems of case selection, including both preliminary case screening and the legal commitment process; systems of custody and treatment; and systems of transition and release.

Within each of these systems, the policy requires organizational systems, resources, operational criteria, and decision rules – factors considered in the operational analysis presented in Chapter 5. For current purposes, however, our primary concern is whether, and under what conditions, the combination of inputs and activities assumed by the conceptual model are capable of producing the required outputs. This capability may be examined on the basis of two key criteria – the empirical evidence regarding technological capacity (technical viability) and the positions of the courts (legal viability).

Table 3 presents the key technical and legal assumptions to be tested in each area. At the conclusion of this section, we will revisit these assumptions, and the extent to which they are fulfilled based on the evidence as presented.

Table 3: Summary of Strategic Assumptions Associated with SVP Civil Commitment Policies

Activity System	Technical Assumptions	Legal Assumptions
Case Selection	SVP case selection criteria can be operationally defined and reliably measured, and can meaningfully differentiate SVP's from broader population of sex offenders.	Criteria for commitment are sufficient to support civil nature of commitment, and can be consistently applied in a manner that satisfies constitutional requirements.
Custody and Treatment	Current technology is available to maintain safe and secure custody of SVP's and to ensure efficacious treatment outcomes for committed SVP's	The courts will grant sufficient latitude to states with regard to custody and treatment provisions
Transition and Release	"Reduced dangerousness" can be reasonably assessed by qualified professionals based on validated methods; Viable models of community supervision and re-integration are available.	The courts will grant sufficient latitude to states in the design, timing and implementation of transition programming;

Case Selection

Considering the rather broad net cast by policymakers, the process of case selection is central to the SVP civil commitment strategy. In terms of the conceptual model, case selection consists of two major sets of activities – initial assessment, which is intended to select potential commitment candidates from the broader population of sex offenders; and the legal process, intended to define the group that in fact does meet SVP criteria, and for which civil commitment is legally justified.

On a theoretical level, one might view case screening and identification as a purely technical determination, and the commitment process as a purely legal one. As a practical matter, however, legal and technical criteria are closely linked, and may each be applied in the context of either set of activities. Moreover, although each of the two activity sets produces a discrete output, the practical boundaries between them are not always clear.[10] Accordingly, this portion of the analysis examines the preliminary case identification and legal commitment processes in tandem, considering both the technical and legal issues associated with the case selection process.

Case Criteria: A Blueprint for Assessing Key Assumptions

A critical examination of these two sets of assumptions associated with SVP case selection may be built around the principle criteria applied in making SVP determinations.[11] By examining these criteria, both separately and in tandem, we may gain a general understanding of the conceptual issues surrounding their application.

---

[10] As will be explored in the operational analysis, states vary in their approaches to initial case screening, the timing of clinical evaluations, and how and when prosecutors enter the decision-making process. For greater detail on this variation, the reader is referred to the structural charts included in Appendix B.

[11] Commitment criteria detail for the six focus states is included in Appendix B; for a more detailed review of statutory criteria in other states, see Lieb and Matson (1998).

Table 4: SVP Civil Commitment Criteria

Criterion	Definitional Elements
Events and/or Behaviors	At least one prior qualifying offense
	Imminent release from custody
	Act of harmful sexual conduct by individual not in custody (some states)
Mental Condition	o Mental abnormality or personality disorder o Volitional impairment
Dangerousness	Likely to engage in acts of violence if not confined

Table 4 describes the three main criteria associated with the SVP population: qualifying events or behaviors, mental condition, and dangerousness. Beyond these three categories, statutes also specify a nexus between the specified mental condition and the dangerousness. The remainder of this section considers each criterion in turn, focusing on the technical and legal issues connected with each.

Events and/or Behaviors

As a matter of statutory definition, SVP laws set forth criteria related to prior offense history, including both the required number and the range of qualifying offenses. While the types of qualifying offenses vary from state to state, enumerated offenses typically range from indecent liberties with a child to adult rape, covering a relatively diverse population of offenders.[12]

Although behavioral criteria are typically operationalized in terms of arrest and conviction on a specific listing of offenses, states may also include individuals whose history includes offenses for which the individual has been adjudicated delinquent or found not guilty by

[12] For offense profiles of committed SVP's, see Lieb and Nelson (2001), Janus and Walbeck (2000), Lieb (1996).

reason of insanity.[13] Similarly, provisions pertaining to the "trigger event" associated with a potential SVP generally reference a pending release from prison, but may also involve pending release from juvenile detention facilities or inpatient psychiatric settings. In some states, an SVP review may be triggered even without a pending release or current conviction, but simply on the basis of "harmful sexual conduct."[14]

Viewed in terms of technical application, this particular definitional category creates few substantive definitional or measurement problems. Assuming the timely and accurate provision of appropriate information resources and sufficient bureaucratic systems (both of which are the domain of the ensuing operational analysis), there are few discernible conceptual obstacles to the execution of consistent decision rules in this area. We may therefore fairly conclude that the principle technical criteria (as noted in Table 3) are at least partially met.

Within a legal framework, however, the picture becomes more complex. While on a rudimentary level, the range of offenses and the sources of potential SVP referrals may be construed as a matter of legislative choice, with few explicit legal obstacles, the law's civil nature establishes qualifying events and behaviors as insufficient to justify commitment as an SVP. Selecting cases based solely on past behaviors blurs the line between civil commitment and criminal incarceration, undermining the legal foundations upon which the laws are based.

The most significant early challenges to SVP civil commitment laws focused on precisely this issue, asserting that the laws, while nominally civil, in fact represented extensions of the criminal justice system, and as such violated constitutional prohibitions against double

---

[13] For a summary of state provisions associated with juveniles and psychiatric patients, see Lieb and Matson (1998).

[14] See, for example, Minn. Statutes §253B.02.

jeopardy and ex post facto lawmaking.[15] Ruling on the Kansas statute, the Hendricks court rejected these arguments, concluding,

> "As a threshold matter, commitment under the Act does not implicate either of the two primary objectives of criminal punishment: retribution or deterrence. The Act's purpose is not retributive because it does not affix culpability for prior criminal conduct. Instead, such conduct is used solely for evidentiary purposes, either to demonstrate that a "mental abnormality" exists or to support a finding of future dangerousness..... Nor can it be said that the legislature intended the Act to function as a deterrent. Those persons committed under the Act are, by definition, suffering from a "mental abnormality" or a "personality disorder" that prevents them from exercising adequate control over their behavior. Such persons are therefore unlikely to be deterred by the threat of confinement."

The implications of the Court's wording surrounding dangerousness and lack of control will be examined in greater detail below. For current purposes, however, it is sufficient for us to establish that, while events and prior behaviors may be a somewhat useful "first cut" in narrowing the potential SVP population, legal acceptance of SVP civil commitment has been based on the assumed presence of **other** factors that distinguish the SVP from a broader group of sex offenders who may meet offense criteria.

As such, of the three prongs of the SVP definition, one may fairly conclude that events and behaviors have the weakest direct utility to the civil commitment case selection process.[16] In terms of the legal

---

[15] The double jeopardy and ex post facto arguments connected to SVP civil commitment laws have figured prominently in several cases. Notable examples include *Kansas v. Hendricks* (1997); *State v. Carpenter* (1995); *Martin v. Reinstein* (1999); *Seling v. Young* (2000).

[16] This statement is not to imply that prior offense history has no bearing on an individual's risk for re-offense (i.e. "dangerousness"). Rather, it is intended to make the point that SVP policies' civil (rather than criminal) legal foundations have more to do with mental abnormality and dangerousness than with offense profiles.

criterion specified in Table 3, we may also conclude that events and behaviors are insufficient means of meeting constitutional standards.

Mental Condition

The second definitional component of SVP eligibility, as referenced in the Hendricks opinion, relates to individual mental condition. Here, two specific and related constructs have emerged in the debate over SVP standards – "mental abnormality" and "lack of control." Coupled with the dangerousness standards that will be examined shortly, these constructs should conceivably represent the factors that distinguish the sexually violent predator from the typical violent criminal recidivist. Each carries a set of critical technical and legal issues requiring examination.

Mental Abnormality

There are a number of potential approaches to operationally defining "mental abnormality" for the purposes of civil commitment. The first, quite simply, is to adopt a standard typically applied in traditional psychiatric civil commitment proceedings, equating "mental abnormality" with "mental illness" as defined and understood within the psychiatric profession. Applied in the civil commitment context, this would essentially limit the universe of potential SVP's eligible for commitment to those with psychotic or major mood disorders that predispose the individual to commit acts of sexual violence.

The problem with this approach is that it is far too limited to meet the intent of SVP civil commitment legislation. As noted earlier, the Washington law evolved precisely because the criteria traditionally applied in civil commitment proceedings simply did not apply to sexually violent predators (Boerner, 1992). Hence, SVP civil commitment policies, from their inception, have implicitly called for a significantly broader definition of mental abnormality than that commonly accepted for purposes of general psychiatric civil commitment.

In *Kansas v. Hendricks*, the Supreme Court supported this expanded definition, holding that "mental abnormality" was a legitimate legal construct, subject to legislative definition, and not necessarily a clinical one:

> "....the term 'mental illness' is devoid of any talismanic significance. Not only do psychiatrists disagree widely and frequently on what constitutes mental illness, but the Court itself has used a variety of expressions to describe the mental condition of those properly subject to civil confinement." ("Kansas v. Hendricks," 1997)

So, if the working definition of "mental abnormality" is not necessarily a matter of clinical diagnosis, then what is it? One approach, which has been generally accepted by the courts, involves the construct of "psychopathy." Assessed using a set of commonly-employed psychological instruments, psychopathy refers to a constellation of three sets of factors – interpersonal, affective, and behavioral. Individuals with high levels of psychopathy may be generally described as grandiose, egocentric, non-empathetic, manipulative, and impulsive (Hare, 1991).

While standardized measures of psychopathy within the SVP committed population have not been aggregated and reported, published data on the committed SVP population indicates that between 60 and 70 percent of committed individuals are designated with some form of personality disorder (Janus & Walbek, 2000; Lieb, 1996; Lieb & Nelson, 2001). Although individuals with personality disorder designations may encompass a broad range of psychopathy levels, this information does provide a useful proxy for the committed population's psychopathic profile. Based on the incidence of reported personality disorder among individuals designated as SVP's, it certainly appears that psychopathy may represent a significant element in the "mental abnormality" equation.

Yet whereas adopting traditional psychiatric definitions of mental illness may restrict the laws' reach beyond policymakers' intent, adopting psychopathy as a working definition may cast too wide a net. Incidence of personality disorders among the nation's incarcerated population has been estimated at up to eighty percent – a figure that may be even higher among those found guilty of past violent offenses (Cunningham & Reidy, 1998).

Further, if we divide the potential SVP population into two offender categories – child molesters on one hand and rapists on the other -- one may argue that the nature of the offense virtually ensures that there will be some basis for establishing mental abnormality. The past behavior of child molesters will almost invariably support some finding of pedophilia or a related disorder, and the offenses committed by rapists will likely be closely associated with psychopathy and associated personality disorders. Viewed in this context, one may easily argue – as some have -- that "mental abnormality" as put forth in SVP laws and as accepted by the courts, is implicitly circular in nature as applied to the target offender population (Wettstein, 1992).

In light of these circumstances, it appears that the mental abnormality requirement, as validated by the courts, brings little additional discriminatory value to the process. Coupled with the previous finding that the designated offenses also do little to narrow the pool of potential SVP commitments, it appears that our quest for meaningfully limiting criteria remains largely unfulfilled to this point.

Lack of Control

Beyond the construct of mental abnormality, a second prong to SVP mental condition criteria involves the concept of "lack of control" – an idea that has figured prominently in sex offender civil commitment since the inception of sexual psychopath statutes over 60 years ago. The nation's first sexual psychopath law, adopted in 1939 by Minnesota, refers to "utter lack of control" as one of three criteria for commitment. [17]

---

[17] Minnesota's "utter lack of control" standard was at the center of a successful challenge to the state's law in 1994 (In Re Linehan), leading the state to adopt a

More recently, the "lack of control" concept, and the requirement that states establish the existence of volitional or emotional impairment as part of civil commitment proceedings, has continued to engender significant debate in both legal and clinical circles (Hamilton, 2002). Organized psychiatry has long maintained that "lack of control" is an untenable concept, and that distinguishing an "irresistable impulse" from an "impulse not resisted" remains beyond the scope of professional judgment (Group for the Advancement of Psychiatry, 1977). Indeed, this argument was central to the case made by the State of Kansas before the US Supreme Court in October of 2001 (see Crane v. Kansas, 2002), and featured prominently in amicus briefs filed with the court on both sides of the case (American Psychiatric Association, 2001; Association for the Treatment of Sexual Abusers, 2001a).

The Court's ruling in the Crane case, issued in the spring of 2002, agreed that while an "absolutist" approach was unworkable, that finding of "some" volitional impairment was required. The Court failed, however, to clarify a workable definition or standard for lack of control, effectively ceding these determinations to state and federal district courts. In the months following the ruling, courts throughout the country addressed the "lack of control" issue, generally yielding opinions supporting wide latitude in applying the concept.[18] One federal court ruling in Arizona concluded:

> "If the state establishes not only that a person is dangerous, but also that a mental illness or abnormality caused the dangerousness, the state has met its burden to show a lack of control (In re Leon G, 2002)"

---

supplemental new law with less restrictive criteria (See Minn. Statutes Ch. 253B. 02 subd. 18c). Nevertheless, the original 1939 law remains in force, and as a matter of practice, civil commitments in Minnesota are generally committed under both the old and new standards. Detail on the Linehan case and its effect on state policy are included in Appendix A.

[18] See, for example, State v. Laxton (2002 WI 82); In re Leon G. (26 P. 3d 481); Commitment of W.Z. (173 NJ 109).

In terms of the technical assumptions framing this analysis, the above-referenced ruling effectively relegates "lack of control" to a rhetorical concept with little substantive bearing on the case selection process. Just as our earlier review established the concept of "mental abnormality" as driven largely by the nature of the individuals' prior behaviors, the "lack of control" criterion may in turn be viewed as similarly circular in its logic and application.

Dangerousness

Thus far, the definitional constructs that we have evaluated have proven to be of limited utility in distinguishing SVP's from the broader population of sex offenders. Criteria related to events and behaviors, as matter of definition, are relatively straightforward, but are clearly insufficient to adequately distinguish the SVP population and support the civil nature of the laws. The concepts associated with mental condition -- 'mental abnormality' and 'lack of control' – in theory could restrict the population and provide legal justification for the civil commitment strategy, but remain amorphously construed as matters of both technical and legal definition. Moreover, as we have seen, the broad interpretation of these constructs by the courts leads to potentially circular logic concerning the characteristics of the "commitment-eligible" population, further diminishing the constructs' practical utility.

Considering these circumstances, we are therefore left with one final definitional element in our quest for limiting principles -- the idea of dangerousness (or, put in causal terms, the likelihood of future acts of sexual violence).

Legal determinations of dangerousness have typically fallen to psychologists, psychiatrists, and related professionals who are assumed to possess specialized knowledge and technology that makes their assessments superior to those that might be made by a layperson. Otto (1994), notes that technical capacity and legal admissibility are independent concepts, setting forth two questions that may be adapted in the context of the current inquiry:

1. Do mental health professionals have any ability to differentiate levels of dangerousness among the population of sex offenders?; and
2. Assuming that this ability exists, should the legal system seek professional input in relevant legal proceedings?

Do mental health professionals have any ability to differentiate levels of dangerousness among the population of sex offenders?

Hanson (1998) has noted three plausible approaches to assessing risk of sexual re-offense among populations of prior sex offenders – **guided clinical approaches**, in which empirically validated risk factors are gathered and applied based on professional judgment; **pure** actuarial **approaches**, in which risk factors are gathered and weighted based on structured and empirically-validated instruments; and **adjusted actuarial approaches**, in which actuarial results are critically examined and modified to account for case-specific circumstances.

General evidence regarding violence prediction has indicated that mechanical actuarial approaches demonstrate greater predictive accuracy than clinical judgment (Grove and Meehl, 1996; Grove et.al. 2000). Moreover, proponents of pure actuarial approaches have argued that adjusted actuarial methods dilute the efficacy of the instruments, compromising predictive reliability in the process (Quinsey, Harris, Rice, & Cormier, 1998).[19]

Yet while actuarial instruments have proven to be effective means of predicting general violence among certain populations, evidence suggests that factors predicting **general** violence in the population may

---

[19] These findings build on a significant prior body of research and legal theory indicating that "experts" may be no more effective at making predictions of violence than laypersons presented with the same set of facts (Ennis & Litwack, 1975).

differ significantly from those that predict **sexual** violence (Hanson, 1998). Moreover, while the empirical study of risk factors for sex offense recidivism dates back nearly 40 years (Quinsey, Harris, et.al., 1998), specialized actuarial risk assessment for sex offenders has emerged only recently, concurrent with the enactment of SVP civil commitment statutes and community notification laws (Campbell, 2000). As a result, some have maintained that actuarial methods applied in the context of SVP civil commitment may be based on instruments that have not been sufficiently tested and validated (Campbell, 2000; Hart, 2000).

In light of these limitations, evidence suggests that there is little basis to assume the superiority of actuarial methods over clinical assessment in predicting likelihood of sexual re-offense (Petrila & Otto, 2001). Indeed, as a matter of practice, application of unadjusted actuarial methods are rarely, if ever, applied in the assessment of risk by mental health professionals (Hanson, 1998; Petrila & Otto, 2001).

Returning to the first question posed above -- do mental health professionals have any ability to assess risk/predict dangerousness in the context of SVP civil commitment proceedings? Certainly, it would be inaccurate to suggest that mental health professionals possess no particular ability to assess risk for purposes of SVP civil commitment. Yet it is also clear that the empirical foundations for predictions of future sexual violence remain in an evolutionary state, and that the certainty of professional judgments must be examined in light of this circumstance. In sum, the message is that professionals making these determinations should proceed only with caution and awareness of the inherent limitations.

Should the legal system seek professional input in relevant legal proceedings?

For purposes of assessing the conceptual viability of SVP case selection processes, the matter of whether the system should seek such input may be less important than the fact that the system does seek the input of experts to assess dangerousness, and that it appears to grant those experts a good deal of latitude in the process.

Despite the technical limitations noted above, and despite the existence of established legal standards associated with scientific validity ("Daubert v. Merrell Dow Pharmaceuticals," 1993; "Frye v. United States," 1923), there are indications that the legal threshold for admissibility of "expert" predictions of future violence in SVP proceedings is somewhat lower than the empirical threshold just described.

Citing a number of cases (see for example "People v. Poe," 1999; "State v. Kienitz," 1999), Petrila and Otto (2001) suggest that courts considering SVP cases rarely apply Frye and Daubert rules with any real force, focusing more on preponderance of evidence than on a critical review of scientific principles:

> "(the courts) appear content to characterize concerns about the reliability and validity of assessment techniques as going to the weight of the *evidence* – a matter for the discretion of the trial court…even if a court questions the reliability of a particular instrument in a particular case, the tendency is to find evidence "in the overall record" sufficient to establish that a defendant meets SVP criteria. This suggests that an expert who relies on both actuarial instruments and "clinical judgment" as bases for his or her opinion will be best equipped to meet a legal challenge."[20]

Considering that the courts appear to grant relatively broad latitude to professionals offering predictions of dangerousness, it is not surprising that investigators have failed to identify a uniform legal standard of dangerousness for purposes of SVP civil commitment (Janus & Meehl, 1997).

---

[20] Considering this, it would appear that the use of "blended" approaches -- that is, the use of actuarial tools adjusted on the basis of general clinical impressions as a means of justifying commitment – may be more a matter of strategic pragmatism than of empirical judgment.

Implications for Conceptual Viability

In our earlier consideration of problem tractability, we established that the viability of SVP civil commitment relies, in part, on states' ability to place meaningful boundaries on the group targeted for commitment. The analysis presented in this section indicates fairly significant technical barriers to case selection, noting continued debate over empirical evidence, amorphously construed definitional constructs, and lingering ethical concerns within relevant professional circles.

Yet despite these technical limitations, the courts have generally granted wide latitude in applying standards for mental abnormality, lack of control, and predictions of dangerousness. In turn, while they have adopted certain limiting principles, the courts have generally validated and supported commitment practices across the states, presenting few major obstacles to the case selection and commitment processes.

Hence, while the criteria employed to circumscribe the population leave much to be desired, it appears that they have generally been established as 'good enough' to pass constitutional muster. Accordingly, the support of the courts – a critical factor associated with the commitment process – may be reasonably assumed, at least with regard to the standards applied for purposes of commitment. In this respect, the policies may be viewed as having passed a critical test.

As we took towards next chapter's operational analysis, the manner and the extent to which the policy is applied (i.e. commitment patterns and practices) remains only minimally circumscribed as a matter of law and professional consensus. Hence, the level of direction provided to those charged with implementing the policy may be assumed to be relatively low, relegating the process of case selection to a matter of high operational delegation. Whether this flexibility translates into an asset or a liability for SVP civil commitment policies may be debated on theoretical grounds, but ultimately presents a critical question for our operational review.

Custody and Treatment

Having considered the issues surrounding the identification and commitment of individuals as SVP's, we now turn to the systems involved in managing the SVP population following commitment. Management of the SVP population involves two distinct, but inter-related functions – custody, involving the maintenance of control over the individual, and treatment, involving provision of services aimed at modifying thoughts and behavior and, in some cases, permitting re-integration into society.

While next chapter's operational analysis will address a range of organizational and resource issues associated with custody and treatment, this review focuses on fundamental technical and legal issues, and explores the implications of those issues for the policies' underlying conceptual viability.

Technical Assessment

Of the two activities contemplated by the model – custody and treatment -- the custodial function is fairly straightforward from a technical standpoint. Assuming provision of suitably secure facilities and properly trained staff, there are relatively few discernible technological barriers to ensuring a safe and secure custodial environment.

The treatment function, in contrast, produces a range of technical issues related to the probable efficacy of treatment interventions for the SVP population. These issues may be assessed through a review of the relevant literature pertaining to general treatment efficacy for sex offenders, applied to subset of individuals assumed to be targeted for SVP civil commitment.

Treatment of sex offenders has generated a considerable amount of research attention during the past two decades (for recent research overviews, see Grossman, Martis, & Fichtner, 1999; U.S. General Accounting Office, 1996). While precise estimates of treatment success are confounded by a range of methodological factors, general evidence indicates that offense-specific, comprehensive programs, based on cognitive-behavioral, relapse prevention, and organically-based treatments may reduce sex offense recidivism by up to 8 percent for certain populations of sex offenders (Hall, 1995).

Applied to sexually violent predators committed under SVP laws, however, the picture is considerably murkier. Several characteristics of civilly committed SVP's have been cited in the literature as having potential bearings on treatment effects. First, while some SVP's are diagnosed with paraphilic disorders that may be amenable treatment in some cases, many others may have no psychiatric condition other than antisocial personality disorder, which is considerably less treatable (Zonana, 1997). Second, SVP's, by definition, are repeat offenders, a group at greater risk for treatment failure than first-time offenders (Hanson and Bussierre, 1998). Third, the vast majority of committed SVP's are committed following a lengthy prison sentence. Unless a treatment trajectory was established during this period of incarceration, treatment experts have pointed out that the chances for treatment success greatly diminish with time (Becker & Murphy, 1998).

Primarily for these reasons, certain members of the sex offender treatment establishment have expressed either reservation (Becker & Murphy, 1998) or outright condemnation (Schwartz, 1999) towards SVP civil commitment, noting that SVP's may be among those least amenable to treatment, especially when such treatment is only provided following their criminal incarceration.

These concerns, coupled with the already low rate of treatment success within more tractable groups of offenders, point towards significant technological limitations associated with this portion of the conceptual model. This circumstance also presents a critical series of issues to be addressed in the ensuing operational analysis, requiring a close examination of the means and resources employed in the delivery of treatment services, rates of treatment participation and success, and the "return on investment" associated with provision of treatment services.

Legal Assessment

Given the noted disparity in technological limitations between the custodial function (with no indications of insurmountable technical issues) and the treatment function (which may encounter significant technical barriers), our inquiry may be logically extended to ask why it is that policymakers would choose to integrate a treatment function into the design at all. Here, the respective legal parameters associated with custodial and treatment functions become paramount.

Examining treatment in a legal context, we must distinguish between two specific issues related to treatment – the individual's Treatmemt to treatment, and the individual's right to treatment. The former is primarily a matter of technology effectiveness, dependent on both the characteristics of the individual and on the efficacy of available treatment modalities. As described above, it remains highly probable that the potential SVP population would be significantly less "treatable" than a broader population of sexual offenders.

The individual's right to treatment, in contrast, is fundamentally a constitutional matter, independent of whether that treatment is likely to be effective. In a major case out of the Western District of Washington, the federal court has noted that committed SVP's "cannot simply be warehoused and put out of sight; they must be afforded adequate treatment."("Turay v. Seling," 1991) Further, the courts have ruled that the fact that treatment has a minimal chance of working does not relieve the state of the obligation to provide that treatment ("Seling v. Young," 2000).

Moreover, the right to treatment, beyond its emergent clinical programming requirements, is a cornerstone of a much broader set of legal requirements surrounding conditions of confinement. In the words of the Supreme Court, "due process requires that the conditions and duration of confinement bear some reasonable relation to the purpose for which persons are committed" ("Seling v. Young," 2000). Hence, while the provision of therapeutic programming should be evident, treatment rights for SVP's also require the maintenance of a therapeutic environment. The concept of a therapeutic environment, in accordance with professional standards, may encompass a range of factors, including the physical plant, facility rules, and operating procedures (Marques, 2001; William M. Mercer Inc., 1999). Indeed, this broader concept of treatment requirements as something s have all figured prominently in Washington's *Turay v. Seling* litigation described above.

Implications for Conceptual Viability

Examining the relevant data concerning treatment programming for the SVP population, two things seem apparent. First, the limited efficacy of sex offender treatment in general, coupled with the presumed profile of the SVP population, indicate that treatment success is likely to be the exception rather than the rule. This, in turn, is likely to produce an incrementally growing population, and an attendant set of substantial organizational and resource demands. Second, despite this limited likelihood of treatment success, legal requirements associated with both treatment programming and the maintenance of a therapeutic environment, are likely to be significant.

These factors present SVP civil commitment policies with several pivotal questions. How do programs approach their dual roles as custodians and treatment providers? How are they structured to maximize the probability of treatment success? What are the associated resource requirements, and levels of program investment? Are resources sufficient to maintain legal standards? Do program structural characteristics or levels of investment have any noticeable effect on treatment participation or outcomes?

These questions and others will be addressed in the ensuing operational analysis. For current purposes, however, we may establish that the divergence between technological capacity and the therapeutic requirements stemming from the policies' fundamental legal premises, present significant organizational and resource challenges.

Transition and Release

The third and final series of activities associated with the SVP civil commitment strategy involves the systems involved in transition and release from custody. Where our consideration of the case selection process involved a close examination of legal dispositions and their associated criteria, and where our review of custody and treatment focused on programmatic requirements, this stage of the process involves elements of both. The process of transition and release from custody includes both a determinations concerning appropriateness for release and a group of program provisions required to balance public safety concerns with the goal of community re-integration. These two aspects of transition and release will be considered in turn.

Appropriateness for Release

From a technical perspective, there are two plausible approaches to assessing readiness for release. First, as previously noted, we can view the transition and release process as part of the continuum of care – something "earned" through treatment compliance and the cognitive and behavioral changes that come with treatment progress. Second, we may view release through the prism of "dangerousness prediction", relying in large part on actuarial or adjusted actuarial methods, as explored earlier in this analysis.

The first is consistent with the phased program approach associated with the relapse prevention model commonly employed in sex offender treatment programs (Association for the Treatment of Sexual Abusers, 2001b; Marques, 2001), in which treatment program professionals maintain some measure of authority to grant conditional release privileges based on clinical progress assessments. While this approach is consistent with general professional practice, as a practical matter SVP statutes have been constructed with a system of "checks and balances" that effectively preclude the unilateral determination by the treatment team that the individual is eligible for conditional release.

The second approach, and the one more clearly aligned with existing statutory guidelines, is linked to the same methods applied in the initial screening and commitment process, notably through evaluations conducted by reviewers who are independent of the treatment team. In this scenario, an examiner recommending release needs to establish that an individual previously found dangerous enough to justify commitment, no longer meets the requisite dangerousness threshold.

Such determinations, however, are significantly confounded by what Grisso (2000) describes as the "tyranny of static variables" – a circumstance stemming from the reliance of sex offender risk assessment practice on immutable factors such the nature or frequency of prior offenses or victim characteristics. Basing commitment on static factors effectively makes "improvement" logically impossible, relegates treatment to a futile exercise, and compromises any efforts towards effectuating release. Hanson (1998) confirms this, indicating that "we have much more evidence to justify committing offenders than we have for releasing them." [21]

Transitional Program Provisions

The provision of a viable means of appropriate and structured community release represents a critical element to sex offender treatment programs (Marques, 2001). This type of programming typically involves the continuation of treatment activities, provision of suitable secure housing and employment, and a phased granting of privileges and autonomy.

From a purely technical standpoint, one may contend that there are no implicit technical barriers to implementing transitional programs for released SVP's. Viable collaborative models of sex offender community supervision have emerged in recent years, utilizing individualized case planning, specially-trained officers, technological

21 While research into dynamic factors associated with risk of recidivism among sex offenders has emerged in recent years, assessment instruments applying such variables remain in a nascent state (Hanson & Harris, 2000)

means of surveillance, and a range of conditional release provisions (Center for Sex Offender Management, 2000).

Placed in a political context, however, the "success" of such programs is typically qualified by the caveat that the intervention will not <u>always</u> succeed in preventing recidivism. As explored at the outset of this conceptual analysis, SVP civil commitment policies emerged from an explicit belief that societal risk was higher than the public was willing to accept, and that special provisions were required to protect society from a particularly dangerous subset of individuals. While a political analysis of risk is far beyond the scope of the present study, it appears reasonable to assume that SVP programs, with their significant costs and their promise of protecting society from the "worst of the worst" may be held to a fundamentally different standard than general community supervision programs.

In this context, one may put forward a similar question to that posed in our consideration of treatment programs – if the risk is so high, why bother at all with transitional programming?

There are essentially two answers to this question, one pragmatic and the other legal. From a purely pragmatic perspective, despite the rarity of release, we may reasonably assume that some SVP's will be ordered released by the courts, either because they have been found to have made sufficient treatment progress or due to legal technicalities. In such circumstances, structured means of transition and release are simply more likely to ensure public safety than the alternative of unsupervised release.

From a legal vantage, transitional programming is a critical factor in validating the policies' claim of non-punitive intent. As referenced above, professional standards indicate that transitional provisions are integral to sex offender treatment programming. Consistent with these standards, at least one major federal court has ruled that the "light at the end of the tunnel" represents a vital component to the provision of constitutionally adequate treatment ("Turay v. Weston," 1994). In this case, described in detail in Appendix A and explored further in next chapter's operational analysis, the State of Washington has been forced through the imposition of fines to embark on a series of exceptional measures to develop a viable Less Restrictive Alternative (LRA) program as a means of transitional release.

Implications for Conceptual Viability

Our review of the transition and release portion of the conceptual model indicates that release decisions are likely to remain a relatively rare occurrence. Beyond the fact that the ability of treatment providers to unilaterally recommend release is generally precluded by the statutes, the standards of commitment are heavily weighted towards static case characteristics, making decisions to release significantly more complex than initial commitment decisions

These likely barriers to release, coupled with the low probability of treatment success within the SVP population, might easily lead to the conclusion that the demand for transitional programming should be modest, manageable, and largely discretionary. However, considering both the legal requirements described here, and the prospect of mounting resource demands associated with a growing committed population that will be explored in next chapter's operational analysis, the development of viable means of structured release represent a critical element in SVP civil commitment policies.

While there appear to be few discernible technological barriers to the development of such programs, the concept of community release in any form remains anathema to the political and conceptual foundations of SVP civil commitment. Accordingly, the operational challenges faced by states as they attempt to mitigate social and political risks while developing and deploying their transitional programs are likely to be significant.

Summary of Strategic Assessment

At the outset of this section, we set forth a series of assumptions related to the strategic viability of SVP civil commitment policies, based on the causal chain specified in the conceptual model. This section has examined the issues and data surrounding these assumptions, and has presented some general conclusions regarding whether key standards have been met. Many of the factors identified will present critical issues for next chapter's operational analysis. The key findings thus far are presented below.

Table 5: Summary of Strategic Assessment

I. Case Selection	
Assumption/Standard	**Assessment**
SVP case selection criteria can be operationally defined and reliably measured, and can meaningfully differentiate SVP's from broader population of sex offenders.	Key definitional constructs have been generally defined, but measurement techniques remain matters of considerable professional debate. Discriminatory value of constructs is questionable. **Standard not met, but mitigated by general legal acceptance**
Criteria for commitment are sufficient to support civil nature of commitment, and can be consistently applied in a manner that satisfies constitutional requirements.	Courts have validated SVP civil commitment standards, and have generally granted wide technical latitude in commitment eligibility criteria. **Standard met.**
II. Custody and Treatment	
Assumption/Standard	**Assessment**
Current technology is available to maintain safe and secure custody of SVP's and to ensure efficacious treatment outcomes for committed SVP's	Custodial function technically straightforward, although efficacious treatment outcomes unlikely. **Standard partially met.**
The courts will grant sufficient latitude to states with regard to custody and treatment provisions	Courts have accepted commitment based on assumed provision of treatment and maintenance of therapeutic environment, and have shown capacity to force compliance. **Standard partially met.**

Table 5: Summary of Strategic Assessment (continued)

III. Transition and Release	
Assumption/Standard	**Assessment**
"Reduced dangerousness" can be reasonably assessed by qualified professionals based on validated methods;	Reliance of risk assessment technology on static factors makes it easier to justify commitment than to support release. **Standard not met.**
Viable models of community supervision and re-integration are available.	Models and technologies of community supervision exist, but have been deemed insufficient to protect society from SVP's. Population may require extraordinary measures. **Standard partially met.**
The courts will grant sufficient latitude to states in the design, timing and implementation of transition programming.	Courts have given fairly wide latitude to date, but have shown capacity to order transition programming provisions. Probably too early to tell. **Standard partially met.**
Overall Assessment: Despite significant technical issues, initial screening and commitment processes good enough to pass legal muster. Treatment, transition, and release all present significant technical challenges, an uncertain legal landscape, and lingering operational challenges.	

EXAMINING THE SOLUTION

Thus far, this analysis has reviewed the nature of the problem, as well as the implicit assumptions and operational challenges associated with the civil commitment strategy. This final section briefly considers the conceptual model's "back end" – the linkages between the presumed outputs – incapacitation and successful treatment -- with the desired outcome of reduced incidence of sexual violence.

The model presumes two pathways to meeting fundamental public safety goals – an incapacitation pathway and a rehabilitation pathway. The former, accomplished through the commitment process and subsequent custodial activity, clearly represents the more direct path to achieving public safety. Assuming proper facilities and the effective performance of the custodial function, it effectively reduces societal (and therefore political) risk associated with a particular individual to zero, and therefore is quite likely to succeed in reducing the incidence of sexual violence as specified by the model.

The rehabilitation pathway, in contrast, requires a level of change in the target population sufficient to support societal re-integration – change that is likely to be technically demanding and difficult to gauge. Additionally, the route of treatment and release, even when combined with community supervision, will always carry some measure of risk of re-offense, a risk that is likely exaggerated beyond its actuarial likelihood when placed in the political arena.

These factors lead us back to a recurring question -- if the primary policy goals (reduced sexual violence and public safety) can be more effectively and efficiently addressed through incapacitation, what then is the underlying rationale for the rehabilitation pathway?

This question is addressed on many levels throughout this book. In chapter one, we noted the absence of the therapeutic ideal that gave rise to earlier sexual psychopath laws. Earlier in this chapter, we explored the deliberative processes undertaken by the architects of the Washington law, who focused their attention on a case perceived to have "fallen between the cracks" of the criminal justice and mental health systems. Also in this chapter, we have examined the treatment imperative stemming from the *parens patraie* legal theory upon which civil commitment is based, which requires that confinement be based on something other than the need for retribution or deterrence.

The picture that emerges is that the rehabilitative goal likely stems more from legal-strategic pragmatism than from any particular ideology or, for that matter, any particular belief on the part of policymakers that rehabilitation is either attainable or desirable. In this sense, we may bring the conceptual analysis back to a re-consideration of the problem that the policies are intended to solve, and the policy goals that emerge from that problem.

Table 6: Effects of Goal Perspectives on Problem Tractability

Tractability Variable	Technical/Therapeutic Perspective	Public Safety Perspective
Technical Difficulties	**Moderate-Significant Issue** Limited professional consensus on acceptable application of risk assessment for population; Limited professional consensus on efficacy of sex offender treatment, although most agree that there is no "permanent cure".	**Minimal Issue** Risk assessment tools generally capable of meeting basic legal admissibility standards; Treatment efficacy secondary to broader public safety goals
Target group as % of population	**Moderate-Significant Issue** Broad definition could lead to over-inclusive policy - partially mediated by ceding determinations to experts	**Significant Issue** Broad definition could lead to over-inclusive policy, leading to increased resource needs
Diversity of target group	**Moderate-Significant Issue** Presents range of treatment programming challenges connected to varying offender populations and special needs groups; Different populations may need to be separated for safety and security reasons	**Minimal-Moderate Issue** Purpose to protect public, hence treatment needs only to be constitutionally adequate; Different populations may need to be separated for safety and security reasons
Extent of Behavioral Change Required	**Significant Issue** Assuming effective targeting SVP's are among most treatment-resistant Standards for release require demonstration of substantial behavioral change, and actuarial risk criteria based on static variables ("change" difficult to measure).	**Minimal Issue** Treatment success secondary to broader goals

PROBLEM TRACTABILITY REVISITED

In the context of the issues as framed above, we may once again re-visit the idea of problem tractability, considering two alternative approaches to the policy's goals and applying the Mazmanian and Sabatier criteria. As indicated by Table 6, the problem's tractability, and the associated efficacy of the civil commitment strategy, depends significantly on the perspective that one takes with regard to the target population and its expectations for change.

Do we view civil commitment as a temporally limited and selective intervention, or as a quasi-permanent incapacitation mechanism? If adopting a pure public safety mindset, we are dealing with a problem that is reasonably tractable in a technical sense, but potentially resource intensive, due to the loosely defined target population and few assumptions or expectations regarding treatment progress. Alternatively, if we view the problem through a technical/therapeutic lens, we come face to face with a range of technical limitations connected to matters such as treatment efficacy and clinical prediction of risk, producing a highly intractable set of problems. In either case, this circumstance presents significant issues for those charged with implementing the policies.

EMERGENT OPERATIONAL QUESTIONS

The conceptual analysis presented in this chapter addressed a range of issues concerning the technical and legal viability of SVP civil commitment policies. Although the analysis found the policies to be generally acceptable within a legal context, this acceptance was predicated on a number of operational contingencies, linked to significant definitional and technical limitations. Table 7 presents a series of general questions stemming from identified conceptual issues. These questions, which will be addressed at various points in the operational review, provide a vital bridge between the conceptual and operational portions of the analysis.

Table 7: Operational Questions Emerging From Conceptual Analysis

Area of Policy	Major Conceptual Issues	Emergent Operational Questions/ Areas of Concern
Screening and Commitment	Ambiguity surrounding statutory standards and decision rules	What is basis upon which referral and commitment decisions are made? Who influences those decisions, and what are their organizational interests? What role does the allocation of resources play in screening and commitment processes and output levels? What patterns might be observed over time in the areas of referral and commitment?
Custody and Treatment	Limitations of treatment technology and the delicate balance between custodial and therapeutic demands	How are custodial and treatment roles balanced in terms of organizational responsibilities, physical facilities, and programming? What are the emergent resource requirements and patterns of investment? What type of success have states had surrounding treatment engagement and progress among committed SVP's?
Transition and Release	Political and logistical challenges associated with criteria applied in the release process and in LRA programming	What standards have states applied in cases involving potential release of committed SVP's, and what patterns may be observed as a result of those standards? What are the emergent organizational and resource requirements and the patterns of investment associated with LRA and release?

The operational analysis presented in the next chapter is partially framed by these conceptual issues. Focusing on the three activity areas introduced in last chapter's strategic assessment,

CHAPTER 6

Operational Analysis

With the questions just presented as a backdrop, we now turn to consideration of the operational model presented in Chapter 3. Whereas the conceptual review examined SVP civil commitment policies through technical and legal lenses, the operational analysis focuses in on two additional factors – **resource viability**, assessed through patterns of resource investment and likely future demands based on policy trends, and **organizational viability**, as manifested in the adequacy and/or sustainability of agency responsibilities, decision rules, and standards.

Consistent with this focus, this analysis focuses on three broad elements of the operational model as set forth in chapter three -- **operational indicators,** denoted in the model by the shaded arrows and reflecting key process outputs; **organizational factors**, including decision rules and standards and designated authorities associated with specific processes; and **resource factors**, reflecting both resource requirements and levels of investment in operations and infrastructure.

The operational analysis is presented in four sections. The first three sections correspond to each of the main activity areas that comprise SVP civil commitment policies – 1) case selection; 2) custody and treatment, and 3) transition and release. Each section begins with a summary table noting general findings and citing operational factors that both support and threaten the policy's viability. Following the summary table, a supporting narrative examines key organizational and resource issues, and providing an assessment of how those issues might affect the prospects for SVP civil commitment, follows the summary table. The chapter's fourth and final part summarizes the results of the operational analysis, examining interactions between processes, and performing broader organizational and resource assessments of SVP civil commitment's viability as a policy strategy.

ANALYSIS OF CASE SELECTION PROVISIONS

The current analysis defines case selection as encompassing two processes specified in the operational model – the administrative process of case identification and screening, and the legal process of commitment. As explained in the preceding chapter, these two processes are combined for purposes of analysis to account for their significant inter-dependency and for the often blurred lines of distinction between these steps in terms of actual practice.

Table 8 summarizes the major operational findings in this area. The ensuing narrative reviews these findings in greater detail, drawing on the information presented in the six case studies. For case data details, the reader is referred to the supporting documentation included in the appendices.

General Operational Indicators

Before examining specific organizational and resource factors, a general overview of operational trends is warranted. While direct comparative assessment of screening and commitment levels across states is complicated by data limitations (most notably the fact that the operational population baseline varies from state to state), the case data presented in Appendix D provides a general sense of how screening and commitment patterns shift over time.

These shifts may be observed from two dimensions – first, by examining the volume of individuals referred to prosecutors by screeners, of commitment petitions filed, and of SVP commitments; and second, by examining the locus of the "screening burden" illustrating the relative roles that various parts of the screening and legal systems play in refining the caseload. In both cases, states invariably show discernible shifts in key outputs over tim

Table 8: Operational Analysis Summary -- Case Selection Systems

	Operational Indicators	Organizational Factors	Resource Factors
General Findings	Some states exercise initial caution in applying policy & gradually expand utilization. Others embrace civil commitment from outset and reducing utilization over time; Locus of screening burden shifts over time, indicating likely policy learning and/or changes in applied standards.	Screening and case prosecution systems vary in complexity, but are generally structured to sufficiently produce required outputs; Relative roles of actors within system evolve over time -- systems of screening and commitment moderately "self-correcting"; Legal system capacity may be issue	Resource intensity of screening process varies across states; No evidence that "front-loading" significant clinical resources in screening process leads to more effective screening of cases; States generally provide supplemental resources to legal systems to handle SVP cases, although funding mechanisms and extent of state commitment vary
Policy Viability Supports	Trend towards greater screening selectivity in most states	Significant legislative focus on process; systems structured to support utilization of policy (strong mission consistency, adequate decision rules); Agencies and systems appear to learn and adapt practices in response to operational challenges	States appear committed to providing resources needed to pursue commitment, and resource demands stabilize over time.
Policy Viability Threats	Lack of consistent standards to assess whether outputs are of "better quality"	Potential for imbalance of workloads between key systems and associated operational breakdowns	Potential for misalignment of incentives and/or resources across systems

Screening and Commitment Volume

A review of general referral and commitment patterns indicates a good deal of variation among the states. Some initiated their policies in a tentative fashion and gradually ratcheted up utilization, while others came out of the gate relatively quickly, and appeared to moderate commitment activities over time. In the former category, one may place Washington and Kansas, which appear to have kept case filings low while awaiting rulings on the statutes' constitutionality. The latter group includes Wisconsin, where referrals and filings proliferated during the first year and a half of the statute's implementation; California, which sent 300 cases on to prosecutors and filed 200 petitions during the first year; and Florida, which struggled with a case backlog from virtually the first day of the policy, and in late 2002 was still conducting trials from its incoming "Class of '99." In all three of these cases, commitment filings appear to moderate somewhat in subsequent years.[22]

---

[22] These contrasting patterns may be noted by comparing the charts in Appendix D depicting referral and commitment patterns for Washington and California. The case of Washington indicates considerable caution on the part of prosecutors during the policy's initial years, while California prosecutors, as well as those charged with case screening, appeared to embrace the policy from the outset. In subsequent years, California's commitment levels dropped and stabilized, while Washington's saw an upward climb. There are two likely explanations for the distinctions between these patterns -- one historical and the other organizational. From a historical perspective, Washington's law was initiated amidst a much more uncertain legal landscape, whereas California adopted its policy after initial legal victories, particularly in Washington ("In Re Young," 1993). The theory that early adopting states may have held back pending key legal rulings is further supported by the tentative approach adopted by Kansas.[22] Viewed from an organizational perspective, the variation between these two states may also be associated with fundamentally different organizational approaches to screening and prosecutor jurisdiction, as examined in the organizational assessment.

Among the states studied, Minnesota appears to have exhibited the highest level of volatility in its commitment filing practices, witnessing a wave of new commitments upon its 1991 revival of its nascent Psychopathic Personality law, another surge in 1995 after the previous year's statutory revisions, and yet another increase in 2003 in the wake of a high-profile rape and murder.

Relative Case Selection Burden

The likely impact of legal and organizational factors on screening and commitment patterns may also be seen in an examination of relative case selection burden over time. Using California and Washington as illustrations, Figure 4: indicates that the relative roles of screeners, prosecutors, and courts appear to shift over time as policies develop and as standards become clarified.

In the case of Washington, the significant reduction in the white area (representing cases dismissed by the courts at trial) following the aforementioned *Young* decision indicates an increased comfort level on the part of the courts. The Washington graph also points to a critical organizational factor, namely that prosecutors continue to exercise a good deal of discretion, rejecting a substantial proportion of cases sent to them by the End of Sentence Review Committee – the state's screening entity – even ten years into the policy.

This pattern is in significant contrast with that observed in other states examined in this study, including California. As California's chart indicates, prosecution is declined on a relatively limited basis, and the decline in case filings and commitments has been largely driven by screeners rather than by prosecutors. Similar patterns may be noted in other states, including Florida, Minnesota, and Wisconsin.

Figure 4: Relative Case Selection Burden: Washington and California

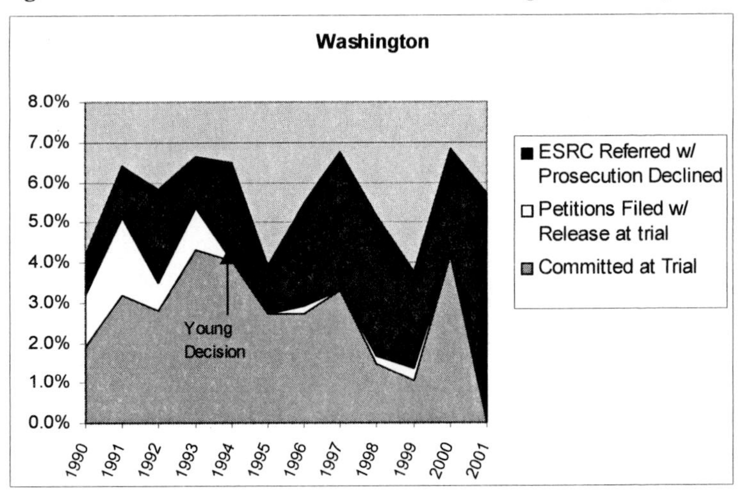

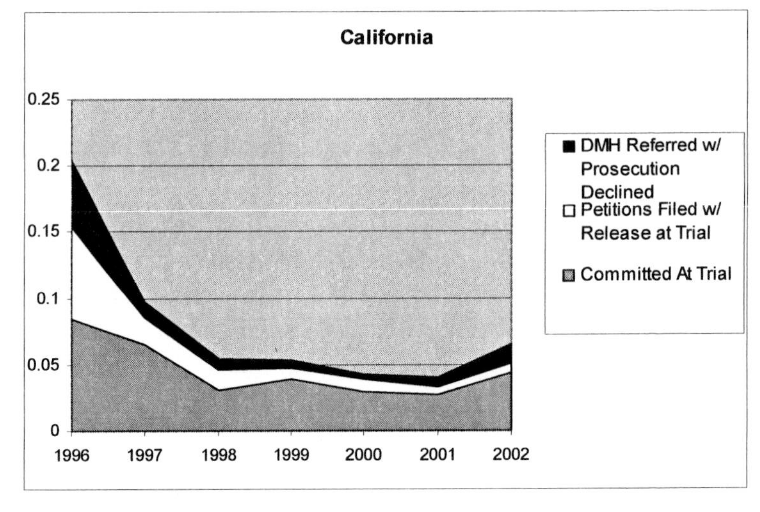

Organizational Assessment

As noted in Table 8, a review of the case study data indicates that threats to the organizational viability of SVP case selection processes are likely to be fairly modest. While states vary considerably in their organizational approaches to case selection and intra-system roles and decision rules often take time to evolve, systems ultimately appear organizationally capable of producing the desired outputs. Nevertheless, the significant number of "hand-offs" between systems produces the potential for organizational breakdowns – a factor that must be considered by policymakers. This organizational assessment first considers how states have assigned organizational roles and responsibilities for the case selection process, and proceeds to examine the manner in which inter-agency issues might affect the policies' future organizational viability.

Organizational Roles and Responsibilities

Table 9 provides a side-by-side comparison of states in two key elements of the case selection process -- the "gatekeeping" function, or the systems through which cases are screened and referred to prosecutors; and the locus of prosecutor jurisdiction, pertaining to legal authorities designated with the ability to file and pursue commitment. Arrangements for the former range from virtually autonomous determinations made by individuals within bureaucratic structures, to multi-agency committees, to intricate consensus rules involving contracted evaluators. Regarding prosecutor jurisdiction, some states have selected highly centralized models relying on attorneys general and/or a limited number of county prosecutors, while others have adopted highly decentralized systems involving county or circuit-based resources. More specific details on these factors are included in Appendix B.

Table 9: Gatekeeping Functions and Prosecutor Jurisdiction by State

State	Primary Gatekeeper(s)	Prosecutor Jurisdiction
Washington	End of Sentence Review Committee (Multi-Agency Group) as agent of Agencies with Jurisdiction. Reviews universe of potential cases. Referral decision based on group consensus.	Attorney General handles all cases w/ exception of King County. State funding provided for both AG and KC prosecutor
Minnesota	Direct referrals from AWJ's (primarily DOC)	Attorney General handles cases for all but two largest counties. Counties absorb portion of costs.
Wisconsin	Direct referrals from AWJ's (primarily DOC)	Attorney General handles cases for all but two largest counties. State funds prosecutors and public defender staff resources, counties have limited cost burden.
Kansas	Multi-Disciplinary Review (Multi-agency) assigns risk levels, Prosecutors Review Committee (under Attorney General) reviews entire case universe.	Attorney General handles cases
California	Dept. of Corrections and Board of Prison Terms send subset of cases for Department of Mental health (DMH) evaluations. Two independent evaluators (contracted through DMH) must concur for referral to take place.	Counties handle cases and reimbursed through state
Florida	Dept. of Children and Families reviews universe of cases forwarded by various agencies with jurisdiction, under guidelines promulgated by agency after public review.	State Attorneys (circuit-based, state appropriated)

The two states with the largest case volume – California and Florida – have adopted systems of initial case screening and case prosecution that diverge significantly from the systems in place in the other states. Regarding initial case screenings, both states have placed the gatekeepers at the "front door" of the mental health system, requiring contracted independent clinical evaluations to be performed under the auspices of state mental health authorities. In contrast, Kansas, Minnesota, and Wisconsin all carry out their initial evaluations under the auspices of their respective correctional agencies, providing various degrees of centralization of the process. Washington, operating through its End of Sentence Review Committee (also housed within the state's correctional agency), conducts a process that combines clinical and administrative reviews to formulate a recommendation to prosecutors.

California and Florida are also distinguished by the fact that these states have entirely decentralized legal filing decisions and case prosecution, placing responsibility and authority exclusively in the hands of regional prosecutors. The other four states each actively involve the Attorney General, and in some cases a small number of county prosecutors, in the filing and commitment process. Those counties that do handle their own cases in these states tend to be those most densely populated, and as such have greater capacity to develop specialized units to handle SVP cases.[23]

In neither case, however, does the specific model employed appear to hamper effective fulfillment of the commitment process. In terms of initial case screening, all states, as a practical matter, include some measure of professional clinical review prior to prosecutor referrals, regardless of whether that review resides with mental health or correctional authorities. Regarding prosecutor jurisdiction, both attorneys general and regional prosecutors have generally appeared capable of developing appropriate expertise in the management of SVP

---

[23] In most cases, states also provide supplemental appropriations to this limited group of counties for operations of their SVP units.

cases regardless of the model employed. Moreover, SVP commitment's fundamental focus as a matter of public safety, coupled with the fact that the proceedings closely resemble criminal trials in terms of procedure and general rules of evidence, appear to ensure reasonable consistency with the missions and expertise of prosecutorial agencies and other portions of the legal system, regardless of where authority resides.

Hence, while the specifics of gatekeeping and case prosecution models may vary, and while some may ultimately prove to be more efficient than others, states ultimately seem to develop case selection systems that are organizationally and legally sustainable.[24] The variation that does exist across systems may be in response to a range of factors, including the size of the state and the need to adapt to existing institutional structures, but is largely incidental to broader questions of viability.

Inter-System Dynamics

Although the individual components of the system appear generally viable, one area of caution involves the number of inter-system hand-offs involved in the case selection process. While most states examined appear to effectively manage the flow of cases through the screening and legal systems, the case of Florida illustrates the significant potential for breakdowns due to lack of systems coordination.

As described in detail in the state's narrative included in Appendix A, Florida faced a significant screening backlog from the first day of its policy. Following a barrage of media coverage and a subsequent trilogy of reports, including one produced by a gubernatorial panel

---

[24] As of early 2005, one state in this study -- Minnesota – has undertaken a review of its case screening practices, after the system failed to identify the perpetrator of a high-profile rape and murder. Notably in this regard, the Minnesota statute contains the least prescriptive screening practice guidelines of the six states included in this study, effectively leaving the system to the discretion of the Corrections Commissioner.

(Jimmy Ryce Act Enforcement Task Force, 2000), a second by a legislative research group (Florida Office of Program Policy Analysis and Governmental Accountability, 2000a), and a third by an independent consultant (William M. Mercer Inc., 1999), the state introduced changes and resources to address these mounting problems with the state's initial screening system. Yet while these modifications may have partially addressed the system's "front door", they did little to account for the capacity of the state's legal system to process the growing number of SVP cases. The result was a mounting backlog in the courts, as indicated by the steadily increasing time to trial noted in Figure 5 below.

Figure 5: Florida Time Between Case Filing and Trial Completion by Quarter

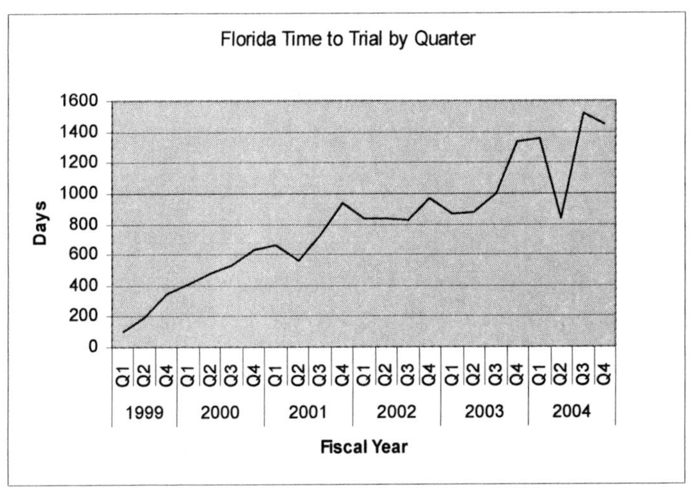

The figure depicts the number of days between initial case filing and trial completion for trials completed between January 1999 and December 2004. The rising trend line implies a steadily growing backlog of cases, which as of the last data point average nearly three years between initial filing and case disposition. During that time, individuals awaiting their commitment trials are generally held in DCF custody, creating a growing number of detainees within DCF facilities.

This case illustrates the significant cross-system interdependencies associated with the SVP civil commitment process, and the associated potential for organizational breakdowns if these interdependencies remain unaddressed. Accordingly, as we turn our attention to matters of resources, the balance of such resources across systems remains a pivotal issue for the policies' viability.

Resource Assessment

The states examined have employed a variety of means for case identification, referral, and commitment. Along with this structural variation comes a range of approaches for system funding, both for purposes of case screening and evaluation and for support of the legal system.

Screening Systems

The resource intensity of the initial screening process varies considerably across states. As described in the organizational assessment, states have taken varied approaches to resource investment in the screening process. Minnesota and Wisconsin have taken a relatively low-cost approach, funding individual positions within their correctional agencies, while Florida and California have each ceded the screening process to their mental health authorities, which in turn subcontract with independent evaluators to screen out cases prior to prosecutor referrals at annual costs exceeding $4 million. [25]

As a matter of relative efficiency, one might speculate that the more expensive and intricate screening process adopted by California and Florida might be justified by a more refined universe of cases referred to prosecutors (LaFond, 2003). Theoretically, a higher-cost screening program might be supported through a higher proportion of referrals ultimately resulting in commitment, and in turn a more efficient system. Yet the current data provides no evidence to this

---

[25] These costs include fees of independent evaluators only, and do not cover costs of in-house evaluation resources, management, or administration. Refer to Appendix C for detail.

effect. In fact, while the commitment rates in California were roughly comparable to those in other states, Florida's relatively resource-intensive screening process is associated with a significantly higher rate of subsequent case dismissals than in many other states.[26]

Yet Minnesota's experience in recent years – notably a significant shift in its screening practices beginning in late 2003 – highlights the volatile nature of case selection practices, and the potential hidden costs of adopting the "homegrown" approach to case screening. Largely due to one tragic case – a high-profile rape and murder committed by an individual who had "slipped through the cracks" of the Minnesota DOC's screening system – the state witnessed a nearly 15-fold increase from 2002 to 2003 in the number of cases referred to prosecutors for potential commitment, as noted in the table below.

Table 10: Minnesota Referrals and Commitments 1997-2004

Year	DOC Referrals	New Commitments
1997	58	25
1998	43	18
1999	32	26
2000	30	23
2001	24	13
2002	13	12
2003	246	18
2004	170	28
Source: Minnesota Department of Corrections		

Equally important, as we will see in the following section, the financial stakes associated with custody and treatment can be significant. Accordingly, there are potentially significant ramifications associated with placing case selection authority in the hands of the

[26] 42% of cases filed by prosecutors that were disposed of as of 9/04 had resulted in dismissal, release, or release at trial (Florida Department of Children and Families, 2004).

agency that will also be charged with managing custody and treatment resources, as is the case in both California and Florida. In such a scenario, there will always be the potential that screening decisions will be driven in part by organizational and resource issues (notably the rate of population growth and the mechanisms for funding that growth), especially given the previously described difficulties in establishing consistent technical criteria.

Certainly, state practices regarding the pre-referral screening process may be a product of many variables. Factors such as the size of the state, the magnitude and geographic distribution of the potential commitment universe, and the vagaries of each state's legal and political landscape all contribute in some form to the choices that states make in this regard. However, considering the capacity for organizational structure and incentives to drive costs and policy utilization, further comparative review of state practices in this area, analyzing both efficiency and policy outputs, appears warranted.

Legal Systems

Regarding funding for legal systems, states adopting civil commitment laws are faced with a series of choices regarding the distribution of the cost burden and the level of supplemental resources that will be provided to prosecutors, public defenders, and the courts for the processing of cases. These choices may have much to do with the rates at which commitments are pursued and the efficiency with which cases flow through the system.[27]

Of the six states examined in this study, California has established the most significant level of financial commitment to its legal system. Specifically, the state has created an open-ended mechanism permitting counties to recoup SVP-related costs, resulting in an annual cost of

27 Although prosecutors would likely be reticent to admit that an SVP filing decision was based on concerns over issues of cost, at least one survey conducted in Minnesota indicates that resource allocation may figure in to the calculus employed by prosecutors when considering potential cases (Minnesota Dept. of Corrections, 2000).

between $9 and $10 million per year, and perhaps more. In terms of relative magnitude, Washington is not far behind – its SVP cases are handled through specialized units within the Attorney General's office and in the King County Prosecutors office, at an annual cost of over $4 million.[28]

In each of these cases, it appears that systems are aligned in a fashion that provides active support to the application of the policy. Where the systems diverge is that Washington's reimbursement is based on annual legislative appropriations, whereas California's system of funding remains essentially an open-ended entitlement. Accordingly, the structural incentives to exercise discretion in case selection are fundamentally different. This may at least partially explain the fact that Washington prosecutors have filed cases on roughly 41% of the referrals they have received to date, whereas California prosecutors have filed cases on 77%. It should be noted, however, that California's case filing rates have shown a rather sustained decline in recent years, indicating that county prosecutors are becoming progressively more selective despite being insulated from issues of cost.

One additional state to examine in this regard is Florida, where the applicable aspects of the justice system depend exclusively on state appropriations. On a comparative basis, funds that have been earmarked for SVP program implementation within Florida's justice system are substantially lower than those provided in Washington or California. It is therefore likely that a significant portion of the SVP workload is being handled by prosecutors and public defenders through deployment of general resources. While this seems to have had no

---

28 As described in Appendix A, Washington's Governor recently proposed eliminating state reimbursement for these costs, and requiring counties to contract directly with the Attorney General to handle SVP cases on their behalf. Beyond the immediate budget savings, this move would have likely resulted in a "chilling effect" on new case filings, reducing state costs on the custody and treatment end as well. The measure was withdrawn prior to reaching full legislative review.

impact on decisions to file – Florida prosecutors have submitted petitions on all but 14 of the 623 referrals received from DCF through June 2002 – it appears to have had a substantial effect on the timely processing of cases, as reflected by the over 350 individuals detained awaiting trial as of that date, and by the time-to-trial data presented in the preceding section.

Summary: Operational Viability of Case Selection Process

In sum, the case selection process appears to be fairly robust from an organizational perspective, with key roles and decision rules adapting over time to effectuate commitment. Moreover, resource demands for case screening and prosecution appear to stabilize over time, and are generally met through either direct appropriations or other means. Working within technical limits, and with the general support of the courts, states have generally been able to structure means to screen, select, and pursue commitment on cases deemed to meet SVP criteria.

Three key areas of caution emerge from this portion of the analysis. First, the technical limitations noted throughout this analysis persist, resulting in the continuing lack of meaningful standards to assess whether states are "hitting their target." While many states have shown more "selective" screening outputs (e.g. lower referral rates), it remains unclear whether this may be attributed to more effective screening of inappropriate cases or to indiscriminate responses to particular organizational or resource restrictions.

Second, as the case of Florida has indicated, effective operation of civil commitment process requires that resources be appropriately balanced across systems. The state's early focus on problems with its initial gatekeeping system, while effective in cleaning up its screening backlog, produced an overburdened court system, potentially affecting the state's ability to refer new cases into the system. Additionally, as we will examine in the next section, the backlog has severely taxed DCF facilities that must accommodate a growing proportion of non-committed detainees in addition to its committed population.

Third and finally, the alignment of incentives and provision of resources across systems remains a pivotal link in the design of SVP civil commitment policies. Particular areas of caution include the potential impact of prosecutor funding levels on decisions to file and the placement of initial screening (and in turn the "key to the front door") in the hands of agencies charged with the custody and treatment of SVP's.

ANALYSIS OF CUSTODY AND TREATMENT PROVISIONS

As with the previous section, this portion of the operational analysis begins with a review of general operational indicators, and examines the organizational and resource issues associated with custody and treatment. Key findings and issues are summarized in Table 11.

General Operational Indicators

This portion of the analysis reviews two sets of indicators that have a potentially significant effect on policy viability – population trends and indicators of treatment participation and progress.

Regarding population levels, all states examined show a pattern of sustained population growth over time, produced by a steady stream of new detainees and commitments and a relatively negligible number of system discharges. Yet while the charts on the following pages invariably reflect consistent cumulative population growth over time, they also show variation across states in both the overall rate of growth and in the ratio of detained to committed individuals. Of the states noted, California has demonstrated a slowing rate of overall rate of growth and a stabilizing number of pre-commitment detainees; Florida and Washington, in contrast, show patterns of accelerated growth over time, and a growing number of detainees; and Minnesota, which had at one point experienced a significant moderating trend, witnessed a surge in commitment activity beginning in 2003, for reasons referenced in the preceding section.

Table 11: Summary of Custody and Treatment Analysis

	Operational Indicators	**Organizational Factors**	**Resource Factors**
General Findings	Census levels steadily increase across states; Committed-Detainee proportion generally increases over time; Tx participation and progress remains limited across all states examined	Custody and tx provisions secondary to commitment process during initial policy planning; Relative agency roles (mental health, corrections) tend to evolve, with correctional involvement diminishing over time; States begin w/ existing facilities but almost invariably gravitate toward stand-alone programs.	Most resource-intensive aspect of SVP civil commitment policies; Program costs compound over time, due to growing population, legal requirements, and shift to standalone facilities; Greater spending on services does not guarantee greater treatment participation and progress.
Policy Viability Supports	Some states showing slowing rate of population growth and modest rates of treatment participation	Mental health agencies eventually find means to carve out a place for SVP programs, and construct viable coalitions of support; Programs provide area of growth for state mental health programs	States have demonstrated willingness to fund SVP program cost increases; States have invested considerably in SVP facility infrastructure
Policy Viability Threats	Population subject to compounding effect due to continued inflow of new commitments and negligible number of system discharges; Relatively few individuals in latter stages of treatment	Low rates of treatment success, and growing proportion of SVP's to traditional mental health patients, may threaten to undermine therapeutic missions of mental health agencies and alienate key constituencies	Treatment programs' low "return on investment" may erode funding stability over time

The observed trends in Washington and Florida may be linked fundamentally to the systems of case selection just explored. In the case of Washington, the relative growth in both the committed and detained population may reflect a growing "comfort level" with civil commitment on the part of screeners, prosecutors, and courts following the tentative restraint that characterized the policy's introduction. In the case of Florida, the mounting size of the detainee population and relatively modest growth of the committed group (at an average rate of approximately 2-3 new commitments per month) reflects the significant case backlog within that state's legal system as explored in the prior section.

Figure 6: SVP Committed and Detained Populations for Selected States

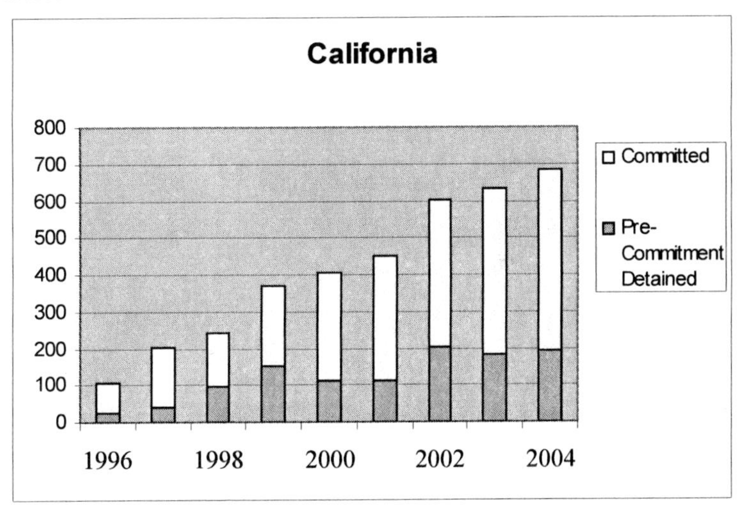

Figure 6: SVP Committed and Detained Populations for Selected States (CONTINUED)

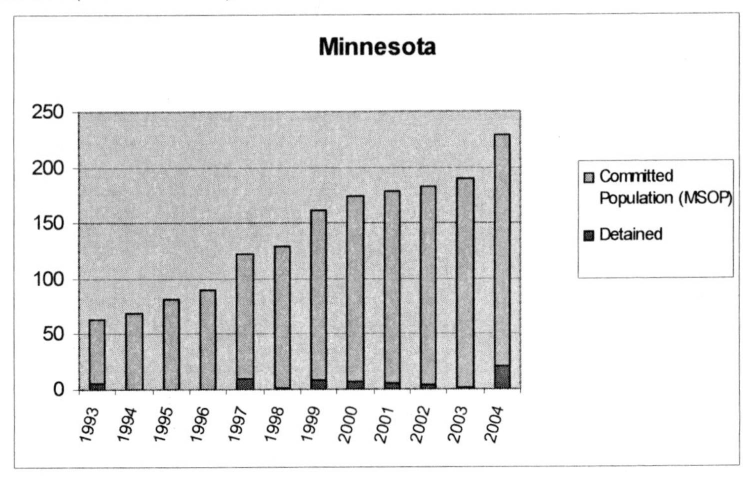

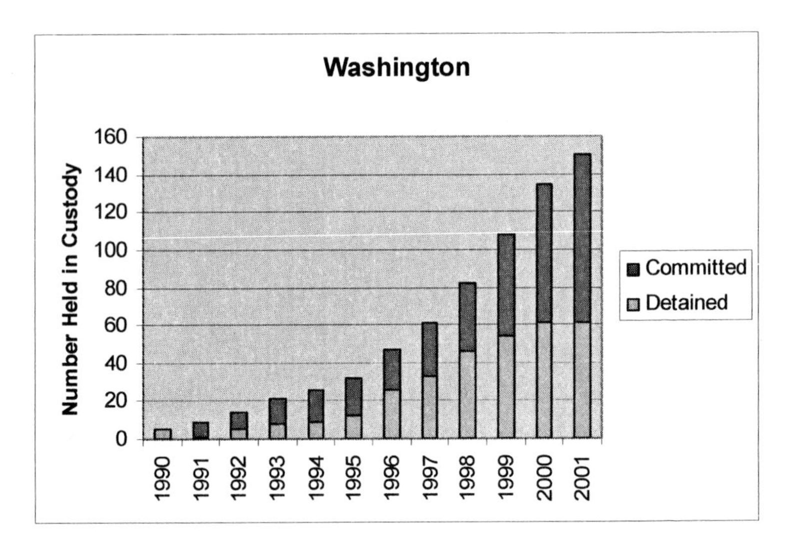

Figure 6: SVP Committed and Detained Populations for Selected States (CONTINUED)

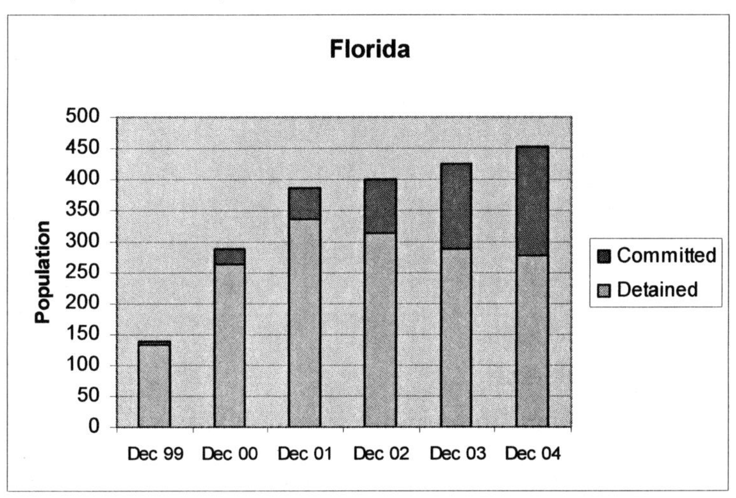

Regarding treatment participation and progress, the charts presented in Appendix C indicate that some states have achieved modest success in engaging individuals in treatment, while others have not achieved such results. The Minnesota, Washington, and Wisconsin programs have developed and maintained treatment participation rates of between 75 and 80 percent, and also have generated a small but growing number of individuals in latter stages of treatment progress. California, in contrast, has had a more modest record of treatment progress, with 80% of its population not actively engaged in treatment and very few in latter stages of treatment.[29]

Although levels of treatment participation and progress may indeed be valid measures of program effectiveness, two factors indicate that these data should be interpreted with caution.

---

[29] Florida's record in this regard remains difficult to gauge, due to both the program's relative immaturity and the disproportionate ratio of detainees in its population. Treatment progress data was not available for the Kansas program.

First, it remains unclear whether treatment participation and progress may be affected by case selection factors – that is, a "creaming" effect. As a theoretical matter, our conceptual analysis revealed that the SVP population – if truly reflecting the most incorrigibly dangerous -- should be extremely resistant to treatment. Coupled with the relative subjectivity and variability of commitment standards, it remains a possibility that those who demonstrate treatment progress in certain states simply might not have met the commitment threshold in others. Viewed in this context, California's low treatment progress numbers may paradoxically reflect a more appropriately selective screening and commitment process than that in place in the other states.

Second, treatment progress itself remains an elusive concept, may be operationalized differently across states, and may have little to do with potential for release. At least one program – Wisconsin – was forced to revise its treatment standards several years into the policy, after policymakers determined that individuals were progressing too rapidly through the stages of its program and were nearing release eligibility. Moreover, as we will see shortly, states across the board have encountered considerable obstacles to release upon treatment completion, rendering the concept of "treatment progress" incidental to broader release decisions.

Organizational Assessment

States have taken varying approaches to the management of their custody and treatment programs, ranging from direct provision by a single agency to approaches involving multiple agencies and contracted service providers. A review of the case studies, however, reveals at certain general themes and patterns, notably:

- A comparatively limited initial focus on this aspect of the policy;
- Patterns of shifting roles, especially regarding correctional agencies; and

- A seemingly inevitable migration from shared facilities to "standalone" program facilities dedicated to the SVP population.

Initial Policy Focus

Custody and treatment, despite presenting significant implementation challenges, has tended to receive relatively little attention during the SVP civil commitment policy adoption process. While substantial legislative attention is focused on identifying dangerous individuals and establishing the grounds that permit the state to retain custody (i.e. the case selection process), the matter of what to do with the population once committed has generally been addressed on a post-hoc basis.

Examining the case studies presented in Appendix A, two key factors point to the relative lack of initial policy focus on the issues of custody and treatment. First, while the statutes go to tremendous lengths to detail the processes for commitment, the issue of custody and treatment is typically addressed only perfunctorily in statutory language. This fact is not at all surprising, considering that the catalyzing forces behind the adoption of SVP civil commitment laws were focused more fundamentally on the policy's incapacitative potential, and not upon any rehabilitative ideal.

Second, with the exception of Minnesota, which adopted its civil commitment policy based on an existing program and law, each of the states reviewed in this analysis experienced significant implementation confusion (and in some cases turmoil) connected to the treatment aspects of their programs. In Washington, we see a program facing a decade-long injunction connected to the adequacy of its treatment program. In Wisconsin, we have a program that jettisoned its treatment program and its clinical director in 1997, after concluding that committed individuals were progressing too rapidly through its program without making the requisite behavioral changes (Taylor, 2001). In Kansas, we have observed a program experiencing early turnover of key management staff and mission conflicts between the Department of Social and Rehabilitative Services and the Department of Corrections (DesLauriers & Gardner, 1999). In California, we witnessed considerable early confusion related to the respective roles of the correctional and mental health departments, related in part to statutory ambiguity. And finally, in Florida, we have seen a program that has struggled to develop a viable privatization model for its service, and has also been faced with pending litigation over the adequacy of its treatment program ("Canupp v. Liberty Behavioral Health," 2004).

With very little explicit guidance (and in cases such as California's, initial conflicting policy directives regarding agency roles), states embarking on SVP civil commitment have thus been required to build their custodial and treatment programs from the "ground-up." The result has typically been an assessment of needs after the policy has been adopted, sometimes pursued by the courts (as with Washington), sometimes undertaken through legislative or other directive (such as Florida), and often leading to a series of uncontemplated requirements and resources.

Shifting Roles

The dual requirements of providing a secure custodial environment that is also conducive to treatment present a critical set of organizational challenges for SVP civil commitment programs. While the "dangerousness" designation and the significant prior criminal involvement of the committed population requires a level of security befitting a prison system, the civil nature of the law and the attendant treatment requirements preclude any provisions that might be deemed punitive in effect. Moreover, although state mental health departments do typically have some experience operating facilities for dangerous persons with mental illness, SVP's as a general rule neither meet the diagnostic profile of the "traditional" psychiatric inpatient population, nor are they likely to respond to existing pharmacological treatments for mental illness. Given these circumstances, and further considering the general lack of policy direction cited above, it is not surprising that agency roles in the provision of SVP custody and treatment appear to shift over time.

While states generally choose to involve their respective mental health authorities in the design and management of treatment programming, most also initially invoke the services of correctional agencies in facility operations, custody, and security. Washington, Kansas, and Florida, for example, each initially adopted models in which the mental health agencies assumed responsibility for treatment, with custody and facility services provided through the prison system. California's legislature apparently had the same idea, mandating in its enabling legislation that the Department of Mental Health operate the treatment program in a facility operated by the Department of Corrections.

In all of these cases, however, the role of correctional agencies appears to diminish over time, with mental health authorities eventually assuming management of facility operations, either directly or through contracted providers. In Washington, Kansas, and Florida, the programs have remained on the grounds of correctional complexes, although the role of correctional authorities has effectively been reduced to the function of perimeter security. In the case of California, a 1996 revision of the original legislation effectively removed the California Department of Corrections completely from any facility role, permitting the DMH to locate the program at Atascadero State Hospital, an public inpatient psychiatric facility.

These diminishing correctional roles may be attributed to a variety of factors. Washington's shift likely had much to do with the ongoing litigation surrounding the conditions and scope of that state's treatment program, and the attendant need for the state to distance itself from any appearance of punitive intent. In the case of Kansas, as in other states, program managers have cited potential mission conflicts between mental health and correctional agencies (DesLauriers & Gardner, 1999). In both Florida and California, it is likely that budgetary considerations may have had some bearing on the organizational shifts – Florida's Department of Children and Families, has managed to gradually ratchet down its annual payments to state's Corrections Department by transferring functions to its contracted provider, and

California's Department of Mental Health appears to have gained significant budgetary windfalls by having new SVP beds funded at the state's loaded rate for inpatient psychiatric care.[30]

Migration to Standalone Facilities

In all six states examined, the SVP population initially shared facility space with either correctional or traditional psychiatric inpatients. Over time, however, in a common pattern observed across these states, the SVP population with its rapid rate of growth gradually began "crowding out" the traditional populations with which they were housed.

In response both to this phenomenon and to the logistical challenges arising from the difficulties of mingling the group with correctional or psychiatric inpatient populations, the states inevitably gravitated towards standalone facilities. Although the timing and specific strategies have varied, all six states examined have proceeded down the path of transitioning their SVP programs from shared facilities to free-standing dedicated sites.

Washington, Wisconsin, and Minnesota have each embarked on their third phases of facility expansion, Florida relocated its services from its initial location to a dedicated 600-bed facility, California has activated its brand new 1,500-bed SVP facility, and Kansas has constructed a new mental health facility for its correctional population, relinquishing that population's prior home entirely to the state's growing population of SVP's.

As examined in the upcoming resource assessment, legislatures have generally supported and provided funding for the shift to standalone facilities, in spite of both significant capital costs and increased operating costs due to diminished economies of scale. Hence, despite the relative lack of initial policy focus on custody and treatment, it appears clear that states indeed have been willing to address demands as they emerge.

---

[30] California's budget arrangement is described in greater detail in Appendix D.

Resource Assessment

As illustrated by the figure below, custody and treatment represent the most significant proportion of SVP program costs. [31] In contrast with case processing expenses, which eventually may level off or perhaps decline in accordance with relatively stable workloads, custody and treatment costs are more likely to increase incrementally with the population, compounding resource demand and increasing these proportions over time. Considering these factors, this portion of the analysis potentially looms large in this study's broader assessment of the viability and sustainability of SVP civil commitment policies.

Figure 7: Allocation of Washington SVP Program Costs

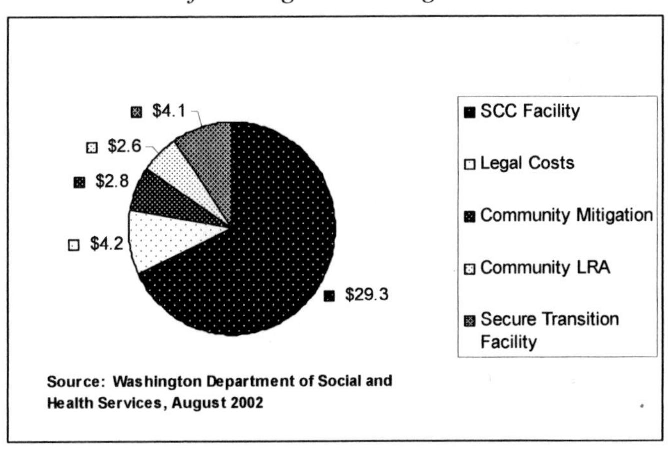

Below, we consider custody and treatment resources by focusing on two types of investment – patterns of investment in **operating resources**, which encompass basic custodial costs, treatment program costs, and recurring costs associated with facility operation and

[31] Washington data is presented for illustration purposes, due to the fact that legal expenses associated with commitment flow through and are tracked by the Department of Social and Health Services, presenting the most complete overall picture of cost allocation across systems. Cost data for other states is included in Appendix C.

maintenance; and patterns of **capital investment**, generally associated with facility expansion or renovation to meet programmatic requirements. After considering each of these factors, the assessment concludes by briefly considering patterns of investment as indicators of the policy's general viability.

Operating Resource Investment

Stripped to a basic level, the operating resources required to operate SVP civil commitment custody and treatment programs are a function of the number of individuals requiring service (e.g. number of required "service units") and by the level of service that the state establishes as necessary to meet fundamental policy goals. Regarding the former, our fundamental interest lies in the relationship between population and costs, and how state resource allocation patterns have responded to the growing SVP population. As for the latter, it is appropriate to ask what comprises "adequate" levels of service and, as a corollary to this, whether treatment program spending produces a "return on investment" sufficient to justify its continuation.

Earlier in this chapter, we established that states have uniformly seen a steady growth in the number of individuals committed under SVP laws. This development, as indicated in the charts presented on the following page, has yielded a steadily increasing allocation of resources on the part of all states examined in this study.

Figure 8: Custody and Treatment Spending and Population Levels in Selected States

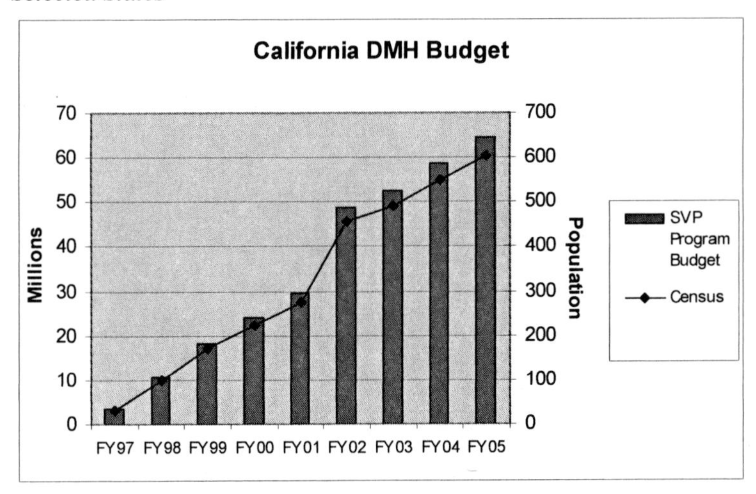

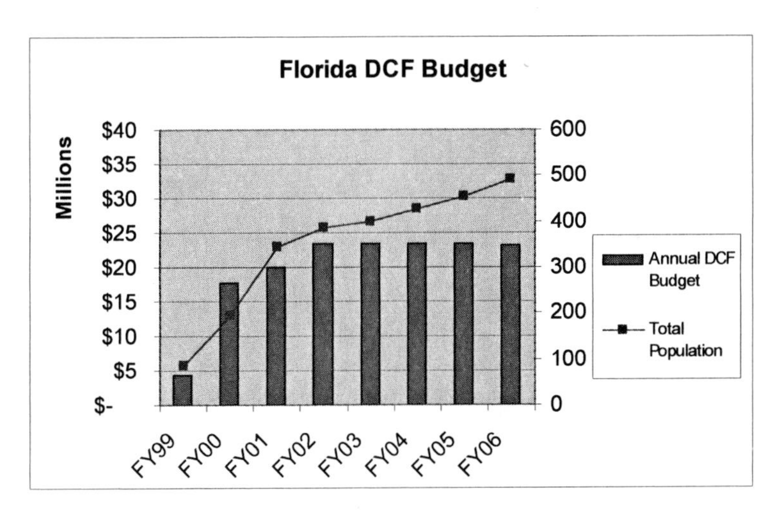

Figure 8: Custody and Treatment Spending and Population Levels in Selected States (CONTINUED)

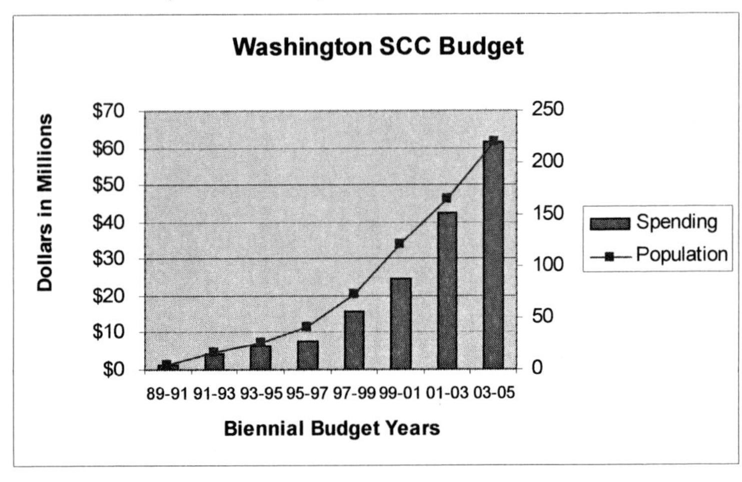

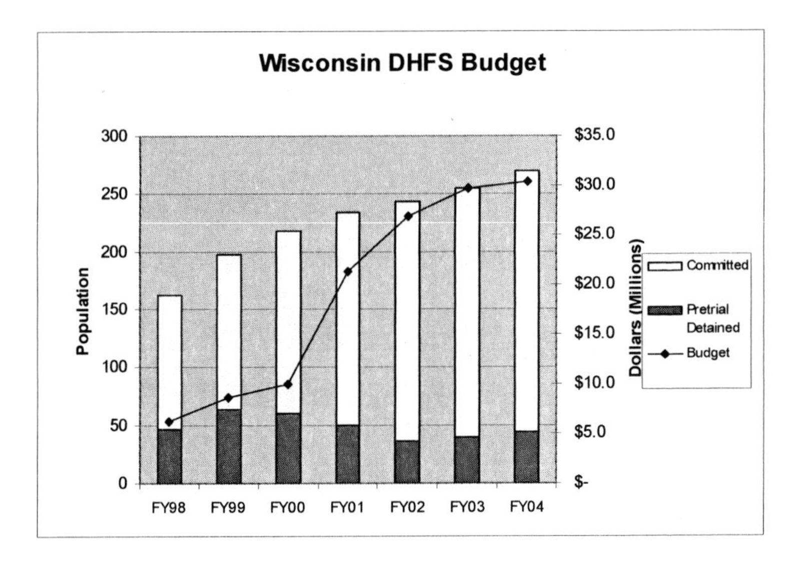

The charts illustrate three patterns of particular note – the sustained and significant growth observed in Washington and California; the "surge" seen in Wisconsin in FY 2001; and the leveling of resources in Florida during FY 2002.

The growth in Washington may be attributed to two main factors – the growing use of its policy in the years since 1996, and the demands set forth by the *Turay* injunction that has driven substantial program reform since its inception in 1994. Notably, the Court in this case began to accrue fines against the state in 1998 – fines that have been held in abeyance pending the state's success in addressing perceived inadequacies in its treatment system. Concurrent with this court action, the state's spending on custody and treatment may be observed as growing at a faster rate than its SVP population.

In California, the data indicates a direct 1:1 relationship between resource growth and population growth – a pattern that may be attributed to that state's funding model that links legislative appropriations directly to the size of the SVP population under the care of the state's Department of Mental Health (DMH). As revealed by a detailed analysis presented in Appendix C, these appropriations are likely independent of actual incremental costs of care, producing a growing DMH budgetary windfall for every newly committed SVP. This arrangement, coupled with the fact that California DMH also maintains a good deal of control over the system's "front door" (in contrast with most other states), presents particular questions regarding the impact of budgetary incentives on programmatic decisions, particularly when viewed in the context of the agency's need to offset losses in operating revenue associated with its decline in the "traditional" inpatient psychiatric population under its care.

The case of Wisconsin indicates a substantial surge in its spending levels in the year following the opening of the state's new SVP facility at Sand Ridge. Similar patterns, which are likely attributable to lost economies of scale, may be observed in Minnesota and Washington in the years following their moves to new facilities. Given that states inevitably seem to gravitate towards standalone status as programs develop, this factor is particularly salient to an assessment of the policies' resource viability.

Florida -- the one state that appears to have capped appropriations to its SVP civil commitment program – remains the newest and the least developed. Whether Florida will succeed in limiting its cost growth without inviting litigation remains to be seen. If it succeeds, it may certainly represent a model for other states to follow. However, the state's rapidly growing SVP population, coupled with its reliance on a private, for-profit treatment vendor that was the sole respondent to its most recent solicitation, is likely to place considerable financial pressure on the state as time goes on. At this stage, there is little evidence to suggest that Florida will be able to avoid future cost growth without either curtailing commitment rates levels or exposing the state to costly litigation.

Earlier in this analysis, we established that states, either through their own initiative or through litigation, have generally been required to provide a constitutionally adequate treatment program and to maintain an appropriately therapeutic environment, despite evidence that a considerable segment of the SVP population is unlikely to respond to available treatment modalities.

In this context, it is logical to critically examine the "return on investment" (ROI) connected to treatment programming. More specifically, given the high costs just described, and further considering the significant technical limitations associated with likely treatment efficacy, what specific beneficial results may be tied to investment in custody and treatment?

On a very basic level, the "return on investment" may be viewed simply as states' ability to pursue their SVP civil commitment policies and to accrue the associated public safety benefits. That is, investment in the treatment program at a minimally adequate level is part of the general cost of doing business. Viewed in this context, ROI has no specific relationship to the outcomes of treatment – whether individuals receiving the service improve over time is merely incidental – the criteria for "success" is simply the program's ability to withstand legal challenges and permit the policy to move forward.

However, given the range of state spending levels on their treatment programs, and further considering indications that SVP's typically become stalled in the system, we must also focus on the relative efficacy of treatment program investment – specifically, do higher levels of spending necessarily translate into more positive results?

The general finding, in a nutshell, is that significant resources are expended on SVP civil commitment treatment, often with very little to show in the way of appreciable treatment progress. While some states, such as Minnesota and Washington, have demonstrated limited success in moving individuals through their phased programs, these programs have remained extremely limited in their ability to effectuate release. Across other systems examined, the majority of committed individuals continue to either refuse to participate, or remain involved in the most basic phases of treatment. The most striking example is California, which ranks among the most expensive programs in the analysis, and has a mere 4% of its population beyond the second phase of its 4-phase program. Accordingly, the limited efficacy of treatment for SVP's may be viewed as having a potentially profound effect on the overall viability of the policies.

<u>Facility Investment and its Effects</u>

One pattern that cuts across all six states examined here is the inevitable demand for facility expansion. Washington, Wisconsin, and Minnesota have each embarked on their <u>third phases</u> of facility expansion. California has commenced construction on a 1,500-bed facility at a cost of $349 million. Florida, after a series of fits and starts, appears ready to embark on its plans for a 600-bed facility that is likely to be at capacity by the time it is eventually constructed. Kansas, one of the fastest growing programs on a proportional basis, is on the verge of crowding out the "traditional" population in its host facility, requiring construction of a new site to house those patients.

In terms of assessing resource viability, the implications of new facility investment are threefold. First and most apparently, states invariably incur significant capital construction costs associated with implementation of their civil commitment policies. Further, the tendency of "early adopting" states to return to the trough every few years for a new infusion of facility expansion resources indicates that facility demands may be easily underestimated.[32]

Second, beyond the direct costs associated with facility construction, the seemingly inevitable shift from "piggy-back" to "standalone" status for SVP facilities appears to bring with it substantial increases to operating costs, as indicated most notably in our analyses of Wisconsin and California.

Third and finally, facility investment may also carry a range of less tangible implications for the implementation of SVP civil commitment policies. On a programmatic level, one must ask whether capacity expansion and investment encourages use of the policy, especially in cases such as California, where the "gatekeeping" agency reaps budgetary windfalls from population increases, and where the size of the Department of Mental Health's planned 1,500-bed facility has encountered particular skepticism among legislative analysts (California Legislative Analyst's Office, 2001). On the political front, the continued patterns of facility investment in states such as Minnesota, Wisconsin, Washington, and California may be viewed as an indicator of the policy's significant level of support from lawmakers and the executive. It may also, under certain circumstances, generate renewed political support for the policy by mobilizing affected constituencies, as in the case of Coalinga, California which lobbied hard for the state's SVP facility and the jobs that it stands to bring to the community.

---

[32] In fact, as noted above, Florida's planned 600-bed facility is likely to be full by the time construction is completed, indicating that states with newer policies are likely subject to similar under-estimation of needs. Only in California, where the facility's cost and size has in fact been criticized as being <u>too</u> far-reaching, does under-estimation appear not to be a factor.

<u>Investment and Policy Viability</u>

As noted above, the extent of resource support over time represents a critical indicator of both the policy's relative level of political support and its ability to withstand socioeconomic change – variables directly related to the policy's long-term viability. Given that SVP civil commitment policies generally emerged during a time of economic growth and associated state budget surpluses, their level of sustenance during the current period of economic contractions becomes an especially critical variable.

Through the case studies, we see that legislatures and governors have shown a fairly high level of support for the policies, even in the face of growing costs and shrinking state revenues. In Wisconsin, the program was exempted from across-the board cuts affecting human service programs in the state, even following a near-doubling of the SVP program's budget in the past two years. In Washington, the legislature has gone to extraordinary lengths to invest the resources necessary to comply with court-ordered requirements and keep the program viable. While the Governor recently proposed targeted reductions of state funding, those proposals were essentially "dead on arrival" in the legislature. In California, a legislature and governor facing a $17 billion budget deficit in 2003 continued to provide the DMH with its caseload-driven funding for treatment services, and invested over a third of a billion dollars in a new facility that will dramatically increase overall operating costs. All states have invested, or are planning to invest, in significant facility expansions to accommodate the SVP population, and all except one have provided the resources necessary to keep pace with a continually expanding population.

Ironically, the one state that appears to have taken steps to pro-actively address mounting costs by freezing appropriations may be the one least likely to afford it. Florida, which funnels the majority of its resources through a private vendor, is highly affected by market forces beyond its direct control. The failure of its recent solicitation to produce any bids beyond that of the incumbent vendor is likely to result in substantial costs above and beyond funded levels. The one means available to reduce costs – reduction of service levels – is likely to compromise a program that remains in a developmental stage, potentially exposing the state to the type of court-ordered future costs experienced in Washington. The odds of such litigation in Florida are further supported by the state's continued lack of structured release provisions, and the pending lawsuit in Illinois – a program also relying on the state's vendor, Liberty Healthcare ("Hargett et. al. v. Baker et. al.," 2002).

Further, the impact of the limited "return on investment" noted above on the policies' ongoing viability may be profound. The great unknown factor in this equation is how the standards applied by the courts and lawmakers will shift over time if progressively expensive treatment programs fail to produce a greater rate of "success." On the legal front, the current parameters of "constitutionally adequate" treatment may be subject to revision, with the courts paying increasing attention to programs' track records. This, in turn, may drive costs even higher as states are forced to further raise the bar on treatment standards. On the legislative front, it may simply be a matter of time before policy makers begin to question the magnitude of expenditures in the context of the comparatively meager results. This, in turn, may gradually erode the base of political support that the programs have relied on for their growth and sustenance.

Summary: Operational Viability of Custody and Treatment

This portion of the analysis has identified several key issues potentially affecting the viability of SVP civil commitment policies.

First, despite the fact that custody and treatment creates the largest portion of the policy's resource demand, we have see that this portion of the policy receives relatively little initial policy attention. In turn, the demands and program provisions or generally addressed on a post-hoc basis, and in some instances driven by litigation or the threat of litigation.

Second, the technical limitations cited in the conceptual review have a very real effect on the organizational and resource demands associated with the policy. In contrast with the case selection process, in which the wide berth granted by the courts mitigates the effects of technological limitations, the limited efficacy of sex offender treatment technology has a great deal to do with how cases flow (or fail to flow) through the system. This, in turn, profoundly affects the rate of population growth, presents certain threats to organizational sustainability, and steadily compounds the aggregate resource demands associated with implementing the policy.

Third and finally, although custody and treatment program costs have to date been politically well-sustained, it is not clear that this pattern will continue. Certainly, many states have exhibited a general willingness to invest in new facilities, and to appropriate funds to meet legal requirements and to accommodate population increases. Yet considering projected cost growth, mounting strains on state budgets, and the marginal effectiveness of treatment spending in promoting change within the target population, it remains quite likely that SVP custody and treatment costs will invite growing scrutiny in the years ahead.

ANALYSIS OF TRANSITION AND RELEASE PROVISIONS

The operational model's third and final element involves the provision of transition and release. The related findings of the operational analysis are summarized in Table 12 on the following page.

Table 12: Operational Analysis Summary – Transition and Release Systems

	Operational Indicators	Organizational Factors	Resource Factors
General Findings	Supervised release and/or less restrictive alternative programs utilized on a limited basis System discharges remain rare occurrence, even in states with the "best" treatment programs	All studied states with exception of Florida operate some system of supervised release and/or less restrictive alternative Housing represents major challenge to LRA/SR programming SR and LRA provisions vary based on case characteristics, but generally entail significant organizational resources	LRA and SR costs highly variable, based on individual needs and legal requirements LRA and SR costs-per-individual may far exceed costs of custody and treatment, due to both legal/political requirements and to limited economies of scale
Policy Viability Supports	N/A	Ability of some states to develop of LRA and SR programs as adjuncts to treatment programs	Effective transition programming may eventually produce lower cost alternative to total confinement
Policy Viability Threats	N/A	Risk aversion among those empowered to effectuate release Logistical barriers to facility siting and program operations, stemming from political difficulty of "selling" idea of release	Potential for costly legal mandates associated with transition and release programming Significant costs associated with rigorous supervision of released SVP's in response to political costs of policy failure

General Operational Indicators

While some individuals in the states examined manage to have their commitments overturned on legal grounds, release through structured progression through treatment remains an exceedingly rare occurrence. The pie chart below, based on data provided in mid-2002 by the Minnesota Department of Human Services, illustrates this phenomenon quite clearly. The figure indicates that only one individual out of approximately 180 admitted to the program, and out of 28 discharged since 1995, has been provisionally released from the state's treatment program, with all other program "discharges" involving either trans-institutional placements or death. These data are especially notable considering that Minnesota's treatment program and transitional programming systems are among the most well-developed of the states included in this study.

Figure 9: Disposition of Minnesota System Discharges, 1995-2002

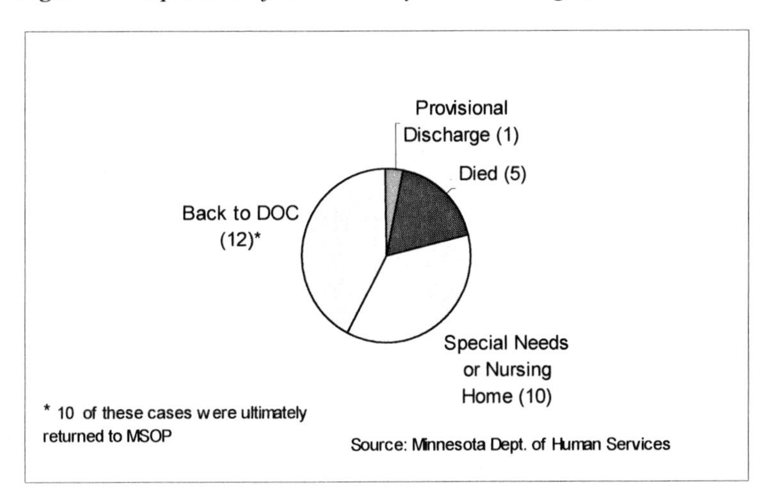

Although the data from other states is fairly incomplete, it does appear that the pattern observed in Minnesota likely holds true in other states as well. Wisconsin, while maintaining it's the number of individuals in supervised release status at between 10 and 14 individuals since at least 1998, reports that about one third of these individuals have typically been held in custody while awaiting community housing, and none have graduated to unsupervised status. Washington, whose LRA program has been developed under the close scrutiny of the federal court, reported 3 individuals in their secure community transition facility as of April 2003 (Washington Dept. of Social and Health Services, 2003), and ## on LRA. California, the largest commitment program in the nation, had not yet released one treatment graduate into its community release program as of March 2003 (Konrad, 2003). Florida, which remains the only state in the study that has yet to develop a structured program for transitional release, had released five committed individuals who have been determined by the courts to no longer meet commitment criteria as of March 2003 (Florida Department of Children and Families, 2003).

Organizational Assessment

As referenced in the conceptual analysis, the transition stage represents a critical link in the continuum that characterizes the relapse prevention models employed in most sex offender treatment programs. Moreover, the courts have made it clear that the "light at the end of the tunnel" represents a vital component to the provision of constitutionally adequate treatment. The key organizational challenges associated with transition and release therefore relate to the required balance between the programmatic goal of community re-integration and the policy's fundamental public safety mandate.

<u>Housing and Program Provisions</u>

The first significant challenge facing states involves the development of geographically and programmatically suitable housing for individuals in transitional release. Considering that SVP policies have commonly emerged from the pending release of sex offenders into particular communities, it is not at all surprising that siting of transitional facilities produces considerable organizational challenges.

States with more active supervised release programs – notably Wisconsin and Minnesota – have developed facilities adjacent to their treatment programs, allowing these programs to take advantage of existing program resources.

Washington, while also establishing a Secure Community Transition Facility (SCTF) on McNeil Island (the same Department of Corrections complex that houses the state's secure SVP unit), has further been required by *Turay* to establish community-based SCTF facilities as well.[33] Following a multi-year planning process, and pursuant to legislative action, Washington ultimately developed a series of complex siting guidelines and community mitigation strategies in response to the court order. As part of this process, the state mandated that counties with five or more committed individuals to site and plan for SCTF facilities of between 3 and 15 beds, and permitted the state to assume the siting process should the counties fail to comply (Washington Dept. of Social and Health Services, 2002).

The second key area presenting organizational challenges to transition and release efforts involves the provision of appropriate supervision and treatment. As mentioned above, co-locating transitional programs with total confinement institutions represents one potential strategy, although as illustrated in the case of Washington, states may be limited in their ability to apply this approach. The alternative – a decentralized approach that disburses programs to multiple locations throughout a state – requires developing multiple networks of treatment providers and supervision resources. Thus far, none of the states examined have succeeded in developing such a

---

[33] Although some states have managed to develop such co-located transitional programs, the political dynamics of constructing total confinement institutions (which offer reasonable protection to the surrounding community) are fundamentally different from those associated with transitional release facilities (which involve some measure of interaction between facility residents and the community).

network, although California appears to have embarked on such an effort as of early 2003 (Konrad, 2003).

A Cautious Approach

One thing that does seem clear is that states to date have generally employed a cautious, tentative approach to transitional services, placing substantial restrictions on individuals who are deemed eligible for release. Those states studied with the most experience in this area – Minnesota and Wisconsin – have each constructed dedicated SR facilities that are effectively extensions of their SVP treatment programs, although neither has succeeded in transitioning individuals back into the community in any significant manner.[34] Washington, operating under court orders to develop and implement a viable Less Restrictive Alternative (LRA) program, has experienced similarly limited success in this area. Further, the state's experiences thus far has indicated that transitional release program case plans may require exceptional measures to address community concerns, including 1:1 supervision for facility residents while working in the community, to supplemental police protection in the area surrounding the facility.

Perhaps the most vivid illustration of states' ambivalence surrounding the release process may be found in the California case of Patrick Ghilotti, who in 2001 became the first committed SVP to successfully complete the state's treatment program .[35] Ghilotti's discharge was blocked by the state's mental health commissioner, who sought to overrule the opinions of treatment staff and independent evaluators recommending release. Although the courts ultimately determined that the commissioner acted beyond his statutory authority in blocking Ghilotti's discharge, the state was permitted to set forth a series of stringent terms and conditions for release. Ghilotti ultimately chose to remain committed rather than agree to the terms and

---

[34] It should be noted that one state not included in this study, Arizona, has also developed a significant supervised release program based on a similar model.

[35] The details of the Ghilotti case and its associated references may be found in the California narrative included as part of Appendix A.

conditions put forward by the state and accepted by the courts. While Ghillotti remains confined, a second individual nearing release in California at the time of this writing has had that release delayed as the state attempts to finalize its sources of community supervision and treatment (Konrad, 2003).

Resource Assessment

The resources associated with transition and release, while including the costs of legal proceedings, are heavily concentrated on costs associated with programming and facilities. Examining state experiences in this area, it appears that transition related costs are highly variable depending on individual case needs, and in many cases may in fact significantly exceed the costs of secure custody and treatment.

Regarding cost variability, Less Restrictive Alternative and/or Supervised Release service plans may include a range of provisions, up to and including 24-hour, one-to-one supervision. Beyond staffing and supervision, these costs are also dependent on such issues as available housing, community mitigation requirements, and ongoing treatment needs. A Wisconsin legislative fiscal bureau report notes that the cost in that state may range from $2,600 per month ($31K annually) to $10,800 per month ($130K annually) (Wisconsin Legislative Fiscal Bureau, 2001). Beyond the noted organizational issues associated with program implementation, the emergent volatility in resource requirements presents particular challenges to policy planners and implementers, that are likely to grow over time as more individuals approach release eligibility.

As for the magnitude of costs, it appears that LRA and SR programming can be extremely expensive, often far exceeding the costs of facility-based commitment. As the Washington experience has indicated, public safety concerns quite typically require extraordinary conditions of release that often exceed the costs of inpatient commitment. Figure 10, based on information provided by the

Washington Department of Human Services, compares the costs-per-person associated with incarceration, civil commitment, and the state's LRA, indicating that the average cost of community-based supervision may be greater than four times the cost of commitment.[36]

Figure 10: Washington's Relative Costs of Commitment and Transition

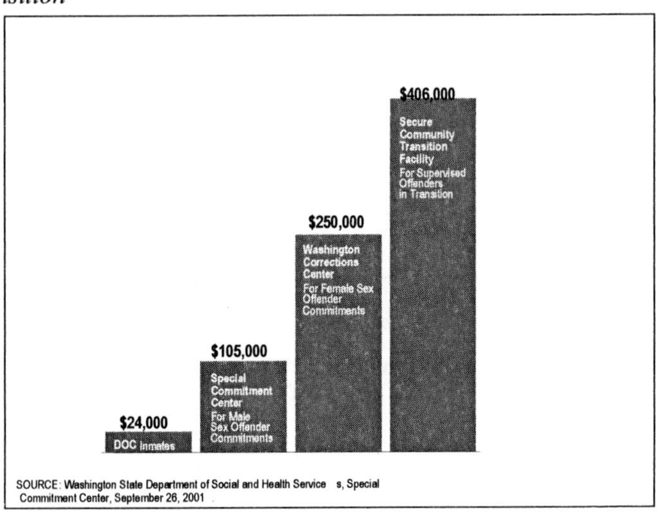

SOURCE: Washington State Department of Social and Health Services, Special Commitment Center, September 26, 2001

Summary: Operational Viability of Transition and Release

Considering the factors described above, the emergent challenge to the organizational viability of transition and release hinges on programs' capacity to balance individual treatment demands with the policies' fundamental public safety mandate. Specifically, **can transition and**

[36] These high costs are often associated with limited economies of scale as programs "ramp up" their supervised release programs. A 2003 report out of California indicates that the state plans to spend approximately $1 million in Fiscal 2004 to cover the costs of its new contracted supervised release program for SVP's, which as of March 2003 was planning for only one client (Associated Press, 2003).

release systems be structured to both create a viable means for release and to provide the requisite level of community protection?

Based on states' experience to date, it appears premature to draw firm conclusions surrounding this question. With the numbers of release eligible individuals comparatively small, LRA and SR programmatic demands have more typically driven by case-specific requirements than by any type of broader strategic focus. Accordingly, while some states are gradually gaining experience in this area, their capacity to develop viable and stable systems of community re-integration for committed SVP's remains a largely open question.

Despite this broader uncertainty, three key things do appear clear:

1. The demands for more structured systems of transition and release are likely to grow over time, as states are pressured by the courts to release committed SVP's nearing the end of their treatment;
2. The prevailing *modus operendi* for transition and release is one of caution, focusing first and foremost on community protection and only secondarily on facilitating pathways of societal re-integration for SVP's;
3. This cautious approach to community risk reduction comes with a substantial and highly unpredictable price tag, requiring resources that in many cases may in fact exceed the costs of commitment. The potential variability and magnitude of costs associated with housing, supervision and treatment for individuals in transition significantly is likely to complicate future planning and development.

Whether the prevailing risk-averse approach to transition and release will diminish over time, and whether it will continue to serve as an impediment to successful release programming remains to be seen. Ultimately, the operational viability of transition and release depends on whether programs can become more resource-efficient over time, without sacrificing public safety or (perhaps more critically) the *public perceptions* of public safety at the core of the policies' political rationale.

OPERATIONAL ANALYSIS SUMMARY

Table 13: Summary of Operational Viability

	Organizational Viability	Resource Viability
Case Selection	**Low-Moderate challenge** Variation in approaches, but states generally able to produce required outputs and gain organizational compliance	**Low-Moderate challenge** Moderate and fairly stable resource demands
Custody and Treatment	**Moderate-high challenge** Basic custodial functions fairly straightforward, but limited tx efficacy could undermine long-term organizational viability	**Significant challenge** Substantial and steadily growing resource demands
Transition and Release	**Significant challenge** Release anathema to policies' underlying rationale, and transitional programming presents substantial logistical and political challenges	**Significant challenge** Currently moderate overall demands, but high cost of entry and unpredictable unit costs

Reviewing the data presented throughout this operational analysis, SVP civil commitment's operational viability may be closely linked to the degree of focus that policymakers have placed on each of the policies' key functional areas.

The case selection process – or the means by which individuals are identified and committed – of the three areas examined, is most closely aligned with the policies' conceptual focus of incapacitating those who are deemed too dangerous to release into society. Accordingly, these processes are often delineated in detail through enabling statutory language, and are fairly stable over time. While states vary across certain structural characteristics, and while practice may be moderately complicated by particular legal and technical restrictions, case identification and commitment systems appear at least moderately sustainable from both an organizational and resource standpoint.

Systems of custody and treatment, in contrast, are typically addressed only perfunctorily in statutory language, are often initially developed in an ad-hoc fashion, and appear to evolve in reaction to emergent legal and operational demands. While these systems generally gravitate towards a state of organizational equilibrium, this is invariably accompanied by exponential growth in resource demands. Whether resources will remain sufficient to support the policies' ongoing implementation, and whether organizational stability can be retained in the face of constricting resources, present pivotal questions concerning the policies' long-range viability.

Transition and release systems remain the least organizationally developed aspects of SVP civil commitment policies – a fact that is not at all surprising, considering that the policies emerged out of powerful public demands to keep sexual predators **out** of the community, and not based on any particular interest in societal re-integration. This lack of structured organizational focus on transition and release, coupled with substantial resource demands associated with ensuring community protection when individuals are released, presents a further challenge to SVP civil commitment's operational viability.

CHAPTER 7

Summary and Conclusions

THE VIABILITY OF SVP CIVIL COMMITMENT POLICIES

This book and its associated analyses have aimed to provide an assessment of SVP civil commitment policies and their future viability, by critically examining the policies' range of activities and processes through technical, legal, organizational, and fiscal lenses.

The conceptual analysis identified several significant issues surrounding the policy's technical foundations, notably those concerned with predictions of risk and the efficacy of treatment technologies. In terms of case selection processes, these issues were largely mitigated by the finding that applicable technology, while imperfect, is generally to be "good enough" to meet fundamental legal standards. As long as commitment is based on an assumed purpose of treatment and a reasonable level of certainty regarding potential for re-offense, there appear to be few conceptual barriers to the commitment process. Regarding treatment and potential for release, however, the practical effects of technological limits were found to be much more significant. The prospective profile of the SVP population, limitations in treatment efficacy, reliance on static factors as the legal basis for commitment, and the potential for significant political barriers to release, all combine to create a system focused more on incapacitation than on working towards release, presenting substantial operational challenges.

The operational analysis shifted our focus to matters of organization and resources. In the organizational realm, we established that, despite variations in state practices, feasible organizational models do exist that can effectively support and promote the effective implementation of SVP civil commitment policies. These organizational strengths are confounded by two sets of limitations – technical limits, which affect all three stages of the policy, and resource limits. Deficiencies in enforceable and measurable technical standards also make the policies particularly prone to over-use, creating further resource demands.

A Matter of Resources

As indicated by the six case studies and throughout the conceptual and operational analyses, it appears that SVP civil commitment policies have generally delivered on their fundamental promise of protecting society from a subset of sexual offenders. States have succeeded in developing legally tenable and organizationally viable processes for commitment and maintenance of custody, despite certain technical limitations. Hence, considering legal, technical, and organizational issues in a vacuum, one may fairly conclude that SVP civil commitment policies are here to stay.

The matter of resources, however, stands to significantly complicate matters as time goes on. Notably, the policies generally came of age during the mid to late 1990's -- a time of unprecedented economic growth. During that period, states appeared willing to make considerable investments in programming and facilities, and in so doing bolstered the policies' organizational and legal foundations. Moreover, the limits of treatment technology have been rendered largely incidental by the fact that states have willingly funded population growth stemming from those limits.

Viewed in this context, one may argue that the policies have remained organizationally and legally viable precisely because states have generally been willing to make appropriate investments in facilities and treatment programming. Hence, while resource levels to date have generally proven capable of counteracting technical shortcomings and responding to legal and organizational demands, it remains to be seen whether the policies may unravel once those resources are no longer sustainable.

Avenues for Addressing Resource Viability

In the end, the question of resource allocation looms large in our assessment of whether SVP civil commitment policies will remain legally and organizationally viable. With the fundamental concepts and organization of SVP civil commitment policies apparently passing constitutional muster, mounting costs loom as perhaps the most substantial barrier to the policies' long-term viability.

The available avenues to controlling these costs may be linked to the three activity systems explored throughout this analysis – reducing the number of admissions produced through the case selection process; reducing levels of service associated with custody and treatment; and increasing rates of discharge by expanding the focus on transition and release. Each alternative, however, produces its own set of questions.

The first avenue to cost control, quite simply, involves reducing reliance on the policy by selecting fewer individuals for commitment. Indeed, some states are showing signs of doing just that. Yet although the overall numbers of referrals and commitments have declined in certain states, the often subjective nature of screening and commitment determinations makes it difficult to determine whether case selection processes are actually becoming more discriminating, or if they have simply reduced their output levels. With the political costs of failure as high as they are in this instance, it remains to be seen how far screeners, prosecutors, and the courts will be willing to raise the functional threshold for commitment – the surge in Minnesota's utilization of the civil commitment strategy during 2004 is a case in point.

On the custody and treatment end, reductions in service levels create their own form of risks. Not only do they inhibit the potential for structured paths to release, but they also expose states to potential litigation that could result on tremendously onerous and expensive program requirements. While this analysis has shown that high treatment resource levels may not always produce better treatment results, the centrality of maintaining program standards to the policies' overall legal viability considerably limits states' ability to cut back significantly on treatment provisions.

Regarding the third means of cost control, increasing the rates of release and expanding the role of transitional programming, requires both an exceptionally well-oiled treatment program and investment in rather elaborate Less Restrictive Alternative (LRA) programs. Not only does this typically require exceptional initiative on the part of the states, but it also entails significant (and as yet largely unknown) additional resource outlays to mitigate the societal risks posed by community release. Release, simply put, remains a politically risky, relatively untested, and potentially expensive prSVP civil commitment policies:role of resources inoposition.

AN ALTERNATIVE ASSESSMENT

The concepts of technical, legal, organizational, and resource viability were selected as major criteria for this analysis based on the theoretical foundations set forth in earlier chapters. Certainly, these four standards, while providing a strong basis for assessing the prospects for SVP civil commitment, are lacking in certain respects. For example, although the case study narratives presented in Appendix A describe the policies' broader socio-political context and implementation chronologies, some of these data were not fully accounted for in the analytic framework.

To partially mediate these limitations, Table 14 presents the findings of this analysis in an alternative framework. Mazmanian and Sabatier (1989), whose model of policy implementation is referenced elsewhere in this book, set forth six criteria for effective implementation. While these criteria do not capture the full scope of the implementation factors considered n this analysis, they do provide an alternative means of summarizing many of the key findings.

Table 14: Review of SVP Civil Commitment Policies Based on Mazmanian/Sabatier Criteria

Mazmanian-Sabatier Condition	**Assessment**
Enabling legislation or other legal directive mandates policy objectives which are clear and consistent or at least provides substantive criteria for resolving goal conflicts.	Goal of protecting society is clear – "end game" is much more difficult to assess; Statutes contain no mechanisms to address implicit goal conflicts, with resolution ceded to implementers and to the courts. *General Assessment: Low-Moderate*
Enabling legislation incorporates a sound theory identifying the principle factors and causal linkages affecting policy objectives and gives implementing officials sufficient jurisdiction over target groups and other points of leverage to attain, at least potentially, the desired goals.	Adequacy of causal theory depends largely on perspective regarding goals and objectives – theory stronger from public safety perspective than from technical/therapeutic one; Jurisdiction over target groups well-established through empowering systems of delegation. *General Assessment: Moderate*
Enabling legislation structures the implementation process so as to maximize the probability that implementing officials and target groups will perform as desired. This involves assignment to sympathetic agencies with adequate hierarchical integration, supportive decision rules, sufficient financial resources, and adequate access to supporters.	Commitment procedures fairly well-structured and hierarchically integrated; Standards for "performing as desired" unclear; Decision rules involve high level of delegation to implementers and courts; Financial resources and commitment generally adequate to high, but at significant risk as programs grow *General Assessment: Moderate*

Table 14: Review of SVP Civil Commitment Policies Based on Mazmanian/Sabatier Criteria (CONTINUED)

Mazmanian-Sabatier Condition	Assessment
Leaders of the implementing agency possess substantial managerial and political skill and are committed to statutory goals.	Available evidence indicates skilled and dedicated program management staff; Emergent coalitions of implementer agents with vested interest in policy (such as private vendors and contractors); Potential for conflict between clinical treatment managers and policy makers regarding policy's goals and priorities. *General Assessment: Moderate-High*
The program is actively supported by organized constituency groups and by a few key legislators (or a chief executive) throughout the implementation process, with the courts being neutral or supportive.	Policies receive high levels of legislative and public support, as long as system does not release dangerous individuals into society; Courts have, with some notable exceptions, generally supported and validated policies. *General Assessment: High*
Relative priority of statutory objectives is not undermined over time by the emergence of conflicting public policies or by changes in relevant socioeconomic conditions which weaken the statute's causal theory or political support.	Policies have remained comparatively robust over time *General Assessment: High*

To summarize, SVP civil commitment policies appear to contain several key elements for implementation success. They emanate from a strong and persistent public perception of a problem. They have garnered near-unanimous support from political leaders, who have invested considerably in program infrastructure, even during a time of fiscal retrenchment. They have received strong support and validation from the courts, with a few notable exceptions. They have in many cases recruited high-caliber professionals to manage their treatment programs, and appear to have achieved reasonable levels of hierarchical integration and support from key sovereigns.

These strengths, however, are offset in part by a series of fundamental limitations in the policies' conceptual and operational assumptions. They are affected by an underlying conceptual ambiguity, manifested in unclear objectives and amorphous definitional constructs. They are affected by a structural complexity, manifested in changing patterns of practice, and compounded by limitations of available technology. Most critically, they are affected by growing resource-intensity, driven by a compounding population effect, extraordinary costs of standard compliance, and no viable "end game" for dealing with the committed population.

This combination of factors – highly-developed means of political and institutional support, high reliance on marginally effective technology, and lingering conceptual inconsistencies – has produced a set of policies in which the financial costs may be high, but the political costs of disengagement may be higher. Looking to the future, the most significant challenge to policymakers appears to be the transition of SVP civil commitment from a "catch-all" strategy to an extremely limited element in a broader policy structure concerning the management of sex offenders. In the absence of such a transition, the policy is likely to sink from its own weight.

LIMITATIONS OF STUDY

This study has attempted to present a broad-based review of SVP civil commitment policy across time and across multiple states. As an exploratory analysis, the principle aims were to provide descriptive information regarding program evolution, practices, and trends for a select number of states, and to develop and apply a series of constructs and variables that may be used in future assessments of the policies.

Clearly, there are certain implicit limitations to the adopted approach. First, as noted earlier in this document, data incompleteness and inconsistencies across states in many cases precluded direct comparison of state practices. Some of these inconsistencies stemmed from structural variation (that is, the way in which data is classified and collected), and some from basic lack of centralized data.

Second, while the study attempted to draw from a broad cross-section of state experiences, the six cases presented by no means reflect the full spectrum of state experiences. Indeed, certain states that were not selected possess unique characteristics that may be worthy of examination. A study of investment patterns, for example, might direct attention to the Texas experience, in which appropriations and the program's reach were pro-actively capped by the legislature. The evaluation assessment might consider Virginia, which has three times delayed the implementation of its SVP law following legislative review. The examination of structural provisions might assess the experience of Massachusetts, the only state in which the SVP program does not include involvement of the state mental health agency. Future studies should no doubt consider the experiences of these and other states.

Third and finally, the present study was constrained by the relative immaturity of SVP civil commitment policies. Even Washington, which has operated its program for over ten years, remains in a transitional mode. Accordingly, the study's portrayal of where these policies are heading is based on a mere "snapshot" in time, and will likely require ongoing revision as the policies evolve further.

FINAL THOUGHTS: SVP CIVIL COMMITMENT IN THE CONTEXT OF RISK

In her essay, *Risk and Justice*, the cultural anthropologist Mary Douglas writes:

> "A risk is not only the probability of an event but also the probable magnitude of its outcome, and everything depends on the value that is set on the outcome. The evaluation is a political, aesthetic, and moral matter" (Douglas, 1992)

In a critical respect, the story of SVP policies and their implementation is the story of risk -- the societal risk associated with the unknown future actions of sex offenders; the political risk associated with the actions or inactions of public officials or their agents; the legal risk associated with the constitutional tightrope walked by SVP civil commitment policies; the financial risk associated with a steady flow of new commitments and the negligible number of system discharges.

The idea of risk – not just in an actuarial sense, but in the broader context as framed above – permeates every aspect of SVP civil commitment policies, accounting for both the policies' most limiting obstacles and their most integral strengths.

On a conceptual level, the social construction of risk concerning perpetrators of sexual violence provides the basis for the policies' exceptional levels of support from policy makers and the general public. It also accounts for the policies' most fundamental conceptual limitation, namely a lack of definitional specificity concerning the target population, the means to be employed in identifying them, and ultimately the goals to be achieved by the civil commitment strategy.

In terms of implementation practice, we cannot ignore the prominent role that this broadened construction of risk plays in the everyday decisions connected to the civil commitment process. With prediction of dangerousness at the forefront of the policy, with statutes crafted in a manner that broadly delegates the rules and standards for such prediction, and with technical limitations relegating predictions to little more than informed conjecture, implementers are forced to employ their own "risk calculus" to commitment and release decisions. In such a situation, the "political, moral and aesthetic" consequences of failure to act are significantly greater than those of acting, creating immense incentives for those involved in the process – corrections officials, psychologists, prosecutors, judges, juries – to push the process as far as the law will allow. Although the courts have accepted the laws within general boundaries, this acceptance does not strip the law of its moral and political pretext, nor does it speak to the policy's significant long-term resource demands.

In light of these circumstances, it is notable that referral and commitment rates in several states appear to diminish with time. Evidence suggests that part of this may be attributed to bureaucratic initiative, policy learning, and associated refinements in the criteria applied by case screeners. It may be equally attributed, however, to a rising sense that the policies' mounting costs severely limit its utility as a long-range solution, and the corresponding need for a more global view of sex offender management.

Appendices – State Case Study Detail

Drawing from a range of sources, this series of appendices includes individual assessments of the six focus states, presented in four parts:

- A series of historical narratives, describing both the adoption and subsequent evolution of the state's SVP civil commitment policy (**Appendix A**);
- Reviews of the key structural elements guiding the policy's implementation, including decision rules and the roles of various agencies and individuals (**Appendix B**);
- Presentation of key operational indicators reflecting the implementation practices and policy outputs in each state, both cumulatively and across time (**Appendix C**); and
- A series of budget assessments reflecting patterns of resource allocation and spending connected to SVP policy implementation (**Appendix D**).

The historical narratives are intended to fulfill two primary purposes – to provide the reader with a general context with which to view the ensuing structural, operational, and budgetary reviews, and to present data that informs the conceptual analysis of SVP civil commitment policies' conceptual foundations. Consistent with this dual purpose, the narrative focuses on key events and forces that both led up to the adoption of the statutes and guided the policy's evolution. Particular focus is placed on matters such as citizen mobilization, the extent and nature of the deliberative processes undertaken by policy formulators and implementers, and pivotal legal actions and court decisions. The data for this section is drawn from a range of sources, including legislative documents, official reports, media accounts, and journal articles. In some cases, information has been added or corroborated through informal interviews with relevant individuals.

The goal of the structural reviews is to identify and classify the core organizational and procedural characteristics of SVP civil commitment initiatives within each state. In accordance with the demands of the operational analysis presented in Chapter 4, the concern here is both on formalized structure, as set forth in statutory guidelines, and more informal guidelines and processes adopted by policy implementers in their pursuit of program goals. Data for the structural reviews has been gathered from statutes, administrative codes, internal agency policies and procedures, official reports, and clarifying interviews with program principles.

The operational indicators represent the *dependent variables* applied in the operational analysis. The primary focus of this section is the examination of program outputs that can be observed across time, shedding light on the relative effectiveness of the implementation process. While variation in both process and data availability across states requires a measure of flexibility regarding the particular indicators that may be examined, effort is made to present state information in a manner that permits inter-state comparison. The majority of the operational data presented and analyzed in this section was provided by implementing agencies, including departments of corrections, prosecuting attorneys, mental health agencies, and independent boards responsible for aspects of the implementation process. In some cases, particularly those involving discrepancies or gaps in available information, additional data was pulled from secondary sources, including legislative reports and journal articles.

The budgetary assessments present data regarding patterns of investment in the programs across time, and describe the systems of funding that states have adopted to support the implementation of their SVP civil commitment policies. The data presented in this section is based on information provided by agency budget divisions (and in some cases from the state's executive budget agency), and on legislative documents including staff reports and appropriations bills.

APPENDIX A: STATE NARRATIVES

Washington

The Washington SVP statute, which took effect July 1, 1990, was the first law in the nation providing for civil commitment of sexually violent predators following their release from incarceration. As with each of the SVP civil commitment laws examined in this study, the law's development and passage can be traced to a particular sequence of societal and political events.

Precipitating Events and Policy Response

In the summer of 1988, a convicted rapist named Gene Raymond Kane was transferred to a work release program in downtown Seattle, after serving thirteen years in prison. Two months after his transfer, on September 26th, Kane raped and killed 29-year-old Diane Ballasiotes. While the tragic event might have easily receded from the public consciousness, it was kept alive by the victim's mother, Ida Ballasiotes, who wrote a letter to Governor Booth Gardner, vowing to "mobilize forces to get change and reform"(Siegel, 1990).

That December, as a group called "Friends of Diane" staged rallies and circulated petitions, the state was shaken by a second attack, as Gary Minnix, a severely retarded man on furlough from a state psychiatric hospital, raped and slashed a 23-year-old woman in Pierce County (UPI, 1990). Then, five months later, came a third event – one that would transform Ida Ballasiotes' mission from a burgeoning reform movement to a massive citizen mobilization.

In May 1989, a 7 year-old boy was abducted, sexually assaulted, mutilated, and left for dead in the woods near his home in Tacoma, Washington. Within a day, authorities had arrested Earl Shriner, a mentally retarded man who had been released from prison in 1987 following a 10-year prison sentence for the abduction and assault of two teenage girls. Media reports over the ensuing days revealed a series of disturbing events concerning Shriner's case over the two years following his release, including a number of arrests and the futile attempts by both the mental health and criminal justice systems to protect society from a man known to be dangerous (Boerner, 1992)

Within four days of the attack, the Shriner case had reached the front pages of newspapers in Olympia, with Governor Gardner noting the inadequacies of the legal system and calling for a change in state law, and legislative leaders calling for an immediate special legislative session on the issue (Siegel, 1990).

Over the next several weeks, citizen mobilization reached unprecedented levels, with Ida Ballasiotes joined by a group galled the Tennis Shoe Brigade, founded in part by Helen Harlow, the Tacoma boy's mother, which organized a march on Olympia calling for a legislative special session. The Governor's office was barraged with mail, leading an aide to comment that the over 1,000 calls and letters received in response to the attack was the most correspondence the office had ever received on a single issue in so short a period of time (Boerner, 1992). Reflecting on the events several months later, Norm Maleng, the King County Prosecutor who would eventually lead the Task Force that developed the Washington SVP law, commented that "the degree of outrage and mobilization is unprecedented in recent history"(Siegel, 1990).

On June 15th, approximately four weeks following the incident, Gardner issued an Executive Order creating the Governor's Task Force on Community Protection (Washington Office of the Governor, 1989). The 24-member task force included representatives of the criminal justice system, legislators, treatment professionals, and, critically, Helen Harlow, Ida Ballasiotes, and Trish Tobias, another victims' advocate. Reflecting the strong political unanimity over the issue, the Democratic Gardner appointed Norm Maleng – the King County Prosecutor and his Republican opponent in the 1988 Governor's race – to head the task force, avoiding the growing call for legislative hearings (Siegel, 1990; Boerner, 1992).

The Executive Order directed the Task Force to report to the Governor and the legislature by December 1st, examining the following issues:

- The effectiveness of the criminal justice system and mental health civil commitment process in confining persons who are not safe to be at large;
- The relationship between these two systems;
- The feasibility of developing a specialized facility to house the most high-risk individuals;
- Approaches for predicting future behavior of those who may commit violent acts, and for legally codifying the criteria for confinement.

The work of the Task Force is chronicled in considerable detail by David Boerner, a law professor and former prosecutor charged by the Task Force to draft the civil commitment legislation. Boerner's account of the Task Force's work during the summer and fall of 1990, sheds important light on the considerations that led to the development of Washington's Community Protection Act of 1990. The picture that emerges from this account is of a group of recommendations born from an implicit tension between legal pragmatism and the community's demand for immediate and dramatic reform.

On one hand, Boerner describes in considerable detail his painstaking approach to potential constitutional barriers to the concept of post-incarceration civil commitment. Recognizing from the outset the likely legal challenges that would follow, Boerner sought to explicitly limit the law's scope to an extremely select group of individuals (like Earl Shriner) for whom a "last resort" measure was required.

On the other hand, Boerner goes to considerable lengths to describe the profound influence that Ballasiotes and the other victims advocates had upon the final product:

> "The pain that sexual violence produces was the reason that the Task Force was created; it was also present on the Task Force. The presence of Helen Harlow, Ida Ballasiotes, and Trish Tobias as Task Force members made it impossible to view these issues as abstract legal issues...their presence made us constantly aware that whatever we did, or chose not to do, would have a direct, tangible impact on individuals."

The task force submitted its report on November 28th. Its recommendations, with minor modifications from the Governor, were submitted to the legislature within a month.

As the measures were debated, official objections were raised by civil liberties groups and by psychiatry groups, including the Washington State Psychiatric Association (Reardon, 1992), but on the whole, response was muted. The ACLU explicitly elected not to testify at the legislative hearings, and the Task Force's loan civil liberties advocate stated his political assessment was that "there was no point opposing this" (Siegel, 1990).

Washington's Community Protection Act of 1990, as drafted by Boerner and approved by the Task Force, was presented for legislative vote on February 5, 1990. During the vote, Ida Ballasiotes sat in the gallery observing the proceedings. As she stated later, "We were watching to see if anyone opposed the bill. We were prepared to publicize the names of those who voted against it" (Siegel, 1990).

Lawmakers passed the bill by unanimous vote, with an effective date of July 1, 1990.[37] Ida Ballasiotes would be elected to the Washington House of Representatives in November 1992.

Initial Experience and the First Challenge

According to data provided by the Washington Attorney General's office, several potential civil commitment cases were referred to prosecutors and declined prosecution in the summer of 1990.[38] The

---

[37] Washington Laws of 1990 Ch. 3 Sec. 1001-1013

[38] Unless otherwise specified, cited Washington case processing data is based on independent analysis of a data run provided in May 2002 by the Attorney

first petition was filed in August by Clark County, with the case subsequently dismissed by the presiding judge.[39]

Then, during the last week in August, two referrals that would ultimately lead to the program's first commitments crossed the desks of two county prosecutors. One of those referrals – a convicted rapist named Andre Young – was forwarded to King County Prosecutor Norm Maleng – the chair of the Community Protection Task Force. Reporting on the filing of Young's commitment petition in October 1990, a local television report commented that Maleng "believes he has found the perfect criminal to test this law"("Protecting Society From Sexual Predators," 1990).

Committed in March 1991, Young immediately appealed the ruling to the State Supreme Court. In August 1993, the Court handed down a 6-3 ruling upholding the law's constitutionality. Through this ruling, the Washington law had withstood its first major constitutional challenge.[40]

General's Office, indicating the names, dates of referral, disposition/current status, filing dates, and commitment dates of individuals considered for commitment between 1990 and 2001. The analysis excluded cases that are currently pending filing determinations.

[39] In the months following the passage of the statute, both the King County prosecutor and the AG office issued guidelines for the filing of SVP cases, leading to one reviewer to speculate that "even prosecutors recognize the law's reach is hopelessly expansive." (La Fond, 1992)

[40] Following the Washington Supreme Court ruling, Young filed a habeus corpus petition in U.S. District court, leading to a 1995 ruling that the punitive nature of Young's detention in fact violated the U.S. Constitution (Young v. Weston, 1995). While this subsequent ruling threw into doubt the future of civil commitment in Washington, the Hendricks decision affirmed the basic practice. Following Hendricks, the Young case itself eventually reached the U.S. Supreme Court, which affirmed both the constitutionality and civil nature of Young's commitment (Seling v. Young, 2000).

Programming and Challenges to Conditions of Confinement

Between 1991 and 1997, new commitments remanded to the custody of the Department of Social and Health Services (DSHS) were housed in a vacated prison unit in the confines of the Monroe Reformatory, a Washington Department of Corrections facility. The 30-bed unit, designated as the Special Commitment Center (SCC), while technically leased by the DSHS from the DOC, depended heavily on the correctional system for security and basic facility operation (Washington Dept. of Social and Health Services, 2001).

The conditions at Monroe were a significant factor in the Washington civil commitment program's next major legal challenge. In June 1994, the U.S. District Court, in the Western District of Washington, placed an injunction on the DSHS, mandating a range of treatment, programming, and physical space provisions required to bring the program into constitutional compliance ("Turay v. Weston," 1994) . The case's fundamental issue concerned whether the Washington system had established a punitive environment that belied the law's nominally civil designation.

As part of the injunction, the Court appointed Dr. Janice Marques, a sex offender treatment expert and an official with the California Department of Mental Health, as a Special Master charged with overseeing the program's progress towards compliance. On December 13th, Dr. Marques issued her preliminary report – the first of nineteen reports produced between 1994 and 2001 -- citing a range of program challenges ranging from the development of a basic treatment model to addressing a four-year history of mistrust and lack of rapport between residents and staff.[41]

The court orders and special master reports associated with the Turay case present a rare "insider's view" of the personalities, sentiments, and struggles associated with the implementation of Washington's treatment program. The picture that emerges is of a system in a continual state of transition and, occasionally, significant

[41] See Turay v. Weston: First Report of the Special Master, December 13, 1994

conflict, especially during the early years of the injunction. The reports, for example, document the hiring, power struggles, and ultimate resignation of a court-appointed in Ombudsman in 1996-97, the entry and aggressive attempts at reform of a new Superintendent and clinical director beginning in early 1997, and several instances of turnover of key positions.[42]

Driven in part by the Turay injunction, and in part by a caseload surge in the wake of the 1997 Kansas v. Hendricks ruling, the state relocated its Special Commitment Center and its 62 residents to a vacant Department of Corrections facility on McNeil Island in April 1998 (Washington Dept. of Social and Health Services, 2001). No sooner had the facility been occupied, however, the state was compelled to examine alternative siting options. Responding to a series of plaintiff and defense motions in December 1998, the Court stated, "the crowded physical plant at SCC remains a serious obstacle to providing constitutionally adequate mental health treatment."[43]

In its 1999 session, the Washington legislature allocated funding for the siting and design of a free-standing facility on McNeil Island. After a year of planning and design, the new construction project was scrapped in favor of an alternative proposal that involved the renovation and expansion of an existing correctional facility. The budgeted costs of constructing the 404-bed facility, were estimated at approximately $87 million (Washington State Office of Financial Management, 2001).

In November of 1999, in the midst of the construction planning, the Federal Court cited the state with contempt of court for failure to meet the requirements of the Turay injunction. The contempt order conveyed the Court's general sense of fundamental structural flaws in the program's implementation structure, implying that the state had yet

---

[42] The Ombudsman, who was eventually replaced, has since emerged as one of the program's most outspoken and vocal critics.(Campbell, 2001)

[43] See *Turay v. Weston*: Order Amending Order of 11/25/98, Denying Motion for Stay Pending Appeal: December 23, 1998

to adequately reconcile the policy's dueling goals of incapacitation and treatment:

> "The State of Washington, through its DSHS (which operates the SCC) and its DOC (which operates the McNeil Island Correctional Center), has failed to devote the resources necessary to achieve compliance. This is the chief cause. Instead of doing what must be done, the state has treated SCC as an unwanted stepchild of a medium-security prison......"

Later in the order, the Court states:

> ".....the defendants persistently have failed to make constitutionally adequate mental health treatment available to the SCC residents, and have departed so substantially from professional minimum standards as to demonstrate that their decisions and practices were not and are not based on their professional judgment."

As part of its order, the Court established that economic sanctions would accrue at a daily rate of $50 for each resident (for a total of approximately $5,000 per day, based on the census of 100 at the time) until the program made sufficient progress towards the requirements.[44]

The Pursuit of a "Less Restrictive Alternative"

A significant issue at the time of these sanctions pertained to the state's failure to develop a viable "Less Restrictive Alternative" (LRA) program. The centrality of an effective LRA, cited by Marques and other treatment experts as fundamental to the efficacy and viability of a treatment program, is summarized by Dwyer:

> "A continuing major flaw in the SCC program is the lack of what experts on both sides have called the light at the end of the tunnel. Mental health treatment, if to be anything more than a sham, must give the confined person hope that if he gets

---

[44] See *Turay v. Seling*: Findings of Fact, Conclusions of Law and Order, November 15, 1999, U.S. District Court (Western District of Washington)

> well enough to be safely released, he will be transferred to some less restrictive alternative." [45]

Washington's efforts to develop an LRA, chronicled extensively in court documents produced between 1997 and 2001, was considerably hampered by an inability to locate appropriate housing sites. In response, the 1999 legislature directed the DSHS to develop guidelines for the siting and development of LRA facilities. These guidelines, produced by DSHS in October of 2000, set forth the parameters for a complex series of rules and procedures providing for extensive public review, equitable geographic distribution of LRA facilities, considerable (and arguably prohibitive) siting restrictions, and systems of financial mitigation for communities (Washington Dept. of Social and Health Services, 2000).

The 2001 legislature, in response to the DSHS report, adopted a series of statutory modifications pertaining to the siting, staffing, operations, and release provisions pertaining to community transition programs. These measures, in large part, were designed to respond to the needs of two audiences – the federal court, which was requiring pro-active steps to develop an LRA, and Washington's communities that demanded assurances that public safety would not be compromised. As explored below in our consideration of the program budget, reconciling these two sets of demands has required an extraordinary dedication of resources amidst of a period of significant economic retrenchment

By the summer of 2001, many of the initial issues concerning the program had been substantively addressed, with the major pieces of "unfinished business" connected to the new facility and to the development of a dedicated LRA facilities. In September, Marques tendered her resignation as Special Master (Duran, 2001). In her final

---

[45] See *Turay v. Seling*: Findings of Fact, Conclusions of Law, December 20, 2000, U.S. District Court (Western District of Washington)

report to the court, she referred to LRA's and community transition programming as "the most important piece of unfinished business in the SCC program."[46]

Minnesota

Minnesota, in contrast with the majority of states that repealed their original "sexual psychopath" laws during the 1970's and 1980's, has retained its law permitting the indeterminate commitment of "psychopathic personalities" to the present day. The law, adopted by the Minnesota legislature in 1939, defined its target population as individuals exhibiting:

> "emotional instability, impulsiveness of behavior, lack of customary standards of good judgment, or a failure to appreciate the consequences of personal acts......which renders the person irresponsible for personal conduct with respect to personal matters and thereby dangerous to other persons." (Minn Stat §526.09)[47]

Examining the language in the 1939 statute, particularly the clause regarding personal irresponsibility, it becomes quite apparent why the law may have fallen into disuse. Indeed, while the law was one of only three in the nation to remain on the books through the 1980's (the District of Columbia still retains its sexual psychopath law, and Massachusetts would repeal its law in 1990), it had fallen into only sporadic use in the two decades prior to February 1989.

That month, in response to a series of sex crimes committed by repeat sex offenders, Attorney General Hubert Humphrey III convened

---

[46] See *Turay v. Seling*: Nineteenth Report of the Special Master, June 25, 2001, U.S. District Court (Western District of Washington)

[47] In response to an early constitutional challenge to the law, the Minnesota Courts further clarified the psychopathic personality as one who "by habitual course of misconduct in sexual matters, evidences an utter lack of power to control his sexual impulses." (Pearson v. Probate Court, 1939)

a Task Force on the Prevention of Sexual Violence Against Women. The 1989 Task Force Report linked the release of many sex offenders to the establishment of "truth in sentencing" guidelines and the associated abolition of indeterminate sentencing in 1980, and pointed out that the 1939 psychopathic personality commitment law was the only legal means available to keep people confined if they still posed a danger to society. The group recommended that indeterminate sentencing be re-instated for dangerous sex offenders, and suggested that prosecutors consider utilizing the psychopathic personality law where it might be applicable (Minnesota Attorney General, 1989).

During the 1989 legislative session, Minnesota lawmakers rejected a return to indeterminate sentencing, but set forth two major sentencing reforms aimed at sexually dangerous individuals. The first was a designation of a new class of individuals known as "Patterned Sex Offenders" – individuals with prior sex offense convictions -- who would be subject to significantly increased prison sentences.[48] The second involved establishing a system of "dual commitments," permitting judges to identify potential psychopathic personalities at the time of original sentencing, and to simultaneously impose a criminal sentence and designate the individual as a "psychopathic personality." Such a measure would essentially permit an individual to be remanded to the custody of the Department of Human Services upon completion of his or her criminal sentence with no further legal proceedings required.

Despite these legislative changes, neither measure appears to have been implemented in any significant way. A 1994 legislative report, citing ambiguity in the statute, indicated that only two "dual commitments" had been effectuated during the five years since the law's enactment (Minnesota Legislative Auditor, 1994), and a series of later studies by multi-agency task forces found similar under-utilization

[48] The "patterned sex offender" statute might be viewed as a precursor to the "two strikes" and "three strikes" laws that would proliferate throughout the U.S. in the 1990's.

of the patterned sex offender provisions (Minnesota Dept. of Corrections, 1998).

In 1991, however, approximately one year after Washington's new civil commitment law took effect, Minnesota commenced a series of initiatives marking a significant shift in policy, and essentially making Minnesota the second state to pursue a policy of post-incarceration civil commitment of sex offenders. Like Washington, the 1991 shift in Minnesota's policies, as well as a subsequent statutory modification in 1994, may be traced to a limited series of cases that attracted the widespread attention of citizens and public officials.

Precipitating Events and Initial Policy Change

In the wake of a July 1991 abduction, rape, and murder of a university student by a twice-convicted sex offender named Scott Stewart, the Department of Corrections produced a report calling for a review of all sex offenders scheduled for release from DOC custody. The report delineated a rudimentary risk assessment protocol, and systems for referring high-risk cases to county prosecutors for possible commitments under the psychopathic personality statute (Wood, 1991).

In the latter months of 1991, ten individuals were referred to county prosecutors and committed as psychopathic personalities under the DOC protocols – up from one the previous year. By September of 1993 – two years following the promulgation of the DOC guidelines – 47 new individuals had been committed, and another 23 cases were pending (Minnesota Legislative Auditor, 1994).

As the commitments continued into 1992, the legislature indicated its clear support for this new policy direction by codifying the new DOC practice, requiring the Commissioner of Corrections to review all upcoming releases for possible civil commitment. Lawmakers also included a range of provisions aimed at facilitating the legal process of civil commitments, empowering the court system to appoint a panel of judges to hear psychopathic personality cases, and requiring the Attorney General to provide prosecution services, at no charge, as requested by the counties (Minn Laws of 1992, Ch 571).

The following year, in response to the growing PP population, the legislature again affirmed its support for the expanded commitment policy by authorizing funding for the Department of Human Services to construct new facilities to house the new influx of civil commitments. In 1994, the Department of Human Services opened its 100-bed Moose Lake facility for individuals committed as psychopathic personalities. It also opened a newly constructed 50-bed wing to the Minnesota Security Hospital in St. Peter. The combined cost of construction for the two facilities was $28 million (Minnesota Legislative Auditor, 1994).

Emergence of a New Law

Yet as Minnesota prepared for this resurgence of new commitments, another high-profile case was waiting in the wings – one that would pose a significant threat to the continued viability of the state's new policy direction.

In 1993, a convicted rapist and murderer named Dennis Linehan appealed his PP commitment to the Minnesota Supreme Court, challenging the standards set forth by the psychopathic personality law. In its July 1994 ruling, the Court ruled that Linehan did not meet the criteria set forth under the state's psychopathic personality law, in that he did not exhibit the required "utter lack of power" to control his sexual impulses ("In Re Linehan," 1994).

The Linehan ruling, coupled with another case in which a commitment had been overturned due to a failure to meet the statute's criteria ("In Re Rickmyer," 1994), set off an immediate political firestorm. Throughout the summer of 1994, media reports about Linehan's pending release abounded. Public perceptions concerning the urgency of the crisis were fueled by the speculation that Linehan was merely the tip of the iceberg, and that he would soon be joined in his quest for release by several of the 68 other individuals held by the state as psychopathic personalities (Halvorsen, 1994). Public officials quickly joined the fray. The Governor's chief of staff, apparently unaware of the constitutional implications of his statement, called for "changing the basis of commitment, moving it more toward penalty and away from the presumption of rehabilitation (Whereatt, 1994b).

Within two weeks of the Linehan ruling, the legislature convened an emergency Task Force on Sexual Predators to study the law's loopholes and make recommendations that would ensure that Linehan and the others remained confined. Governor Carlson personally appeared before the Task Force in mid-August, and along with Attorney General Humphrey presented draft legislation that would widen the net of individuals that could be civilly committed under Minnesota law (Whereatt, 1994a). Media accounts from the time, commenting on the bipartisan and unilateral spirit of the push towards reform, note that Carlson, Humphrey, and the legislature were all bracing for fall elections.

The new legislation did not replace the existing psychopathic personality law, but rather supplemented it through the designation of a new class of individuals known as "sexually dangerous persons" – from a definitional perspective, a group somewhat reflective of Washington's "sexually violent predators." Additionally, the 1939 psychopathic personality law was re-codified to incorporate the clarifying standard set forth by the Minnesota Supreme Court in an early challenge to the psychopathic personality statute.[49]

---

49 See State ex rel Pearson v. Probate Court (1939). As a practical matter, prosecutors have typically proceeded with simultaneous commitment petitions under both the recodified PP statute and the newer SDP statute, and have successfully committed the majority of individuals in such a manner (Janus and Walbeck, 2000). The fundamental distinction between the "new" law and the 1939 statute – as described by the 1998 civil commitment study group – was that the old law contained a requirement that the committed individual contained an "inability to control" standard that was essentially unworkable in the context of current state of knowledge regarding risk assessment. The new law, in contrast, relaxed this standard, requiring instead that the person have a history of harmful sexual conduct and a mental disorder or dysfunction that makes the person likely to engage in further harmful sexual conduct. Moreover, the law explicitly stated that "it is not necessary to prove that the

The SDP law was enacted in a special session, in accordance with the draft legislation, on August 31st., barely one month after the Linehan ruling. The measure passed 65-0 in the senate and 133-0 in the house, and was signed into law within a matter of hours by Governor Carlson. The law took effect immediately. Within a matter of days, Ramsey County Attorney Tom Foley – two weeks prior to a September primary run for a Democratic U.S. Senate nomination – filed petitions to have both Linehan and Rickmyer recommitted (Gustafson, 1994).

Implementation of the Revised Law

As the first commitments under the new law proceeded, the Task Force released its final report in February 1995. While clearly supporting the new policy direction, the Task Force Report reflected a general view among the group that the SDP legislation was a temporary and inadequate long-term response to the issue of managing sexually dangerous individuals. The report, for example, cited the legal system's failure to adequately utilize measures such as patterned sex offender sentencing, and concluded by stating:

> "......as a matter of general principle, the Task Force believes that even though Minnesota does have the sexual psychopathic commitment process that can be used for certain offenders when it is appropriate, the long-term goal of policymakers should be to diminish the use of the mental health system and increase the use of the criminal justice system to deal with these offenders. This will save the state scarce financial resources and at the same time make those individuals criminally responsible for their behavior, which should be Minnesota's long-term goal." (Minnesota Dept. of Corrections, 1998)

---

person has an inability to control the person's sexual impulses" (Minnesota Dept. of Corrections, 1998).

Despite this sentiment, however, civil commitment was rapidly becoming an increasingly more prevalent means of managing the state's sex offender population. An analysis of the Minnesota program published in 2000 indicated that the number of civilly committed individuals grew from 3% of the "sex offender incapacitation burden" in 1989 to 13% of the burden in 1998, projecting the figure to grow to 25% within ten years (Janus & Walbek, 2000). By 1998, a total of 122 individuals were in the DHS custody, with just under 95 held at Moose Lake and another 27 housed in a second facility in St. Peter, Minnesota on the grounds of a state forensic psychiatric hospital.[50]

With the population growing at approximately 20 per year, the legislature authorized in a 1998 special session a 50-bed addition to Moose Lake. While this addition had been contemplated when the facility was constructed, the new beds were now projected to be needed by early 2000, six years earlier than originally planned (Schlank, 1999).

Re-Assessing the Practice

The same year, in the wake of the Hendricks decision, the legislature again convened a Task Force to study and make recommendations regarding the use of civil commitment. The mandating legislation required the commissioner of corrections, in consultation with the Department of Human Services, to examine and make recommendations pertaining to the current systems of confinement, treatment, and commitment of the SDP and PP populations.[51] The legislature stipulated that the task force consider and report on the financial costs of the existing system, and on alternative approaches including modifications to sentencing laws. While the precise concerns of the legislature cannot be unequivocally stated, the greater-than-planned growth of the PP/SDP population and the associated costs was likely a considerable factor.

The group consisted of three representatives each from the Department of Corrections and the Department of Human Services, and

---

[50] Source: Minnesota Dept. of Human Services

[51] See Minnesota Laws 1998, Chapter 367, Article 3, Section 15

four legal system representatives -- an assistant attorney general, a county prosecutor, a district court judge, and a public defender. Designated as the Civil Commitment Study Group, the group released its report in December of 1998. While the report included a detailed review of Minnesota's civil commitment practices, its explicit recommendations amounted to limited modifications of the PP/SDP civil commitment process per se. The report did, however, sound a fiscal alarm, forecasting that the cost of the current system would increase from approximately $17 million in 1998 to $24 million in 2000 and $76 million by 2010 – sustained increases averaging approximately 20% per year (Minnesota Dept. of Corrections, 1998).

In this context, the report presented a series of alternative sentencing and programmatic approaches, echoing the 1994 Task Force's suggestion that long-term policy pertaining to sex offender treatment and management should be focused on the criminal justice system rather than in the system of civil commitment. Among the alternatives put forth were an increased focus on the state's relatively under-utilized provisions for sentencing patterned sex offenders, a shifting of treatment needs assessment processes from the "back door" to the "front door" of the criminal justice system (in effect echoing the 1989 "dual commitment" legislation), and an extension of the DHS-run Minnesota Sex Offender Program (MSOP) into the Department of Corrections as a means of diminishing the need for post-incarceration commitment.

During its 2000 session, the legislature once again took up the issue of managing high-risk sex offenders, convening yet another study group – again under the auspices of the Department of Corrections, but this time with more extensive involvement of the judiciary, prosecutors, and the state's sentencing guidelines commission. In contrast with the 1994 and 1998 task forces, which were charged primarily with refining the system of civil commitment, the work group established in the summer of 2000 was directed by the legislature to adopt a more global view, essentially picking up on the alternatives presented by the CCSG two years earlier.[52] The report again noted the under-utilization of Patterned Sex Offender statutes, inferring that prosecutors had fallen into a pattern of using civil commitment as a long-term, rather than as a temporary, solution (Minnesota Dept. of Corrections, 2000).

Examining the multiple task force and other reports issued between 1989 and 2000, a picture emerges expressing both recognition of continued reliance on civil commitment as a policy strategy, and a general sense of frustration stemming from the continued failure of the criminal justice system to keep pace with demands presented by the sex offender population.

This general sentiment appears to be reflected in both distinct policy shifts and a discernible trend regarding Minnesota's PP/SDP caseload during the late 90's. Data provided by the Minnesota Department of Corrections indicated a steady decline in the number of referrals to prosecutors, from 58 referrals in 1997 to 27 referrals in 2001. Moreover, the Minnesota legislature authorized over $1 million in its 2002-03 biennial budget to expand the reach of correctional-based sex offender treatment programs, pursuant to the recommendations of the 1998 task force.

Another Swing of the Pendulum

Minnesota's period of moderate reliance on its civil commitment program, however, would come to an end in late 2003, following the nationally-publicized abduction and murder of North Dakota college student Dru Sjodin.

The December arrest of alleged perpetrator Jose Rodriguez, who had been discharged from Minnesota Department of Correction custody earlier that year after serving a 23-year sentence for aggravated rape, focused attention on the effectiveness of DOC's screening systems.. Within a month, the DOC had all but abandoned its case screening process, referring the names of all "Level 3" sex offenders to county prosecutors for potential civil commitment, and causing the number of

---

[52] See Minnesota Laws of 2000, Chapter 359

DOC prosecutor referrals to jump from 13 in 2002 to 246 in 2003[53]. This surge in referrals translated into in increase in the DHS population from 190 in June 2003 to 229 in June 2004 and 265 by December 2004.

In August 2004, Governor Tim Pawlenty appointed a panel, headed by a retired Minnesota Supreme Court judge and directed by a state representative, to perform a top-to-bottom assessment of the state's system for managing sex offenders. Simultaneously, the legislatively-appointed Sentencing Guidelines Commission undertook its own review of sentencing policies regarding sexual offenders.

Both groups – the gubernatorial panel and the Sentencing Guidelines Commission -- released their reports in January 2005, signaling another round in the state's ongoing debate over the management of sex offenders, including the adequacy of the state's criminal sentencing policy and the role and mechanics of civil commitment (Governor's Commission on Sex Offender Policy, 2005; Minnesota Sentencing Guidelines Commission, 2005). Notably, the Sentencing Commission's rejection of open-ended sentencing directly contradicted the conclusions of the Governor's Commission, which called for a retreat from the determinate sentencing guidelines adopted by the state in 1980.

Additionally, among its recommendations, the Governor's Commission report called for the legislature to amend the civil commitment statute to establish an independent board to review all potential civil commitments prior to discharge from correctional custody, and to also review all candidates for transitional release or discharge. While these recommendations' ultimate disposition remains unknown, they appear to reflect a policy still in a state of evolution nearly 15 years following its introduction.

---

[53] Personal communication with William Donnay, Minnesota Department of Correction, February 2005.

Wisconsin

In October 1992, the Wisconsin Department of Corrections released from its custody a convicted murderer and child rapist named Gerald Turner. At the time of his release, Turner had served just under 18 years in prison for the Halloween 1973 abduction, rape, and murder of a 9-year-old girl (Associated Press, 1992).

The release provoked immediate uproar from the suburban Milwaukee community to which Turner was released, with focus eventually shifting to the administration of Governor Tommy Thompson. Critics, including the Democratic Attorney General Jim Doyle, faulted Thompson's corrections department over its procedures utilized for calculating Turner's early release (Mayers, 1994). During the course of the next year, the Thompson administration was forced to defend its release policies before a court of appeals, which eventually sent Turner back to prison on a temporary injunction (Associated Press, 1994).[54]

With Doyle leading the attack on the Thompson administration's policies, and both Thompson and Doyle facing re-election challenges in 1994, the debate over the management of sex offenders such as Turner turned rapidly partisan. In December 1993, a Republican state senator named Alberta Darling put forth a bill, dubbed the "Gerald Turner bill," aimed at confronting the problem of sexual predators. While the bill contained several elements, the provisions connected to civil commitment were placed front and center in the controversy (Schneider, 1994).

On March 13th, one of Doyle's deputies appeared before the senate committee considering the bill. In her testimony, she put forth an opinion that the law would not pass constitutional muster, expressed concern about ceding of criminal justice matters to the mental health

[54] The political fall-out from Turner's release was not limited to squabbling among state officials – within days of the release, U.S. Senator Robert Kasten would seize the events to level a "soft on crime" attack against his opponent Russell Feingold (Callender, 1992).

system, and questioned the legal practicality associated with prediction of future risk (Schneider, 1994).

The bill's failure to pass the joint finance committee the following week (on an 8-8 vote) led to a barrage of partisan recriminations, with Senator Darling and her Republican colleagues blaming Doyle for the bill's defeat and accusing Doyle of "standing in the way of keeping people locked up for life" (Pommer, 1994). Doyle countered with a letter to Darling, citing both the inadequacies of the bill and the Thompson administration's handling of the Turner case:

> "By calling (sic) the 'Gerald Turner Bill' and blaming me for its defeat, you hope to shift the blame for the Gerald Turner debacle as well as your failure to get this bill passed...Let's be clear about one thing: I didn't let Gerald Turner out of prison to commit another crime. The Republican administration let Turner out against my advice...." (Pommer, 1994)

The letter prompted the State's Republican Party Chair Dave Opitz to accuse Doyle of a "litany of lies" – a statement that led in turn to the head of Wisconsin's Democratic party dubbing the Turner case "Tommy Thompson's Willie Horton case waiting to happen," and speculating that the Republicans had formed a "hit squad" of Darling and Opitz, intent on blaming Doyle for the "Turner mess." The legislature adjourned on March 25th having failed to pass Darling's bill (Pommer, 1994).

By mid-April, as the media coverage continued, Doyle requested that Governor Thompson call a special session of the legislature to reconsider the measure, indicating that he now supported civil commitment of sexual predators despite "serious flaws" in Darling's bill. Thompson called the session on May 18th , and the following day, the Joint Finance Committee – the same group that had failed to pass the bill with an 8-8 tie in March, passed the measure by a vote of 14-1. Thompson signed the bill into law the following week, with Doyle at his side (Capital Times, 1994).

<u>Implementation Experience</u>

The initial Wisconsin program utilized two facilities for the evaluation, housing, and treatment of potential and committed SVP's. Initial commitments for purposes of court-ordered evaluations were housed at the Mendota Mental Health Institute, the state's forensic evaluation facility. Upon a permanent order of commitment, SVP's were housed at the Wisconsin Resource Center, a 300-bed psychiatric treatment facility utilized for inmates of the Wisconsin Department of Corrections requiring psychiatric treatment.

In 1997, noting the rising caseload, and expressing concern that the SVP's were "crowding out" the WRC's regular patient population, the legislature authorized $30 million in borrowing to fund a 300-bed dedicated facility for the SVP population, a figure that was increased to $39 million following preliminary design estimates (Wisconsin Legislative Fiscal Bureau, 1999c).

The following year, however, the program faced a potential crisis in its treatment program, as several patients neared completion of the 8-trimester program, which had been adapted from Minnesota's MSOP model. Concluding that the individuals had progressed through the program too rapidly without making the necessary behavioral changes, the WRC jettisoned its treatment protocol, fired its clinical director, and informed the affected individuals that their release would not be forthcoming. Eventually, the state adopted a program developed by David Thornton in the British prison system, and hired the internationally-known Thornton to run the program (Taylor, 2001).

By the spring of 1999, the SVP program had grown to 200 individuals – 180 housed at the WRC and 20 at Mendota. Amid projections that the SVP population would reach 280 (virtually the entire WRC capacity) within two years, the Governor's proposed budget for the Fiscal 2000-2001 biennium, submitted to the legislature in early 1999, included provisions for a major funding infusion to support the new dedicated SVP facility, the Sand Ridge Treatment Center (Wisconsin Legislative Fiscal Bureau, 1999c). An $8.1 million annual increase proposed during the 1999 funding cycle, coupled with a further increase of $5.8 million included in following biennial budget adopted in 2001, essentially doubled the general operating costs associated with the SVP program within a period of three fiscal years.[55]

The 1999 budget cycle also included provisions for folding several SVP program costs that had been funded on a temporary basis pending the Hendricks ruling in to the state's general program revenue cost base. This included allocations for the Department of Corrections' dedicated SVP screening unit (Wisconsin Legislative Fiscal Bureau, 1999b), and resources for the prosecution and appellate representation costs incurred by the Attorney General and the district attorneys of Brown and Milwaukee counties (Wisconsin Legislative Fiscal Bureau, 1999a). Equally important, the budget included provisions for a significant infusion of resources for the DHFS supervised release program, including the short-term siting, leasing, and operation of a transitional facility (Wisconsin Legislative Fiscal Bureau, 1999d).

In January 2002, Governor Scott McCallum presented to the legislature a "Budget Reform Bill" that included – among other provisions – a 3.5% across-the-board reduction in the fiscal year ending June 30, 2002, with the reduction growing to 5% in ensuing fiscal years. Within the Department of Health and Family Services – an agency responsible for a range of services ranging from community mental health to Medicaid to public assistance and child welfare services – the Governor's sole exemption to the across-the-board cut was the funding allocated for the operation of the SRTC and WRC facilities (Wisconsin Office of the Governor, 2002). The response from the legislature reflected a slightly moderated approach to the issue, requiring a 1% reduction in these programs, but permitting the agency to re-allocate the cuts elsewhere (Wisconsin Legislative Fiscal Bureau, 2002).

---

[55] Figures based on information provided by the Wisconsin Department of Health and Family Services

Supervised Release Challenges

The next series of challenges faced by the Wisconsin program involved the implementation of the supervised release provisions authorized during the 1999 legislative session. Following approximately four years of planning for a dedicated supervised release facility in Milwaukee County, the issues surrounding community-based placement for previously committed SVP's were brought to a head by the 2003 court-ordered supervised release of an individual named Bill Lee Morford.

Although the program had been transitioning individuals into supervised release as early as 1995, Morford's pending placement within the City of Milwaukee prompted a flurry of community, bureaucratic and legislative activity concerning the process applied to place released SVP's into the community. As the Morford case unfolded throughout 2004, the cases of two other individuals slated for supervised release in the community brought further attention to the intricacies involved in pursuing a viable supervised release strategy (Associated Press, 2004).

In response, the Wisconsin legislature established an advisory committee to present a strategic plan for the selection and siting of supervised release facilities, and ordered the DHFS to submit to the committee a report and recommendations specifically concerning the location of such a facility in Milwaukee County.[56] DHFS submitted its report in June 2004, recommending construction of new 10-12 bed facility and setting forth guidelines for its siting (Wisconsin Department of Health and Family Services, 2004). As of February 2005, the selection of an appropriate site was still underway.

Kansas

In the summer of 1993, 19-year-old Stephanie Schmidt, a university student in Pittsburg, Kansas, disappeared after leaving a bar with a former co-worker. Investigators quickly turned their attention to the

[56] 2003 Wisconsin Act 187

co-worker, 31-year-old convicted rapist named Don Gideon, who was also missing. Three weeks following the disappearance, after Gideon was profiled on the television show "America's Most Wanted," the suspect turned himself in to authorities, eventually leading them to Stephanie Schmidt's body in a remote area of central Kansas (Fisher, 1993).

Over the ensuing months, the victim's parents and sister – outraged at the perceived systematic failures that had led to Stephanie's death -- joined forces with a group of public officials and families of other victims to form the Stephanie Schmidt Task Force, aimed at modifying the laws pertaining to sexual predators (McCaffrey, 1994).

At a public press conference held in November 1993 – four months after their daughter's death, Gene and Peggy Schmidt unveiled a legislative package of five bills, ranging from employee screening requirements for businesses to an extension of the death penalty to murders involving sexual crimes. The package's most controversial element, however, involved the adoption of a sexually violent predator civil commitment law modeled on Washington's (Associated Press, 1993)

The Stephanie Schmidt Sexual Violent Predators Act, providing for civil commitment of sexually violent predators, passed the Kansas legislature on April 27, 1994. The remaining four bills presented by the Schmidt's task force were adopted one month later. The civil commitment bill was signed into law by Governor Joan Finney within two weeks of passage, and took effect immediately (McCaffrey, 1994).

Among the individuals on the Schmidt's task force was a Pittsburg attorney named Carla Stovall. As the legislation was adopted, Stovall, a former county prosecutor, was preparing for a fall 1994 run for the Republican nomination for Attorney General. Elected to that office in November 1994, Stovall would soon find herself in the midst of a case that would soon take on national significance, eventually bringing her to the United States Supreme Court to argue on behalf of the SVP law's fundamental constitutionality.

Leroy Hendricks

In August of 1994, a county district attorney filed the first 4 petitions for commitment under the new law, two of which resulted in commitment trials, and one of which resulted in a commitment (DesLauriers & Gardner, 1999). The committed individual was a twice-convicted pedophile named Leroy Hendricks.

Hendricks, along with two other individuals committed in the latter part of 1994, was housed at the Larned Correctional Mental Health Facility, which had dedicated 30 beds for the planned influx of new civil commitments. The facility, although programmatically managed by the Department of Social and Rehabilitative Services, was functionally under the control of the Kansas Department of Corrections.

During the summer of 1995, Hendricks and two other residents filed a habeus corpus petition in district court indicating that treatment services were inadequate.(DesLauriers & Gardner, 1999). While this petition was eventually dismissed, the true legal test of the statute was soon to follow, as Hendricks filed an appeal of his original commitment to the Kansas Supreme Court.

In March 1996, the Kansas Supreme Court issued its ruling on Hendricks' case, maintaining that the Kansas Sexually Violent Predators Act violated substantive due process. The ruling also cited the inconsistency between the law's implicit intent and its purported civil nature, stating that "it is clear that the primary objective of the act is to continue incarceration and not to provide treatment." ("In Re Hendricks," 1996)

In response to the State Supreme Court ruling, Stovall immediately sought injunctive relief from the federal courts. The U.S. Supreme Court issued its 5-4 ruling in June 1997, overturning the Kansas court's decision and essentially ushering in a new stage in the application of SVP civil commitment in Kansas and elsewhere. [57]

---

[57] The details of the Hendricks ruling are described elsewhere in this report, and are copiously described and analyzed in the legal literature (a May 2002 Lexis-

Following the Hendricks ruling, Kansas stepped up its utilization of the civil commitment process. In the almost three years between the adoption of the SVP law and the Hendricks ruling, Kansas had committed a total of 9 individuals to its program. This figure would double within one year after the ruling.

Kansas v. Crane

While the Hendricks ruling represented a watershed in the development of SVP programs nationwide, it by no means represented the end of the legal spotlight for the relatively small Kansas program. In the fall of 2001, Stovall would once again find herself in front of the U.S. Supreme Court, arguing a case that addressed some of the "unfinished business" stemming from Hendricks. As with Hendricks, the Attorney General had turned to the Court seeking reversal of a decision made by the Kansas Supreme Court.

In its 2000 ruling (*In Re Crane*, 2000), the Kansas Court had revisited the standards for commitment implied by the U.S. Supreme Court's ruling in Kansas v. Hendricks. In the Hendricks majority opinion, Justice Clarence Thomas stated that civil commitment is properly applied "in narrow circumstances for the forcible detention of people who are unable to control their behavior." Interpreting this opinion in the context of the case before them, the Kansas Court found that the respondent in the case – an individual named Michael Crane – had been committed without a finding of volitional impairment as required by Hendricks. Simply put, while the volitional impairment criteria may have been sufficient to justify commitment in the case of

---

Nexis search of the term "Kansas v. Hendricks" yielded 346 law review citations). For current purposes, it is sufficient to indicate that the 5-4 Hendricks ruling has generated considerable controversy in the five years since its issuance, and – as will be illustrated in ensuing sections of this analysis -- has fundamentally influenced the diffusion and implementation of SVP civil commitment laws throughout the United States.

Leroy Hendricks, it did not necessarily apply to Michael Crane or, for that matter, to anyone for whom there was no such finding.

On appeal, the U.S. Supreme Court essentially agreed. While the Court did not fully uphold the Kansas decision, neither did it reverse it – the general conclusion reached by the Court by a 7-2 margin (Thomas and Scalia dissenting), was that, while Hendricks set forth no requirement of total or complete lack of control, that some finding of volitional impairment was indeed necessary (*Crane v. Kansas*, 2002).

Despite the relatively limited scope of Kansas' SVP program, the exposure resulting from the Hendricks and Crane rulings has kept Kansas' SVP policy in the political spotlight – both locally and nationally -- even a decade following the legislation's passage. Since 1998, the Kansas program has continued to grow steadily by between 15 and 25 annual admissions to the program, bringing the population to 100 by the end of Fiscal Year 2004.(Kansas Department of Social and Rehabilitation Services, 2005)

In response to this growing population, the state's FY04 budget of $4.5 million was nearly double the level from three years prior. Additionally, in response to the growing SVP population at Larned, the state allocated $16 million in the Department of Corrections budget to construct a new 250-bed secured psychiatric facility in 2003, allowing the state to convert Larned's 250 existing beds for exclusive SVP use (Kansas Division of the Budget, 2002).

California

Precipitating Events and Policy Response

In the spring of 1994, California stood at the forefront of a burgeoning national "tough on crime" movement. In the aftermath of the nationally-publicized disappearance and murder of 9-year-old Polly Klaas, and amid growing national attention over the issue of crime, California enacted the one of the nation's first "three strikes" laws, prompting over two dozen states to follow suit (Austin, Hardyman, Henry, & Clark, 1999).

As California Governor Pete Wilson and State Treasurer Kathleen Brown faced off in a contentious gubernatorial campaign, Brown unleashed a series of television ads attacking the Wilson administration's handling of the parole of a convicted rapist named Melvin Carter (Wallace, 1994). As the ensuing controversy brewed, Wilson put forth a proposal to the legislature to adopt an SVP law, modeled on Washington's, that would provide for civil commitment of sexually violent predators. While the bill passed the California senate by a vote of 33-0, it failed to pass the Assembly Public Safety Committee, and died with the expiration of the 1994 legislative session (California State Senate, 1994).

Within one month after Wilson's victory in the fall election, however, the release of another convicted rapist named Reginald Muldrew to the community of Covina, California, provoked a major public uproar akin to the 1992 Gerald Turner controversy in Wisconsin (O'Neill, 1994). As the citizens of Covina mobilized, Wilson found the public support and impetus to resurrect the SVP bill during the 1995 legislative session.

Within a period of months, the SVP law was taken up again in both houses and with the City of Covina listed as source of the bill, and with Wilson's strong public support and backing.[58] The resulting legislation passed the Assembly Public Safety Committee – the committee that killed the bill during the prior session -- by a vote of 5-0, and was approved by the Assembly by a 67-10 vote (California State Assembly, 1995). In October 1995, Wilson signed the bill into law in a public ceremony staged on the steps of Covina's City Hall, surrounded by crime victims groups and community activists (Decker, 1995).

---

[58] Legislative documents from the 1995 session alternatively note the sources of the bills as the Governor, the Governor's Office of Criminal Justice, and the City of Covina.

Implementation Experience

With the program scheduled to take effect on January 1, 1996, the Governor's Director of Finance submitted in December 1995 a $17.7 million spending proposal for the fiscal year ending June 30, 1996, a figure that annualized to $33.2 million for the following fiscal year. The annualized figure included $10.4 million for the Department of Corrections (CDC) for screening, transportation, and facility lease and security; $22 million for the Department of Mental Health for evaluation and treatment services; and $800,000 for the Board of Prison Terms (the state's parole agency) to support the CDC in screening operations and to conduct "temporary hold" hearings (California Legislative Analyst's Office, 1996).

Reviewing this request, the Joint Legislative Budget Committee, expressing concerns over "significant problems" with the proposal, recommended that the administration temporarily fund the program out of existing revenues. In March 1996, the Legislative Analysts Office echoed the budget committee's concerns, withholding recommendation on the budget request until the agencies responsible for the operation of the program resolved a number of "significant implementation issues." The LAO report expressed four major areas of concern:

1. The participating agencies each based their respective spending plans on differing caseload assumptions;
2. As a result of the discrepancies in the caseload estimates, the submitted program was up to seven times more costly than the spending levels assumed by the legislature when the law was passed one year earlier;
3. The administration had failed to adequately define responsibility for the housing and treatment of committed SVP's, notably location of the facility and the respective roles of the Department of Correction and the Department of Mental Health; and
4. The submitted implementation plan, particularly concerning the locus of facility control and management, contained provisions that were deemed by the Legislative Counsel's Office as inconsistent with the provisions of the legislation.

The LAO report also cited confusion over how and where committed individuals would be housed and inconsistencies between the plans put forth by the Governor and specific provisions of the legislation.(California Legislative Analyst's Office, 1996)

By the time of the 1997 budget cycle, the administration had shifted responsibility for custody and control of committed SVP's from the Department of Corrections to the Department of Mental Health. Reflecting this change, the 1997 legislature adopted an amendment to the original statute, eliminating the requirement that SVP's be held in a state prison, and placing full responsibility for custody and control under the aegis of the DMH. The legislation further specified that Atascadero State Hospital – the state's primary forensic psychiatric facility – be designated as the principal location for housing and treating committed SVP's.[59] Since that time, virtually all SVP's committed under California law have been housed at ASH, a 1,200-bed forensic psychiatric facility housing a range of individuals committed under various provisions of the state's Welfare and Institutions code.[60]

With these fundamental issues addressed, however, California's SVP civil commitment policy was now faced with a series of longer-range issues affecting its future viability. In its first year, 991 potential SVP's had been referred to the Department of Mental Health, far surpassing the volume of cases experienced by any other SVP program to date. By December of that year, 410 of these cases remained pending in various stages of the evaluation and legal process, and 10 had been committed (California Legislative Analyst's Office, 1997).

This volume, coupled with the considerable uncertainty arising from the pending Supreme Court decision in Kansas v. Hendricks, had rendered policy makers virtually unable to make the requisite resource

---

[59] See California Statutes of 1996 (Budget Trailer Bill) Chapter 197

[60] Subsequent legislation, adopted in 1998, specified that the Atascadero facility is to be used only until a permanent housing and treatment facility is made available (see SB 1976, 1998 legislative session).

decisions during the 1997 budget process. The LAO, in its 1997 report to the legislature, noted a substantial range in the potential resources that would be required for treatment services, indicating that anywhere between 30 and 126 new commitments could take place during the coming fiscal year (the eventual number of new commitments for that period would be approximately 70).

The 1997 LAO report also pointed to a series of factors that could eventually lead to significant long-term growth in program costs. First, the report noted a cost of roughly $10 million per year resulting from the designation of SVP laws and the associated costs to counties as a state mandate.[61] Second, the report reflected a realization that, despite the two-year term of commitment provided by the California statute (as opposed to the statutes of other states that viewed the commitment as indeterminate), the probability of indefinite confinement of committed individuals was becoming more and more apparent. Beyond the obvious implications for caseload growth (resulting from a constant flow of new admissions and a negligible, if not non-existent, number of system discharges), the legal costs associated with biennial re-commitment hearings would grow incrementally with the population.

Bed Capacity Challenges

By the end of 1997, contemplating a population surge in the wake of the Hendricks decision, and expressing concerns that the growing SVP population was adversely affecting the delivery of services to the "traditional" population at Atascadero State Hospital, the Department of Mental Health put forth plans to site and construct a new, dedicated 1,500-bed SVP facility. While the promise of the new facility attracted

61 In 1979, California voters approved Proposition 4, which placed strict limits on tax proceeds of local governments. As part of the resulting legislation, the state was required to reimburse localities for any costs arising from a new state mandated program. In 1996, Los Angeles petitioned the Commission on State Mandates claiming that the new SVP law constituted a state mandate. The CSM issued its opinion on the matter in 1998, concluding that counties were indeed permitted to recoup costs associated with SVP proceedings (Commission on State Mandates, 1998).

the interest of several California communities, all but one withdrew amid fears of escapes and the effect of the facility on their civic images (Rainey, 2000).

In August of 2000, the state selected the San Joaquin Valley town of Coalinga to house the new facility and its estimated 2,000 jobs. By that time, however, the projected cost of construction had more than doubled from previous estimates, to an estimated $349 million, prompting the legislature's budget analysts to call for a scaled-back version of the facility with the option of future expansion (California Legislative Analyst's Office, 1997). With the urging and backing of the City of Coalinga, however, the legislature disregarded its analysts' recommendations, and appropriated the full amount -- $349 million – to the project in its FY2002 budget.[62] The project was completed in 2004 at a final cost of approximately $366 million.[63]

Legal Cases Reshape Practice

By 2000, as the California SVP program entered its fifth year, the program had reached a general state of equilibrium. New cases had stabilized at approximately 75 per year, case processing backlogs had reached relatively manageable levels, and legislators and the new Governor Gray Davis had continued to demonstrate a continued commitment to the program's funding. In the ensuing years, however, two cases addressed by the California Supreme Court would present fundamental challenges to the program's structural parameters, ultimately expanding the policy's potential reach.

The first case concerned a civilly committed individual named Patrick Ghilotti, who in late 2000 reached the community transition phase of his treatment program at Atascadero State Hospital. In

---

[62] The City of Coalinga's lobbying for the facility was not without its critics. Upon approval of the new facility, one community activist facetiously quipped, "Welcome to Coalinga – the sexual predator capital of California. I don't think that this is going to encourage a lot of future industry in the area." (Rainey, 2000)

[63] California 2003-2004 Enacted Budget

accordance with statutory requirements and DMH operating practice, Ghilotti's case was reviewed by two independent examiners, each of whom concluded that Ghilotti met the clinical and statutory criteria for release. The pending release produced an immediate barrage of press reports in Marin County, where Ghilotti had been convicted of a series of rapes in the 1970's and 1980's (Chabria, 2002).

In stepped Steven Mayberg, the head of the Department of Mental Health, and one of the few gubernatorial appointees making the successful transition from Wilson's administration's to Davis'. Based on his reading of the law, Mayberg concluded that he had the authority over-ride the opinions of the independent evaluators, and in the fall of 2001, did just that. The interpretations of Mayberg's actions ranged from those who saw it as a calculated political move, possibly linked to the Davis administration's desire to placate the pivotal Marin County voters during the upcoming election cycle, to the alternative view of Mayberg as a protector of the public safety (Chabria, 2002).

Ghilotti appealed the decision to the California Supreme Court, which handed down its ruling in April of 2002 ("People v. Superior Court of Marin County (Patrick Ghilotti)," 2002). While the Court concluded that Mayberg had indeed overstepped his authority in over-ruling the evaluators, it also significantly lowered the risk threshold required for purposes for commitment. While prior practice in California, and in most other states had established the term "likely to engage in acts of sexual violence" in terms of a 50% standard (that is, "likely" means "more likely than not"), the Ghilotti ruling rejected that definition, opting instead to require only a "well-founded risk" of future sexual violence.

While political leaders such as Governor Davis and Attorney General Bill Lockyer praised the ruling (California Office of the Governor, 2002), dissenting opinions within the Court voiced concern that the revised standard did little to differentiate sexually violent predators from "everyday sex offenders," and that the ruling threatened to compromise the significance of the requirement of proof "beyond a reasonable doubt."(McKee, 2002). Mayberg's reflections on the case, however, are perhaps most telling:

> "We're really clear that at this stage there is not a cure for sexually violent predators.....I don't know that I'm necessarily the last line of defense, but I think I have an obligation to be honest and objective, and if I think that there are risks, I have an imperative to articulate that. I sort of have two clients here. I have to figure out how to deal with the sexually violent predator, and also how to prevent traumatization of innocent folks. The toll this kind of inappropriate behavior takes on everyone is huge. And if I'm really a mental-health clinician at heart, we need to look at how we prevent people from being traumatized."(Chabria, 2002)

As the Ghilotti case unfolded, a second major case with implications for the law's reach was working its way through the courts. Guadalupe Torres, who had been civilly committed after serving eight years in prison after pleading guilty to charges of "date rape," appealed his commitment on the grounds that his prior sexual offense was not "predatory" in nature, as defined by the statute. Upholding an earlier court of appeals ruling, the California Supreme Court ruled in May 2001 that a finding of past predatory behavior was not required for a jury to conclude that there is potential for future predatory behavior. Torres' commitment was upheld. ("People v. Torres," 2001)

From an operational perspective, the Torres ruling essentially broadened the pool of potential referrals to prosecutors for civil commitment proceedings, and significantly lowered the legal threshold for commitment eligibility. Indeed, as we will see in the ensuing review of operational indicators, the Torres ruling appears to have had an appreciable impact on the number of cases referred by the California Department of Corrections and the Board of Prison Terms for potential commitment, in turn contributing to a surge in prosecutor filing activity during 2003.

Florida

Precipitating Events and Policy Response

Florida was one of several states that adopted or amended their SVP civil commitment laws in the wake of the Supreme Court's 1997 ruling in Kansas v. Hendricks. The law's passage was due in part to the efforts of Don and Claudine Ryce, a Dade County couple whose 9-year old son Jimmy had been abducted, sexually assaulted, and killed by a released sex offender in September 1995. Following in the path of Ida Ballasiotes, Helen Harlow, and Gene and Peggy Schmidt, the Ryces took up a crusade that brought their personal tragedy into the public domain and ultimately into the halls of the statehouse (McGill, 1998).

As early drafts of the bill – labeled the Jimmy Ryce Civil Commitment for Sexually Violent Predators Treatment and Care Act – circulated through relevant committees, a legislative analyst produced a report sounding a cautionary note. The analyst, working under the aegis of the House Committee on Family Law and Children, stated in her introductory paragraph that " a significant fiscal impact is expected." The report included general survey of treatment and evaluation costs in other jurisdictions – notably Kansas and Wisconsin, concluding that the state could expect to pay approximately $100,000 per year for each committed individual, and that the program could reach 600 committed individuals at a total cost of $60 million per year (Florida House of Representatives Committee on Family Law and Children, 1998).

The report was part of the package submitted to the Human Services Appropriations Committee in February of 1998. By the time the package left that committee, however, the introductory warning regarding "significant program costs" had been deleted from the report, and the cost estimates had been significantly reduced. The revised fiscal impact statement, in contrast with the one that had been initially prepared, implied that the state had a good deal of choice with regard to program models and costs, and estimated that the state could operate a 60-bed unit at a cost of approximately $3.1 million – roughly half of the originally estimated costs. The revised report contained no mention of projected future growth and associated costs (Florida House of Representatives Committee on Health and Human Services Appropriations, 1998).

While the legislation attracted the usual share of legal criticism, and a measure of scrutiny from the press regarding perceived under-estimation of program costs[64], the Jimmy Ryce Act passed the Florida legislature by unanimous vote in April of 1998. The bill, signed into law by Governor Lawton Chiles on May 19th, was scheduled to take effect January 1, 1999. As part of the bill, the legislature allocated $6.4 million to the SVP program for Fiscal Year 1999, including $4.9 million to the Department of Children and Families and $1.5 million to the Department of Corrections (Florida Legislature, 1998).

Pre-Implementation Rumblings

In November 1998, two months prior to the law's scheduled implementation, Florida voters elected Republican Jeb Bush to succeed Chiles as governor. In the midst of the gubernatorial transition period, and as the program's planned implementation date approached, doubts began to emerge regarding the policy's tenability.

A front-page story appearing in the Tampa Tribune on New Year's Day 1999, the first day of the new law, described the looming implementation issues, citing the 182 cases that had already been referred as potential SVP's, and quoting legislators and program managers who cited the apparent under-projection of cases and required resources (Samolinski, 1999a). Three days later, the St. Petersburg Times joined the fray, writing in an editorial:

> " Legislators say these claims (of under-estimation) are overblown. Rep. Alex Villalobos, R-Miami, who sponsored the Ryce Act in the House, said that the projection of hundreds

[64] A Miami Herald editorial appearing April 7, 1998 noted the discrepancies between the program's rhetoric and its proposed funding levels, urging lawmakers to "put up or shut up" (Miami Herald, 1998).

> of commitments are a 'Fig Newton in someone's imagination.' But with the built-in pressures all in favor of civil commitment, Florida should expect a deluge. The Legislature had better start looking for a way to pay for it all. Keeping these people, who have already paid their debt to society, locked up indefinitely is going to be very expensive." (St. Petersburg Times Editorial, 1999)

Implementation Begins

As projected in the press, in its first month the Department of Children and Families faced a substantial backlog of cases requiring review and assessment under the Act (Florida Office of Program Policy Analysis and Governmental Accountability, 2000a). According to a legislative report, the backlog emerged in the wake of a disagreement between DCF and the Attorney General over the population eligible for commitment. While the DCF had interpreted the law as encompassing individuals who reached the 180-day threshold after January 1, 1999, which would have produced a gradual stream of referrals, the Attorney General ruled that the law in fact applied to all individuals scheduled to be discharged from the DOC within the coming 180 days, effectively presenting the DCF with 6 months of planned discharges from the first day of the program.[65]

The press barrage over implementation difficulties continued. The January 31st edition of the Palm Beach Post commented:

> "There was not a whisper of dissent last spring when the **Jimmy Ryce** Act preventing the release of sexually violent felons glided through the Florida Legislature, followed by a photo-op signing by then-Gov. Lawton Chiles. But during the month since the law took effect, a chorus of complaints could

[65] Over the following two years, the statutory timeframe for initiating the process would be extended by the legislature twice – first to 365 days and then to 545 days. Although these changes were put forth with the intent of providing more "breathing room" for the process, they had the short-term paradoxical effect of **increasing** the size of the case backlog, as the universe of potential cases was broadened.

> be heard from those who must make the statute a reality. For prosecutors, it's a logistical headache. To defense lawyers, it's a constitutional outrage. To the psychiatric community, it's a medical sham. To state officials, it's an unwieldy - and potentially expensive - bureaucracy in the making." (Hiaasen & Stapleton, 1999)

Notably, the newly-elected Governor Jeb Bush was quoted as pondering whether lawmakers had "overstepped our bounds." And Don Ryce – the father of Jimmy Ryce and the law's vocal proponent – soon joined the chorus of those questioning whether the state had over-extended the law's reach beyond its original target population (Samolinski, 1999b).

Amidst this turmoil, the DCF was faced not only with a backlogged evaluation and review workload, but with the additional challenge of preparing for the influx of new detainees and commitments. In the early spring of 1999, the DCF took over a former county jail located in Martin County, designating the facility the Martin Treatment Center (Florida Office of Program Policy Analysis and Governmental Accountability, 2000b). Contracting with the Florida Department of Correction for perimeter security, the program entered into a facility operations and treatment services contract with Liberty Behavioral Health, a Pennsylvania-based corporation that had recently begun operating a similar program for the State of Illinois. The DCF also contracted with Wackenhut Corporation – one of the nation's largest private correctional facility management companies – to house and supervise detainees choosing not to participate in treatment, at a facility located in Palm Beach County.

<u>Attempts to Fix the Problems</u>

The legislative session in the spring of 1999 included a range of provisions aimed at stemming the mounting concern regarding the policy's implementation. First, lawmakers responded to the growing calls to properly fund the DCF program. DCF operating budget appropriations for that year included $17 million, encompassing DCF vendor contracts with Liberty, Wackenhut, and contracted evaluators; approximately $1.5 million for an inter-agency agreement with the Department of Corrections; and approximately $500K for central program management services. The FY00 budget also increased base funding allocations for county prosecutors and public defenders for staffing and case-related costs associated with SVP cases. On the facilities front, two appropriations totaling $6 million were allocated for DCF to contract with the Department of Corrections for renovation of two sites – a 144-bed unit for detainees, and an 88-bed treatment facility for committed individuals – located on the grounds of the DeSoto Correctional Complex (Florida Legislature, 1999).

The legislature also directed that the DCF contract with a consultant to evaluate the program, its systems, and its processes. Pursuant to that directive, the DCF entered into a consultant agreement with William Mercer Associates, which in turn enlisted the services of Dr. Judith Becker, a nationally-known expert on sex offender treatment, and Dr. Gene Messer, the Chief Operating Officer of Arizona State Hospital, which two years earlier had begun to operate that state's civil commitment program.

As the Mercer group began its work, the Governor issued an Executive Order on October 7, 1999, creating a Jimmy Ryce Act Enforcement Task Force. The task force was charged with "considering and making recommendations regarding the implementation, administration, and effectiveness of existing legislative mandates regarding the civil commitment of sexually violent predators" (Florida Office of the Governor, 1999). Of the 13 members named in the order, four were through legislative appointment, one was through appointment by the Chief Justice of the Florida Supreme Court, and one was through the Attorney General. The remaining 7 members, including the Task Force chairperson, were either to be immediate members of the Governor's administration or appointed through the Governor.[66]

The Task Force Report, issued on February 1, 2000, acknowledged the problems encountered during the early months of the program, but ultimately concluded that:

> "...the Jimmy Ryce Act, after one year of operation, appears to be sound public policy that provides an adequate framework for implementation. The Department of Children and Families and the other agencies with responsibilities under the Jimmy Ryce Act, have developed a program that is generally functioning well for a complex civil commitment program in its initial year." (Jimmy Ryce Act Enforcement Task Force, 2000)

The report's ten recommendations, many of which were drawn directly from the Mercer Report that had been issued in December, were more heavily focused on the location, building, and operation of treatment facilities than on the review and commitment processes that had plagued the program throughout its first year. Regarding the evaluation and commitment process, the Task Force's sole recommendation, drawn directly from the Mercer Report, pertained to an extension of the statutory timeframe for DCF to complete its evaluations, from 45 to 90 days.

The Task Force report is as notable for what it did not include as for what it did include. First, although the report briefly mentioned potential bottlenecks in the legal process, its recommendations were essentially silent on any type of modifications to the legal system, which by the date of the report's release, had detained 136 individuals,

---

[66] The scope of the Task Force's mandate overlapped considerably with the scope of service defined by the legislature for the Mercer Report. While it would be speculative to attribute motivations for creation of the Task Force, it is notable that the seven members appointed by the Governor effectively gave Bush a controlling stake in the Task Force's report and recommendations, and in turn the public presentation of the Mercer Report's results.

and had only completed 9 commitment trials. Second, the report was tentative with regard to the state's provision of a less restrictive alternative (LRA) program. Despite the Mercer Report's citing the lack of an LRA as a "major concern," and that report's unequivocal statement that "it is imperative that there be a provision for an LRA,." the Task Force report merely suggested that the state "consider the addition of a post-commitment supervision program." To date, there has been no legislative or executive action on this key issue.

Facility Issues

Approximately three months after the release of the Task Force report, a resident of the Martin Treatment Facility scaled a perimeter fence and attempted escape by helicopter, prompting a considerable amount of media and legislative attention. A legislative review of the incident pointed at least in part to a disconnect between the mission of the contracted vendor – Liberty Healthcare – and the Department of Corrections, which maintained responsibility for perimeter security. Beyond the specific issues such as Liberty's insufficient levels of supervisory staff and removal of razor wire that might have prevented the escape, the report cited the problem of "differing missions of the two entities", noting that the DOC emphasizes security whereas Liberty "focuses on treatment" (Florida Office of Program Policy Analysis and Governmental Accountability, 2000b).

At the time of the escape, the DCF and the DOC had already initiated plans to vacate the Martin facility, which both the Mercer Report and the Jimmy Ryce Task Force had found to be inadequate to address the growing population, and to re-locate the SVP facility to an alternative DOC site. In a quest for a more permanent arrangement, the Florida legislature granted statutory authority to the Correctional Privatization Commission, in consultation with the DCF, to oversee the siting, construction, and management of a dedicated SVP facility in the general vicinity of the DeSoto Complex.[67]

The CPC issued its RFP on September 1, 2000. The scope of service set forth by the original CPC plan effectively called for a full privatization of Florida's SVP program, covering the design, construction, lease, and facility operations, including sex offender treatment programming (Correctional Privatization Commission, 2000). While this "soup to nuts" model had achieved relatively wide use in Florida and several other states as applied to prison facilities (McDonald, Fournier, Russell-Einhourn, & Crawford, 1998), the approach had not been tested by any other states for the purposes of civil commitment.

The following spring, the CPC made preliminary award of the contract, worth between $30 million and $50 million in the first year, to Atlantic Shores Healthcare, a subsidiary of Wackenhut Corporation (PR Newswire, 2001). Within a period of weeks, however, the contract award had been rescinded by the governor's office, effectively putting on hold any new facility plans. In December 2001, the legislature rescinded the authority granted to the CPC, instead directing the Department of Corrections to internally develop a plan to construct a new facility adjacent to the DeSoto complex. Concurrent with DOC's planning for the new facility, the DCF issued a new Request For Proposals in January 2002 for the operations and programming of the SVP facility (Florida Department of Children and Families, 2002). The sole bidder on the procurement was Liberty Healthcare, the incumbent provider.

Challenges to Treatment Program Adequacy

Governor Bush's 2003 Budget, submitted to the legislature later that spring, included two notable omissions connected to the SVP program

---

[67] See Chapter 2000-171 Laws of Florida, Section 28. The CPC was established by to contract with private vendors to design, finance, acquire, lease, construct, and operate private correctional facilities.

budget. First, the Governor declined to include in his budget request an approximately $1 million proposal to fund the first stages of DCF's Less Restrictive Alternative program.[68] Second, the budget declined to provide for anticipated program growth, opting instead to level-fund the program for Fiscal 2003.[69] Through this budget strategy, the Florida SVP civil commitment program, arguably the least developed of the six state programs included in this study, attempted to contain the costs of its treatment program while other states struggled with steady and considerable cost increases.

Yet this adopted strategy appears to have come at a significant cost. In May 2004 several residents of the facility filed a civil complaint against Liberty Behavioral Health and the Department of Children and Families in 2004 ("Canupp v. Liberty Behavioral Health," 2004). The plaintiffs held, among other allegations, that the defendants had affirmatively capped treatment capacity at 150 slots -- approximately 36% of the 420 residents held at the facility at that time.

As the Canupp case began to unfold, a series of events in the ensuing months reflected the considerable challenges being faced by a treatment program struggling to keep pace with a growing population in the face of three years of virtually level funding. Two inspector general investigations – the first based on a series of whistleblower complaints, and another initiated to investigate new allegations that surfaced during the first inquiry – exposed several staffing and management issues associated with the state's contracted treatment program, including falsification of incident reports and official records and serious security breaches (Florida Office of Inspector General, 2004, 2005).

---

[68] Funding alone would not be sufficient to establish an LRA, since legislative authorization and guidelines for implementation would also have been required. However, the Governor could have used the budget request to propose such a legislative change, and has clearly declined to do so.

[69] Agency budget request information and Governor's response pulled from http://www.ebudget.state.fl.us/home.asp.

APPENDIX B: STRUCTURAL REVIEWS

Washington

Washington's program structure is described in detail in Table 15. For purposes of comparison with other state programs, several key points regarding this structure should be noted.

First, Washington law provides for several potential sources of potential SVP referrals. Most commonly, these sources involve the pending release from custody of an individual who at any time in the past has been charged with or convicted of a sexual offense. Such pending releases may include individuals scheduled for discharge from the Department of Corrections upon completion of a prison sentence, as well as individuals about to be released from the custody of the Department of Social and Health Services after being held as an adjudicated delinquent (juvenile cases), incompetent to stand trial, or not guilty by reason of insanity.[70] Additionally, based on an amendment to the statute adopted in 1995, a county prosecutor may file a petition on individuals in the community with sex offense histories who commits a "recent overt act" of sexual violence, regardless of whether that act resulted in criminal proceedings.

Second, although the statute stipulates that the "agency with jurisdiction" shall forward referrals directly to prosecutors, operating practice has funneled the screening process through an End of Sentence Review Committee (ESRC), an entity established under separate statute under the direction of the Secretary of Corrections. The ESRC consists of representation of all potential agencies with jurisdiction, including DOC and the applicable divisions of DSHS.

Third, Washington's treatment program, provided through the DSHS Special Commitment Center (SCC), operates in a separate

---

[70] In addition to its role as administrator of the SVP program, DSHS also manages the state's juvenile justice facilities and its forensic mental health system.

facility located on McNeil Island, a complex managed by the Department of Corrections. Although the SCC has become progressively independent of the DOC over the past several years, the facility still relies on the Department for certain facility operations, security, and transportation services.

Fourth and finally, Washington's statute is replete with detailed requirements connected to the establishment, management, and operation of a Less Restrictive Alternative (LRA) Program. Seven sub-sections of the law, mostly added in the legislature's 2001 section, refer to a range of LRA-related provisions, including identification of sites, distribution and mitigation of community impacts, and procedures for petition. As we shall see later, no other state has promulgated as extensive a set of statutory guidelines connected to LRA programming.

Minnesota

The key structural elements of Minnesota's PP/SDP policy are described in Table 16. Partially due to the Minnesota's unique status as an extension of its prior sexual psychopath law, the policy contains several notable characteristics.

First, its system for case initiation – both in terms of defining the "target" population and in establishing systems for screening and referral – is comparatively open and broadly defined. Regarding the population, the statute explicitly focuses on a concept defined as "harmful sexual conduct" rather than predicate offenses as a main criterion for commitment. This focus on behavior, rather than criminal justice system factors, effectively broadens the pool of potential commitments. Minnesota is also the only state that routinely seeks commitments under two potential standards – the sexual psychopathic personality standard and the sexually dangerous person standard.[71]

---

[71] New Jersey also maintains two standards on its books, since it adopted its initial SVP law in 1994 and adopted a new law in 1998 following the Hendricks ruling. As a practical matter, however, New Jersey does not seek

Second, regarding screening and referral systems, the current statute is rather broad, indicating only that the Commissioner of Corrections "shall make a preliminary determination whether, in the Commissioner's opinion, a petition may be appropriate." Between 1998 and 2003, the Department employed a relatively refined system for case identification, involving the administration of an actuarial instrument by correctional caseworkers,[72] record review and clinical interviews by a doctoral-level psychologist, and committee review prior to referral. DOC practice, however, shifted dramatically at the end of 2003 in the wake of the Dru Sjodin murder, at which time the Department began referring all "Level 3" offenders to prosecutors for potential commitment.[73]

Third, Minnesota law involves the placement of series of financial requirements on counties connected to the civil commitment process. Under the law, counties are responsible for all legal costs including 50% of the costs of housing of the individual during the pre-trial period. Subsequent to commitment, counties are responsible for 10% of the housing costs associated with post-commitment housing. Through a subsequent statutory amendment, however, the Attorney General was required to waive its usual fees for representing the counties in PP/SDP commitment hearings. As a matter of practice, the AG provides services for all but the state's two largest counties.

---

commitments under both standards simultaneously, as is the practice in Minnesota.

[72] This instrument, the Minnesota Sex Offender Screening Tool (Revised), was developed internally by the DOC, specifically for SDP screening purposes. Adapted loosely from several common actuarial and psychological testing tools, the MNSOST-R has been utilized in several other states with SVP laws.

[73] Refer to the Minnesota state narrative for details on the Sjodin case and its impact on implementation practice.

Fourth, Minnesota's legal process is unique, in that it is only state examined here that does not provide the option of a jury trial. [74] Additionally, the standard of proof, in contrast with the "beyond a reasonable doubt" employed by most states, is "clear and convincing evidence."

Fifth and finally, Minnesota's two treatment facilities are located adjacent to correctional complexes, the facilities are wholly operated by the Department of Human Services. One of the facilities is operated under the broader umbrella of a secure forensic mental health facility, while the other is a free-standing site. Treatment includes a comprehensive, multi-phase relapse prevention model, and detailed systems for community transition and the attainment of supervised release.

Wisconsin

Wisconsin's SVP civil commitment system is described in Table 17. While Wisconsin's initial screening system is not quite as broadly defined as Minnesota's, the operating practice is somewhat similar. Referrals funnel directly from the agency with jurisdiction (AWJ) to county prosecutors, and the Department of Corrections has established a system and deployed resources providing for psychological evaluations of potential referrals.[75]

As is the case in both Washington and Minnesota, the Attorney General provides legal support for the state's smaller counties in the management of SVP cases. Unlike those jurisdictions, however,

---

[74] Examining this process in its 1998 report, the Civil Commitment Study Group recommended no changes to this law, indicating that respondents had a series of appeal options that precluded the need for a jury.

[75] The Wisconsin Department of Corrections (DOC) oversees the custody of both adult and juvenile offenders. The screening and referral processes are handled by the respective divisions within the Department, with adult cases are screened through the Department's Offender Classification Division, and juveniles through the Office of Juvenile Programs.

county prosecutor positions are funded through state appropriations, as are public defenders. The legislature has earmarked funds in its budget for the state's two largest counties and for the Department of Justice for staff resources associated with SVP cases.[76]

Also like Minnesota, Wisconsin operates two facilities under its Department of Human Services for housing, evaluating, and treating pending or committed SVP's. The Department also maintains between 12 and 14 individuals on supervised release. These individuals have generally not completed all phases of their treatment, but rather have successfully petitioned the court to permit an SR placement. While the state has appropriated funding for the construction of a dedicated supervised release housing facility, siting difficulties have delayed implementation (Wisconsin Department of Health and Family Services, 2004).

Kansas

The Kansas program's key structural elements are summarized in Table 18. Compared with the other states examined here, the Kansas model is relatively basic. Below, we briefly consider the state's screening and referral process and its treatment program.

Regarding the screening and referral process, Kansas has established a "dual gatekeeper" system involving a multi-disciplinary review team (MDRT) administered through the Department of Corrections, and a prosecutors review committee (PRC) administered through the state Attorney General. In contrast with many other systems that permit referring entities to screen out a subset of cases sent on to prosecutors, the Kansas system is structured to permit the PRC to review all potential cases.[77] As a practical matter, however, the PRC

---

[76] Only prosecutor staff resources are funded through the state. Support staff and ancillary costs associated with cases remain a county responsibility.

[77] Certain states such as Florida and Massachusetts are also required to send notice to states attorneys prior to release of anyone who may qualify.

typically focuses its attention on cases established through the screening process to be "high risk."

The Kansas program for custody and treatment is more heavily dependent on the Department of Corrections for its day-to-day operations than any of the six programs investigated in this study. The statute specifying the requirements on and authority of the state's Department of Social and Rehabilitative Services explicitly precludes DSRS from housing SVP's in the same facility as more "traditional" DSRS clients, notably community inpatient psychiatric patients. On the other hand, the statute authorizes the Department to enter into an inter-agency agreement with the DOC, and requires only that SVP's be "housed and managed separately," implying that a separate SVP housing unit within a DOC facility is sufficient. As a practical matter, the treatment program, located within the Larned Correctional Mental Health Facility, relies on the DOC for facility security, food, transportation, and medical care – virtually everything with the exception o f delivery of the treatment program. This level of inter-agency dependence reflects a critical structural dimension with which to view the Kansas program.

California

California's SVP civil commitment program structure, described in reflects several significant departures from the programs described thus far.

The first source of variation pertains to the definition of the target population. Beyond the usual stipulations pertaining to mental abnormality and likelihood of future sexual violence, California's definition restricts SVP filings to individuals with two or more victims and whose sexual violence has been directed at strangers or "individuals with whom a relationship was cultivated for the purposes of victimization."[78] The population is further restricted by a

[78] It should be noted that this seemingly restrictive guideline, which would presumably preclude commitment of incest offenders, for example, has been

requirement that the law may only be applied to individuals currently serving a determinate sentence in the CDC or an individual whose parole has been revoked.

The second critical point of divergence in California's system involves its relatively complex pre-referral screening process, entailing a sequence of reviews involving multiple agencies. Although the program's referrals all emanate from the California Department of Corrections (CDC), the initial CDC review is supplemented by a review by the Board of Prison Terms (BPT), the state's parole agency, prior to a referral to the Department of Mental Health. Both the CDC and the BPT retain dedicated units to handle SVP cases. Of the cases referred to the DMH, the statute requires a minimum of two professional evaluations, conducted by psychologists or psychiatrists who may not be state employees. If the two evaluators do not concur on commitment eligibility, two additional evaluations are performed.[79]

A third point worth noting involves the issue of prosecutorial jurisdiction and cost burdens. Of the five states we have examined thus far, California is the first that does not involve the Attorney General in the direct filing of cases.[80] Additionally, as described in the preceding narrative, counties do not bear financial responsibility for costs associated with prosecuting or defending SVP cases, since they receive reimbursement under a ruling through the Commission on State Mandates. From a structural perspective, therefore, there are few financial incentives against counties' filing of cases. Coupled with the fact that cases referred to prosecutors have received the "blessing" of two or more independent evaluators, one may expect to see few cases in which prosecution is denied.

---

given a relatively broad interpretation by the California Supreme Court (People v. Torres).

[79] Despite this statutory requirememnt, DMH operational practice involves an initial "triage" of cases through record reviews prior to ordering evaluations.

[80] The Attorney General does, however, represent the state in appellate challenges to the state's law.

A fourth critical distinction pertaining to California's commitment program involves the fact that commitments are only authorized for a two-year period, and must be affirmatively extended biennially. This is in contrast with the practices of other states examined here that utilize an indeterminate commitment system. In practice, commitment extensions are routinely filed and granted, producing little functional difference between California and other states beyond the additional workload requirements.

A fifth notable aspect of California's program involves the location of the treatment program. Committed men are housed in a specialized unit within Atascadero State Hospital, a 1,200-bed state forensic facility. Committed women are housed at Patton State Hospital, another DMH facility. While this arrangement means that the program is wholly operated through the DMH, the SVP program remains part of a much larger institution, and in fact retains a staffing pattern more closely resembling a psychiatric inpatient setting than a dedicated sex offender treatment program. As described in the narrative, a new 1,500-bed, free-standing SVP facility is under activation as of this writing, scheduled for opening in September 2005. The staffing pattern submitted by the DMH closely reflects the current system employed at ASH.

Florida

Florida's structural provisions, depicted in Table 20, contain four aspects of particular note. First, Florida's system, like California's, funnels referrals to prosecutors following a screening through its mental health agency. However, in contrast with the California system, which includes a delineation of statutorily limiting elements that permit correctional agency to reduce the number of cases referred to DMH, the referrals that DCF receives from Florida's DOC and DJJ essentially amounts to all pending releases from those agencies with current or prior records of sexual offenses.[81] Another critical distinction pertains to the independence of the examiners – while Florida shares California's model of utilizing contracted consultants, actual recommendations are made by a team that may include DCF staff psychologists, and unanimity of opinion is not a requirement. Further, virtually all of DCF's evaluations are provided by one contracted vendor, rather than a group of independent contractors.

Second, Florida's legal system, including the court system, regional prosecutors, and public defenders, is entirely state funded, and not paid through county revenues. Accordingly, the system is highly dependent on state legislative appropriations to meet its core implementation requirements, including the timely processing of cases.

Third, Florida's system of custody and treatment requires close coordination between DCF, its contracted vendor, and the Department of Corrections. Florida is the only state in our analysis that relies on a contracted vendor for its treatment services.

Fourth and finally, Florida is the only state in our analysis that has yet to develop provisions for supervised release or less restrictive alternatives. Although such a program has been included in DCF budget requests, it has failed to make it into the budget. Moreover, the enabling legislation does not include any provisions or mechanisms for committed individuals to petition for such status, nor does it include any guidelines or authorization pertaining to operation of an LRA program.

---

[81] Potential "Jimmy Ryce" cases are flagged in the DOC's information system during the course of incarceration. Facility-based staff gather documentation on these cases approximately twenty months prior to scheduled release, and forward this documentation to the DOC's Offender Classification unit, which transmits the information to the DCF. The statutory timeframe for DCF referral has been modified twice, from an original 180 days, to 365 days, and most recently to 18 months prior to release.

Table 15: Washington Program Structure

Stage	Statutory Requirements	Operating Practices
Agency With Jurisdiction (AWJ) Referral Wash. Code §71.09.025	When it appears that person may meet criteria of a sexually violent predator (convicted or charged w/ a crime of sexual violence and who suffers from mental abnormality that makes the person likely to engage in predatory acts of sexual violence if not confined), AWJ must provide notice to county attorney in county where person was charged three months prior to release from custody AWJ to submit range of records regarding institutional, psychiatric, and criminal history	Two major AWJ's provide the cases flowing into the SVP system -- the Department of Corrections (DOC) and the Department of Social and Health Services (DSHS). DSHS referrals may include juveniles, mental health incompetent cases, NGRI cases, and MR cases. All agencies funnel their referrals through a centralized entity, the End of Sentence Review Committee, which conducts case screening
End of Sentence Review Committee (ESRC) Determination Wash. Code §72.09	ESRC to be established by Secretary of Corrections to review each sex offender under DOC authority prior to release and assign risk classification level. ESRC is multi-agency body composed of 12 voting members – 4 from the DOC, 5 from DSHS divisions (Mental Health, Juvenile Rehabilitation, Children and Family Services, Developmental Disabilities, and Victim Witness Protection) 2 county prosecutors representatives, and 1 member of the state's Indeterminate Sentencing Review Board.	Operating through a subcommittee structure based on area of case specialization, ESRC reviews all pending sex offender releases, ordering psychological evaluations on a subset of these cases. Cases referred by the subcommittees for further action are reviewed by the full ESRC prior to referral to prosecutors.

Table15: Washington Program Structure(continued)

Stage	Statutory Requirements	Operating Practices
County Attorney Filing Wash. Code §71.09.030	County attorney may file upon receiving AWJ/ESRC notice or unilaterally if individual who had previously been released from confinement commits a "recent overt act" ; County attorneys may request that Attorney General file petition on their behalf.	Prosecution for all but one of the state's counties is handled through a special unit within the office if the Attorney General. King County – the state's largest – handles SVP cases through its own designated unit
Probable cause/ detention order Wash. Code §71.09.040	Judge determines whether probable cause exists to believe that person is an SVP as defined by statute; Upon PC finding, person transferred to DSHS custody for evaluation as to whether person is an SVP	Upon finding of probable cause, the individual is remanded to the custody of DSHS for a clinical evaluation, conducted at the Special Commitment Center (SCC).
Trial and commitment Wash. Code §71.09.050 and §71.09.060	Trial to be conducted within 45 days of probable cause unless continued; Respondent has right to counsel, retention of expert examiners; Jury trial may be demanded by court, petitioner, or respondent; Jury or judge must determine beyond a reasonable doubt that person is SVP; Upon such finding, person is committed to DSHS custody until person's condition has changed making him/her no longer meeting SVP criteria or until less restrictive alternative as established	

Table15: Washington Program Structure(continued)

Stage	Statutory Requirements	Operating Practices
Treatment and Custody Wash. Code §71.09.070, §71.09.090, and §71.09.110	DMH "shall afford the person with treatment for his or her diagnosed mental disorder…that shall be consistent with current institutional standards for the treatment of sex offenders and shall be based on s structured treatment protocol"; Amenability to treatment is not required for a finding that person is an SVP…. treatment does not mean that the treatment be successful or potentially successful"; DSHS responsible for all costs relating to evaluation and treatment for SVP's. Department may pursue reimbursement for these expenses from committed individuals in accordance with provisions of state law.	Treatment program provided at the Special Commitment Center Program based on relapse prevention model and phase system beginning with orientation and proceeding through community transition and conditional release.
Annual Reviews and petitions for conditional release LRA provisions for release added by legislature in 2001 session Wash. Code §71.09.070, §71.09.090, and §71.09.094	Annual review of case required to be submitted by DSHS to the court. Person entitled to retain independent expert if disagreeing with findings of review; Review to include consideration of LRA or conditional release; If person does not affirmatively waive their right to petition, show cause hearing is scheduled; Person may file for conditional release, LRA, or unconditional discharge with or without approval of Secretary of DSHS; If petition supported by DSHS, hearing to be set within 45 days – if petition not supported by DSHS, preliminary "show cause" hearing is required; LRA petition must be supported by identification of specific treatment plan, including housing and community treatment; To deny LRA petition, State must prove beyond reasonable doubt that either the LRA is not in best interests of respondent **or** the proposed LRA does not sufficiently protect the community	

Table 16: Minnesota Program Structure

Stage	Statutory Requirements	Operating Practices
Dept. of Corrections Review Governed by Minn. Stats Ch 244.05 (7)	Commissioner of Corrections "shall make a preliminary determination whether, in the commissioners opinion, a petition under section 253B.185 may be appropriate."	Multi-step review, commencing 14 months prior to release; MN-SOST administration by correctional caseworker; Triage of cases and clinical interviews by Civil Commitment Coordinator; Review of interviewed cases by Multi-Disciplinary Team; Determination on referral made by Director of Sex Offender Programs As of December 2003, all Level 3 Offenders referred on for potential commitment
County Attorney or Attorney General Decision to file Minn Stats Ch 253B.18 and 253B.18	Responsibility for filing resides with county attorney, who may request that the Attorney General provide representation in the case; Petitions may be filed on any individual with at least one prior sex offense conviction who exhibits "harmful sexual conduct" (that is, a current conviction is not required for a petition to be filed – harmful behavior is sufficient)	DOJ handles cases for all but state's two largest counties; Although prosecutors have wide latitude in identifying cases for potential commitment, virtually all filings emanate from DOC referrals
Statewide Judicial Panel Minn Stats Ch 253B.185 (4)	Statute authorizes the supreme court to establish a panel of district judges with statewide authority to preside over SDP/PP commitment hearings	Option has not been exercised, but under consideration

Table 16: Minnesota Program Structure (continued)

Stage	Statutory Requirements	Operating Practices
Review and Hearing for Preliminary Commitment Minn Stats Ch 253B.18	If judge hearing case finds "clear and convincing" evidence that person satisfies PP or SDP criteria, person is committed to DHFS custody for evaluation, which is to be submitted to court within 60 days	Evaluations conducted by DHFS psychologists at St. Peter facility, and include information pertaining to diagnosis and treatment needs.
Indeterminate Commitment Minn Stats Ch 253B.18	Upon receiving evaluation report, if judge finds that person continues to meet criteria by clear and convincing evidence, he/she may issue an indeterminate commitment order, upon which person is remanded to DHFS custody until meeting criteria for provisional discharge.	No provision for a jury trial Respondent may seek review of judge's order through Minnesota Court of Appeals or through federal courts via habeas corpus
Treatment and Custody Minn Stats Ch 246B.02	DHS to establish and maintain secure facility known as the Minnesota Sexual Psychopathic Personality Treatment Center to "provide care and treatment to 100 persons committed by the courts as sexual psychopathic personalities or sexually dangerous persons"	Population served through Moose Lake facility specified in the statute, and a unit at the Minnesota Security Hospital in St. Peter. Both operated by the DHS. Comprehensive, multi-phase treatment program includes both regular and special needs tracks, and a system leading to gradual community re-integration.

Table 16: Minnesota Program Structure (continued)

Stage	Statutory Requirements	Operating Practices
Provisional Discharge	Following successful completion of the core treatment program, committed individuals may petition a Special Review Board for placement in the MSOP's transition stage; Upon agreement of the Special Review Board and the prosecutor in the county of commitment, the individual may be granted unsupervised passes into the community, which are phased in incrementally; Provisional discharge decisions for individuals in transition are reviewed first by the State's End-of-Confinement Review Committee (which oversees the sex offender community notification system), then by the SRB and the county prosecutor in the county of commitment; Should the county and the SRB disagree, the case is mediated through a 3-judge panel.	

Table 17: Wisconsin Program Structure

Stage	Statutory Requirements	Operating Practices
Agency With Jurisdiction (AWJ) Review Wis. Stats Ch. 980.015	AWJ determination that person "may meet criteria for commitment as sexually violent person Referral for cases meeting criteria within 3 months of planned release to Dept. of Justice, DA in county of conviction, and DA in proposed county of release	Governed by Specialized psychological screening unit established in 1999, and funded through legislative appropriations; Multi-step Review, commencing one year prior to release; Initial record screening and End of Confinement Review for selected cases; Psychological evaluation for selected cases
DOJ/DA Review and Petition Filing Wis. Stats Ch. 980.02	Dept. of Justice may file at its discretion; If DOJ does not file, DA may file.	DOJ reviews cases and prepares most initial petitions; Handles cases for all but state's two largest counties upon request of the county; DOJ and two counties provided with targeted state appropriations for prosecutors to handle Ch. 980 cases
Assignment of counsel Wis. Stats Ch. 980.03	Respondent entitled to counsel, which may be appointed if indigent; County must pay for expert defense witnesses for indigent clients	Majority of cases handled through attorneys in Wisconsin Office of Public Defender.

Table 17: Wisconsin Program Structure (continued)

Stage	Statutory Requirements	Operating Practices
Probable cause determination, detention, and evaluation Wis. State Ch. 980.04	Circuit court in which petition is filed must hold PC hearing within 72 hours if person detained; If PC found, person remanded to DHS for evaluation to determine if he/she is an SVP	Evaluations conducted by DHS psychologists in accordance with agency rules and guidelines
Trial and Commitment Wis. State Ch. 980.05 and 980.06	Jury trial to be conducted upon request of petitioner or respondent; Petitioner must prove beyond reasonable doubt that person is dangerous due to a mental disorder that makes it "substantially probable" that he/she will engage in acts of sexual violence; If SVP determination made, person remanded to DHS custody for tx until he/she is "no longer a sexually violent person."	Standards for commitment such as nexus between mental disorder and dangerousness, actuarial thresholds, definitions of "substantially probable", etc. remain somewhat elusive and are focus of numerous pending appellate cases.
Treatment and Custody Wis. Stats Ch. 980.06 and 980.12	DHS to provide "control, care, and treatment" DHS responsible for costs related to evaluation, treatment, and care of all committed individuals	Population served through two stand-alone facilities operated by DHS – the Sand Ridge Treatment Center and the Wisconsin Resource Center; Treatment programming governed by internal DHS operating procedures

Table 17: Wisconsin Program Structure (continued)

Stage	Statutory Requirements	Operating Practices
Supervised Release Wis. Stats.Ch. 980.08	Person may petition court for supervised release following 18 months of commitment, or at least 6 months following denial of prior petition for discharge or supervised release; Director of DHS program may petition at any time; Court order for supervised release requires DHS to "make its best effort" to locate a suitable placement; SR order may be revoked upon DHS request if person violates terms established by court	DHS maintains 12-14 persons on supervised release, and has initiated plans to build 12-bed SR facility in Milwaukee County
Petition for Discharge Wis. State Ch. 980.09	Person may file for discharge with or without approval of Secretary of Human Services; If state (the DA or the DOJ) contests petition, must prove by clear and convincing evidence that person is still SVP	DHS has not recommended any committed individuals for discharge to date.

Table 18: Kansas Program Structure

Stage	Statutory Requirements	Operating Practices
AWJ and Multi-Disciplinary Review Team (MDRT) Reviews Kan. Stats §59-29a03 (2001)	AWJ determination that person may meet criteria for commitment as sexually violent predator (defined as "any person who has been charged with a sexually violent offense and who suffers from a mental abnormality or personality disorder which makes the person likely to engage in repeat acts of sexual violence") requires written notice to attorney general and to multi-disciplinary team; MDRT has thirty days to complete assessment, and is required to notify attorney general of its assessment	Majority of cases emanate from Department of Corrections, which also oversees operation of MDRT; Following an initial record review by the Department of Corrections SVP Administrator, a subset of the cases are referred for clinical assessments, including the completion of the Static-99 (an actuarial risk assessment instrument), completed by contracted psychologists based at the facilities; The MDRT, consisting of representatives from the KDOC, the Kansas Department of Social and Health Services, and the Juvenile Justice, reviews all cases, assigns risk levels (High, Medium, Low) to each, and forwards all cases on to the PRC for further review.
Prosecutors Review Committee (PRC) Review and Filing Kan. Stats §59-29a03 and §59-29a04 (2001)	Attorney General to appoint PRC to assist AG in determining whether person meets definition of SVP; Upon PRC positive determination, the Attorney General may file a petition within 75 days of initial notification.	As matter of practice, the PRC has typically recommended prosecution on cases confirmed by the MDRT as "high risk."

Table 18: Kansas Program Structure (continued)

Stage	Statutory Requirements	Operating Practices
Probable cause and evaluation Kan. Stats §59-29a05	Upon filing, judge to determine whether probable cause exists; Respondent has right to counsel, presentation of evidence, and cross-examination at PC hearing; If PC found, person may be transferred to secure facility for professional evaluation	Evaluations typically conducted on-site by Dept. of Social and Rehabilitative Services (DSRS) at Larned Correctional Mental Health Facility (LCMHF)
Trial and Commitment Kan. Stats §59-29a06 and §59-29a07 (2001)	Jury trial to be conducted upon request of petitioner or respondent; State must prove beyond reasonable doubt that person is a sexually violent predator. Jury verdict must be unanimous; If SVP determination made, person remanded to DSRS custody for care, control , and treatment until the person's mental abnormality has so changed that the person is safe to be in the community at large	Standards for commitment such as nexus between mental disorder and dangerousness, actuarial thresholds, definitions of "substantially probable", etc. remain somewhat elusive and are focus of numerous pending appellate cases.

Table 18: Kansas Program Structure (continued)

Stage	Statutory Requirements	Operating Practices
Treatment and Custody Kan. Stats §59-29a07 (2001)	Control, care, and treatment shall be provided at facility operated by DSRS, which must house patients in a facility separate from other individuals in DSRS custody; DSRS may enter into an inter-agency agreement with the Department of Corrections for the confinement of population, although population must be housed and managed separately; DSRS responsible for costs related to evaluation, treatment, and care of all committed individuals; Statute's population separation requirements more restrictive pertaining to traditional MH population than with correctional population..	Population housed in facility located at Larned State Hospital. Operated by DSRS, which provides treatment services. DOC provides security, food, transportation, and facility support.
Annual Review, Discharge Petitions, Transitional Release Kan. Stats §59-29a07 (2001)	Committed individuals to receive examination of mental condition annually, with report provided to court; DSRS to provide annual written notice to person regarding right to petition court for release; Person may petition for transitional release or discharge. If probable cause found that person's condition has changed, court may set a hearing, which may be conducted before a jury; mState must prove beyond a reasonable doubt that person is not ready for transitional release or discharge.	

Table 19: California Program Structure

Stage	Statutory Requirements	Operating Practices
Criminal Justice System Review **California Dept. Of Corrections (CDC) And Board of Prison Terms (BPT)** Cal. Welfare and Institutions Code (WIC) §6601	Director of CDC to determine whether person "may be a sexually violent predator" CDC and BPT to screen on basis of whether person has committed a sexually violent predatory offense (as defined in statute) and on review of social, criminal, and institutional history. If it is determined likely that person is an SVP, case to be referred to DMH for full evaluation.	CDC Operating Procedures Article 17, Sec. 62130; CDC cases screened by facility-based classification officers, and forwarded to specialized CDC unit established for screening SVP cases; Reviews fundamental statutory criteria: qualifying offense, two or more victims, predatory relationship w/ victims; Positive cases and "maybe" cases sent on to BPT for further review and information; BPT recommendations sent to CDC, which makes referral to DMH; BPT commenced reviewing positive cases only in 2001, following requests from district attorneys; Statutory criteria threshold operationally modified through Torres ruling.
Department of Mental Health (DMH) Evaluation Cal. Welfare and Institutions Code (WIC) §6601	DMH to employ "standardized assessment protocol" assessing mental disorder and risk factors; Person to be evaluated by two psychologists and/or psychiatrists contracted through DMH (may not be state employees); If two evaluators do not concur, two additional evaluators to be brought in. Petition can only be filed if both evaluators agree on determination; If DMH determines that person is SVP, request for petition submitted to county attorney of initial commitment	DMH performs initial screening of cases; Evaluation performed through approximately 50 independent evaluator contracts maintained by DMH statewide; Evaluators typically perform evaluations in CDC facilities prior to CDC discharge. Ghilotti ruling affirmed that DMH cannot unilaterally overrule its evaluators, but that evaluations may be challenged on technical legal grounds. Ruling also established that prediction of dangerousness need not exceed 50% probability.

Table 19: California Program Structure(continued)

Stage	Statutory Requirements	Operating Practices
County Attorney Filing California WIC §6601	States attorney decision to file following receipt of DMH request; Cases to be filed in Superior Court in county of initial CDC commitment.	
Probable cause determination and detention order California WIC §6602	Judge determines whether probable cause exists to believe that person is an SVP as defined by statute; Upon PC finding, person may be placed in state hospital (DMH) upon discharge from CDC	
Trial, commitment, and extended commitment California WIC §6604 and 6604.1	Jury trial to be conducted upon request of petitioner or respondent; Respondent or county attorney may order updated evaluation prior to trial ; Jury or judge must determine beyond a reasonable doubt that person is SVP; Upon such finding, person is committed to DMH custody for two years – after two year period, state must file for an extended commitment to keep person in custody.	As matter of practice, extended commitments are routinely pursued upon expiration of initial or prior extended commitments.

Table 19: California Program Structure(continued)

Stage	Statutory Requirements	Operating Practices
Treatment and Custody California WIC §6606	DMH "shall afford the person with treatment for his or her diagnosed mental disorder…that shall be consistent with current institutional standards for the treatment of sex offenders and shall be based on s structured treatment protocol"; "Amenability to treatment is not required for a finding that person is an SVP…. treatment does not mean that the treatment be successful or potentially successful"	Treatment program provided at Atascadero State Hospital, an 1,100-bed forensic psychiatric facility operated by DMH; Scheduled to move to standalone Coalinga State Hospital 9/05; Program based on relapse prevention model and phase system beginning with orientation and proceeding through community transition and conditional release.
Annual Reviews and petitions for conditional release California WIC §6604	Person entitled to annual examination and review; DMH required to furnish annual written notice of person's right to petition court for conditional release; If person does not affirmatively waive their right to petition, show cause hearing is scheduled; Release to be effectuated through three possible routes: Individual initiates petition for conditional release at annual review; DMH commissioner petitions court for unconditional discharge; or commitment not extended after two years.	Conditional release may be approved by court per plan submitted by DMH. Individual or court may or may not accept submitted terms of conditional release, and may petition court for modification of plan; Indivuduals on conditional release managed and monitored through DMH's Forensic Conditional Release Program (CONREP), which is also used for other individuals committed to DMH custody. DMH/CONREP Policy and Procedure Manual §1250

Table 20: Florida Program Structure

Stage	Statutory Requirements	Operating Practices
Agency With Jurisdiction (AWJ) Review Florida Stats 394.913	AWJ forwards information on all pending releases meeting charge criteria to Multi-Disciplinary Team (MDR) and to state attorney; Dept. of Correction required to refer cases 545 days prior to release; Dept. of Juvenile Justice w/in 180 days; and DCF within days	The universe of potential SVP cases is drawn from three main sources – the Department of Corrections, which produces percent of the referrals, the Department of Juvenile Justice, producing percent of the referrals, and the DCF itself, which produces the balance. The DCF cases are those individuals held in DCF custody due to a previous finding of Not Guilty by Reason of Insanity (NGI) in connection with a sexual offense; Process consists primarily of gathering records on individuals meeting charge profiles. DOC cases flagged in system upon admission to DOC custody w. records gathered prior to point of statutory referral date
MDR Team (Dept. of Children and Families) Review Florida Stats Ch. 394	MDRT to be established by Secretary of the Dept. of Children and Family Services, and to include at least two psychologists and/or psychiatrists; MDRT must offer a personal interview to anyone being considered for commitment; MDRT required to report to states attorney within 90 days	Florida Admin. Code Ch.65E-25; Codified administrative guidelines, adopted in November 2001, call for initial record review by two psychologists or psychiatrists (in practice, virtually always psychologists), and clinical interview if warranted. All decisions made by MDR team on majority basis (unanimity not required). If commitment recommendation made, individual conducting clinical interview must concur; Use of specific actuarial instrument (Static-99) is codified as requirement in evaluations

Table 20: Florida Program Structure (continued)

Stage	Statutory Requirements	Operating Practices
States Attorney Filing Florida Stats Ch 394.914	States attorney decision to file following receipt of MDR report; If person is being held in DCF custody (on temporary hold), petition must be filed within 48 hours, or person is to be released	State attorneys file petitions on vast majority of cases; May also file in cases where SA disagrees w/ MDR recommendation; 48-hour petition requirement rarely required, due to extension of timeframe for DOC notification (see above)
Probable cause determination and detention order Florida Stats Ch 394.915	Judge determines whether probable cause exists to believe that person is an SVP; Upon PC finding, person transferred to DCF upon expiration of incarceration; Court may conduct adversarial PC hearing in cases in which trial is delayed; Respondent has right to counsel, presentation of evidence, and cross-examination of witnesses	Probable cause determinations virtually always found (see data in following section);

Table 20: Florida Program Structure (continued)

Stage	Statutory Requirements	Operating Practices
Trial and Commitment Florida Stats Ch 394.915	Jury trial conducted upon request of petitioner or respondent (Jury of 6); Trial to be conducted within 30 days of PC determination; Respondent entitled to counsel and to a court-appointed expert to conduct evaluation; State must prove by clear and convincing evidence that person "suffers from a mental abnormality or personality disorder that makes the person likely to engage in acts of sexual violence"; If SVP determination made, person remanded to DCF custody until "the person's mental abnormality or personality disorder has so changed that it is safe for the person to be at large."	Trials rarely conducted within 30-day timeframe due to continuances and other sources of trial delays. "Time to trial" indicator explored later in this section; Florida Supreme Court ruling in 2001 has raised questions about admissibility of evidence derived from actuarial methods.
Treatment and Custody Florida Stats Ch 394.917 and 394.9151	DCF to provide "control, care, and treatment" DCF may also "contract with a private entity or state agency for use of and operation of facilities to comply with the requirements of this act."	Population served under contract with Liberty Healthcare, a private, for-profit vendor, at a facility leased through the Department of Corrections. DOC provides perimeter security and transportation, while Liberty is responsible for provisions within the walls, including treatment, internal security, health care, and food.
Supervised Release/LRA	No current provisions for supervised release or Less Restrictive Alternative	Formal agency requests for LRA funding thus far not included in Governor's budget

APPENDIX C: OPERATIONAL INDICATORS

Washington

The figures below indicate the general trends associated with Washington's screening and commitment process, from the program's initiation in 1990 through the end of 2001.[82] Figure 11 conveys volume outputs associated with three sets of actors – the End of Sentence Review Committee (ESRC), which drives the initial referrals; the prosecutors, who initiate the case filings; and judges and juries, which make determinations regarding commitments. Figure 12 depicts the decisions made by these actors as percentages of the cases reviewed by the ESRC. The upper outline of this graph reflects the trend in the percentage of cases resulting in ESRC referrals, with the various shaded areas reflecting case dispositions of cases referred by the ESRC during that particular year.

Figure 11: Washington Referrals,Filings, and Commitments 1990-2001

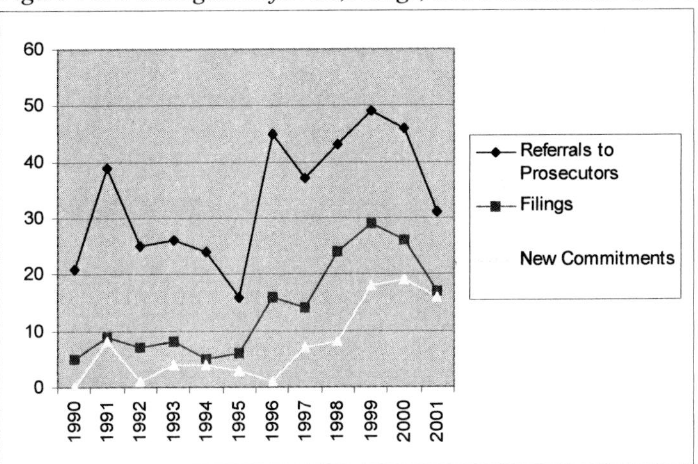

---

82 Data based on case-level information provided by the Washington State Attorney General's office and by the Washington Department of Corrections.

Figure 12: Washington Screening Burden Distribution 1990-2001

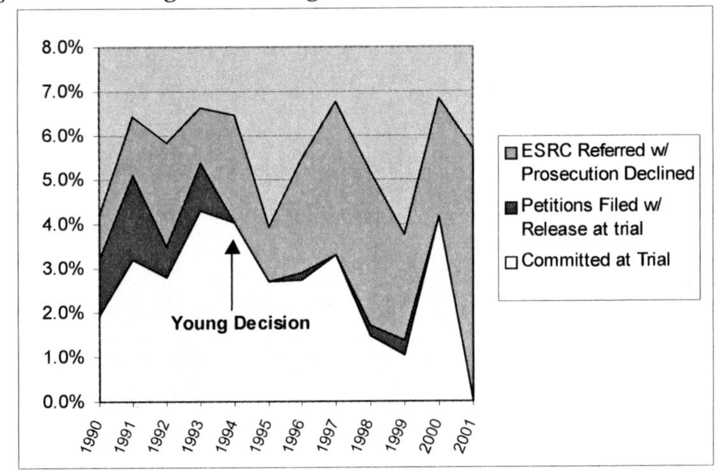

Referring to Figure 11, and adjusting the 1990 data points to account for the fact that the policy was only in operation for six months during that year (making the annualized number of referrals roughly comparable to 1991), we may observe a distinct series of phases.

Initial referrals have followed in essentially four phases – an initial two-year period involving a relatively high number of referrals to prosecutors (1990-91); a four-year period involving a 40% drop from previous levels and a pattern of relative stability (1992-95); a five-year period showing a significantly higher volume of referrals and moderate fluctuation (1996-2000); and finally, a drop in referral activity in 2001. Case filings, in contrast, follow a relatively low and stable pattern of fewer than 10 cases per year throughout the program's first six years of operation, begin to show some upward growth in 1996-97, climb to a peak of 29 cases in 1999, and begin to taper off in 2000-2001. The number of new commitments follows a similar pattern, although begins to show a moderate lag, attributable to increased case processing times, as the number of filings increases.

Examining the period from 1990 through 1995, two aspects of the observed patterns are of particular note – the apparent shift in ESRC screening and referral practices, and the negligible impact that this shift appears to have had on prosecutor filing decisions. Viewed through the lens of general policy implementation, the shift in ESRC practice might be viewed as an implementation "learning curve" – an initial surge, followed by a pattern of relative equilibrium associated with program learning.(Mazmanian & Sabatier, 1989). There is evidence to suggest, however, that the relatively high number of initial referrals stems instead from an explicit policy decision to place the selection of initial cases in the hands of prosecutors, rather than ESRC screeners.(Lewis, 1990)

Regardless of the reasons for this decline, the observed shift in ESRC screening practices appears to have had little or no practical effect on the volume of filings and commitments during the program's first four and a half years. This finding suggests that prosecuting attorneys – both in the attorney general's office and in the offices of the county prosecutors, had established a relatively conservative "comfort level" pertaining to the appropriate types and volume of potential cases, most likely connected to the policy's looming constitutional challenges.

Beginning in 1994, we begin to see a series of shifts associated with major court and legislative activity. The first such shift, as indicated in Figure 11, occurs in the year following the Young decision by the Washington Supreme Court, affirming the statute's fundamental constitutionality. For cases referred between 1990 and 1993, the courts played a fairly significant role in moderating the number of cases ultimately committed. This role is indicated in the chart by the darkly shaded area. For the cases referred in 1994 and onward, however, court decisions to dismiss the case or release the individual at trial became a rare exception. Through its 1993 affirmation of the constitutionality of the statute, the Washington Supreme Court appears to have had a substantive practical effect on the application of the law by judges and juries.

The second major shift that we observe involves a surge in referrals, and a corresponding increase in filing activity in 1996. An associated increase in commitment activity stemming from these referrals ensues in 1997. The most likely catalyst for this surge involved the legislature's 1995 re-visitation of the statute and a corresponding series of statutory amendments. At that time, the legislature considerably broadened the pool of potential commitments, from individuals serving current sentences for sexual offenses to <u>any individual</u> with current or prior sex offense convictions who were either serving sentences or, if in the community, have committed a "recent overt act." ("ARCW Chapter 71.09," 2001)

The third major shift – and one that we will observe in several other states – involves a surge in referrals, filings, and commitments between 1998 and 2000. These increases, an extension of activities stemming from the 1995 statutory changes, were most likely driven by the 1997 U.S. Supreme Court ruling in Kansas v. Hendricks. [83]

Although 2001 saw another series of legislative revisions – primarily in response to injunctive requirements pertaining to treatment and LRA programming – the decline in referred cases and filings for that year may be less attributable to explicit policy changes than to general events within the state and the nation. Major state budget deficits emerging in early 2001, an earthquake in February, and the fallout from major national events in September 2001, may have all contributed to the decline in activities surrounding SVP commitments.

<u>Population</u>

Figure 13 depicts the population trends resulting from Washington's case filing and commitment activities between August 1990 and December 2004. The population is divided into three groups – individuals detained in DSHS custody pending trial, individuals committed following trial, and individuals placed in Less Restrictive

---

[83] Although the Washington Supreme Court's 1993 ruling In re Young had cleared the way for earlier implementation efforts, the effects of the Hendricks decision in Washington was likely considerable. At the time, Young had been successful in his federal challenge to the law, and the case was pending appeal with the Supreme Court. Hendricks provided a viable barometer for the U.S. Supreme Court's position on the issue.

Alternatives under DSHS supervision. Consistent with the data discussed earlier, the overall numbers show rather modest growth through 1995, reflecting a pattern of tentative restraint. Beginning in 1996, however, the population begins a sustained climb that has continued through 2004.

Figure 13: Washington Committed and Detained Population 1990-2004

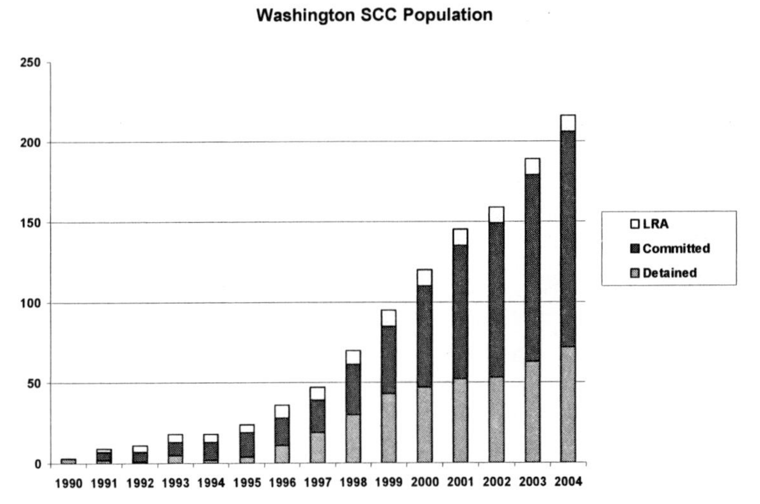

Notably, between 1996 and 1999, the detained population absorbed a growing proportion of the total number committed, implying growing delays in the time between preliminary commitment (probable cause finding) and trial. In short, it appears that the courts and other sectors of the legal system have experienced some measure of change in the timeframes for case disposition, either due to volume or shifts in legal practices.

Treatment Progress

While the system's "front door" continues to drive population increases, the "back door" is dependent primarily on the efficacy of the treatment provided and the ability of the state to effectuate subsequent release. As we will observe in each of the states under analysis, releases through successful completion of treatment remain a relatively rare occurrence. As of March 2005, Washington has ten individuals in Less Restrictive Alternatives – a figure that has remained relatively constant for approximately five years – but has released only one individual from its custody unconditionally.

In this context, data on treatment completions and release is a largely ineffective measure for the purposes of the present analysis. Alternatively, we may examine programmatic trends with regard to treatment participation, compliance, and progress. Through the regular reports to the court, the Special Master assigned to the Turay case began providing treatment compliance information in 1998, roughly coinciding with the program's relocation to McNeil Island. While treatment information prior to that time is not available, the initial assessment indicated a total of 27 individuals participating in treatment, out of 67 committed – a treatment compliance rate of approximately 40%.[84] Over the ensuing three years, the Special Master reports chronicle the evolution of treatment activity at the Special Commitment Center, as indicated in Figure 14: Washington Treatment Participation and Progress.

Washington's main treatment model consists of 6 phases, with the first phase deemed the "orientation" phase" and the sixth encompassing placement in a Less Restrictive Alternative. In addition, the program includes a "Special Needs" track for individuals with severe mental illness or cognitive impairments.[85]

[84] As we will examine later, this rate is quite low by "industry standards". It is therefore sufficient to say that, in all likelihood, treatment compliance prior to 1998 was at or below these levels.

[85] Only the June 2001 report separated the Special Needs group from the main presentation of data.

Figure 14: Washington Treatment Participation and Progress

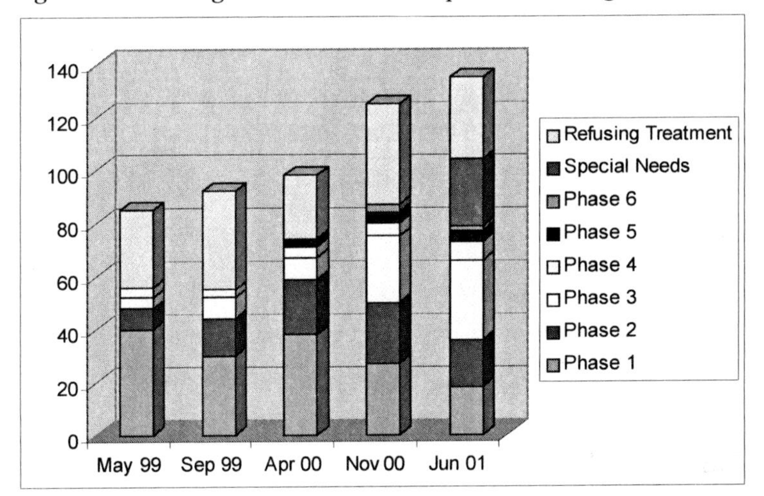

The figure reflects the distribution of individuals in the various treatment phases. It indicates a considerable reduction in the proportion treatment refusers, from just under 50% in May 1999, to 23% in June 2001.[86] It also shows an increase in treatment progress, with the numbers and proportions of individuals in the intermediate and advanced stages of treatment improving over time.

Despite the fact that the Washington program is over a decade old, it appears from these data that the evolution of the treatment program has been a relatively recent phenomenon. SCC program managers, with the support and prodding of the federal court, appear to have had modest success in creating a pattern of forward progress. It would therefore be premature to surmise that the lack of system discharges to date imply that Washington's treatment program is ineffective. The

---

[86] These figures should be viewed with some caution. Treatment refusers are defined in the reports as those who refused to sign treatment consent forms. Another group, most likely a subset of those in Phase 1, involve those who signed the forms but not actively and regularly participating in treatment activities.

question of whether treatment progress represents a viable pathway for committed individuals to gain release, however, remains largely unresolved. Thus far, communities have been reticent to accept placement of individuals following their commitment as a sexually violent predator, despite extraordinary steps taken by the program to facilitate such placements.

Minnesota

Throughout the 1990's, the Minnesota civil commitment program experienced a series of shifts connected to referral and commitment activity.

Figure 15: Minnesota Referrals and Commitment Patterns

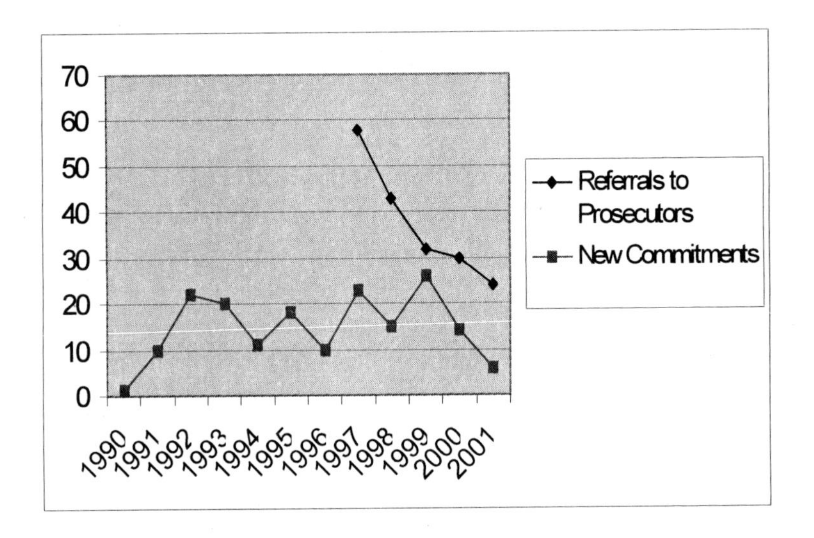

Following the 1991 change in DOC practice and the associated legislative changes during the 1992 session, the initial impact of the policy change is readily discernible. The surge in new commitments – there was just one in 1990 and ten in 1991 – is made even more dramatic considering that the DOC policy change occurred in the latter part of the year. On an annualized basis, the 1991 rate of commitment was comparable or greater to that experienced in 1992.

The fluctuating pattern observed between 1994 and 1997 may quite likely be linked to the shifting legal landscape both during that period, both in Minnesota and nationally. The 1994 decline in commitment activity may be attributable to a "chilling effect" connected to the Minnesota Supreme Court's July 1994 rulings limiting the reach of the statutes, the subsequent surge in cases in 1995 tied to introduction of the SDP statute, and the decline and resurgence of commitments in 1996-97 to the periods leading up to and following the Hendricks decision.

Beginning in 1998, and continuing through 2002, the number of new case referrals from the Department of Corrections begins to show a significant decline. Corresponding with the centralization of the DOC screening process, this decline is also associated with a modest, although unsustained, convergence of referral and commitment patterns, indicating that the process was "correctly" screening a greater proportion of cases.

Table 21: Minnesota Referrals and Commitments

Year	DOC Referrals	New Commitments
1997	58	25
1998	43	18
1999	32	26
2000	30	23
2001	24	13
2002	13	12
2003	246	18
2004	170	28

This trend, however, would reverse dramatically in 2003, as the Department of Corrections referred a total of 246 cases – more than the previous five years combined – to prosecutors. These cases, which included some individuals who were released during prior years, would contribute to a surge in new commitments during 2004, and signal a new series of DOC referral practices with potentially lasting significance for the policy.

Population

Consistent with the commitment trends discussed above, the Minnesota Sex Offender Program (MSOP) witnessed several surges in its population -- between 1991-93, again in 1997, again in 1999, and finally in 2004 in the wake of the Dru Sjodin case described in the narrative. Until this case, which produced a surge of new referrals from the Department of Corrections, the number of detained individuals had remained relatively constant, indicating a fairly balanced flow of cases through the justice system. These population patterns are indicated in Figure 16.

Figure 16: Minnesota Population Growth 1993-2004

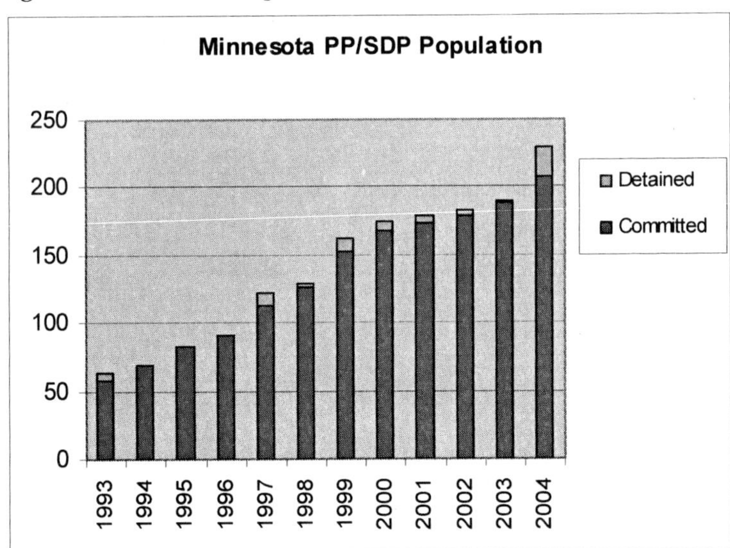

Treatment

As civil commitment policies have developed over the years, the MSOP has emerged as a "model program" in many respects. The program is well-documented in the treatment literature and its detailed policies and procedures are codified in the Minnesota Rules. A "snapshot" of the treatment status of the 2002 population (Figure 17) indicated that 78% were involved in active treatment, with the majority of those cases in the initial two phases. One individual had been provisionally discharged from the program, and five are involved in the transition stage.[87]

Figure 17: Minnesota Treatment Participation and Progress

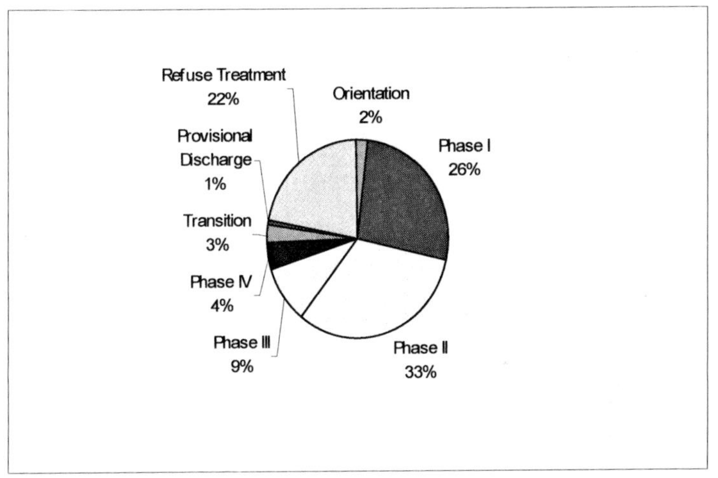

In 2004, MSOP modified its classification system to more effectively distinguish special populations served through its programming, including those with significant behavioral problems, cognitive disabilities, and serious mental illness. As of December 2004, the program reported the status of its current population as indicated below.

---

[87] One other individual reaching the transition stage passed away in 2001.

Table 22: Minnesota Population Treatment Status as of 12/04

Category	Unit/Status	Census (12/04)
General Treatment Population	Initial Treatment Unit	47
	Mid Treatment Unit	48
	Advanced Treatment Unit	25
Specialized Units	Non-Participant Unit	40
	Behavior Therapy Unit	25
	MAP Unit	24
Transition	Supervised Integration	9
Legal Status Pending Populations	Admissions Unit	45
	County Jail	2
Source: Minnesota Department of Human Services		

These treatment figures, viewed in the context of the state's relatively well-established treatment program and the substantial number that have resided in the program for between 5 and 10 years (Janus & Walbek, 2000), indicate the extremely slow route to treatment success. While a limited number of cases are able to progress to transitional release, a substantial portion of the committed population is likely to remain in the program for an indefinite period. As indicated in Figure 18, which depicts the breakdown of program departures between 1995 and 2002, discharge remains the least likely means of exit from the program.

Figure 18: Minnesota System Departures as of 2002

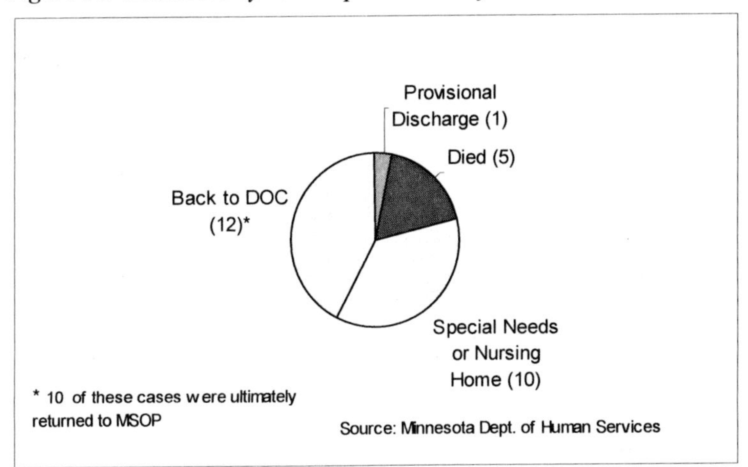

Wisconsin

Screening and Commitment

Figure 19 and Figure 20 reflect the initial screening and referral patterns associated with Wisconsin's Chapter 980 commitment process. The referral trends reflected in Figure 19, based on data provided by the Wisconsin Department of Justice, indicate a progressively more selective process employed by the referring agencies – notably the Department of Corrections – in the identification of potential commitment cases.[88] While the referral pattern shows some modest increases in 1996 and 1998 (the years following the Wisconsin v. Post and Kansas v. Hendricks decisions, respectively), there is an observable

[88] The data presented in this chart is annualized for the purposes of illustration. Specifically, while the actual number of cases referred in 1994 was 45, this figure represented only 6 months of activity. Data for all other years reflect annual actuals.

trend of greater selectivity in the cases that are sent on for potential prosecution.

Figure 19: Wisconsin Referrals to Prosecutors

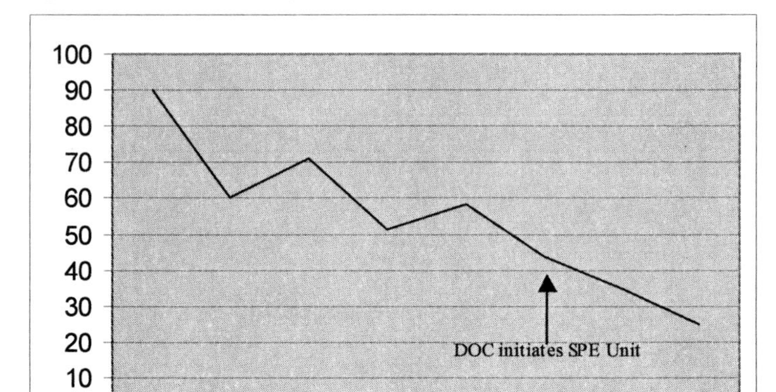

Figure 20 reflects program-to-date (aggregated) information provided by the Wisconsin Department of Corrections Offender Classification Unit. Between the 1994 inception of the civil commitment program and 2001, 46.5% of pending releases had passed through the End of Confinement Review, 21.9% had received psychological "special purpose" evaluations, and 7.2% had been ultimately referred on for potential prosecution.

The observed overall decline in referrals to prosecutors indicates that the percentage of potentially eligible cases referred on from DOC based on current practice is considerably lower than the mean value of 7.2%. This is supported by further data available from the DOC indicating that the overall numbers of sex offenders released from Wisconsin prisons has remained relatively constant throughout the period.

Figure 20: Wisconsin DOC Screening Process

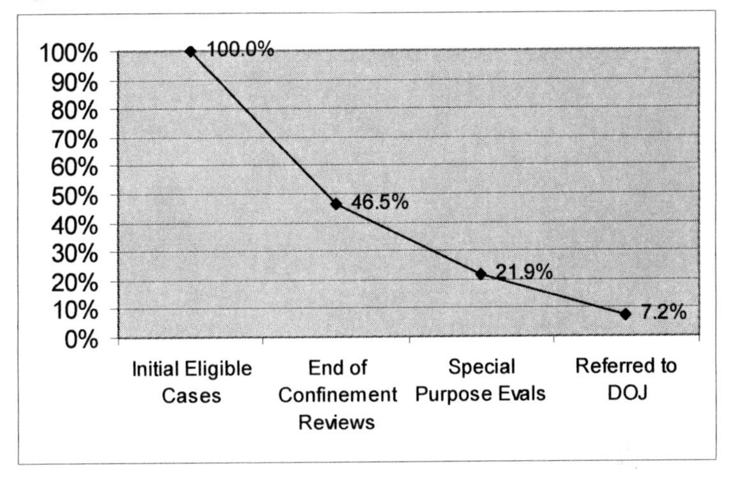

Consistent with a progressively selective screening process, the "quality" of the referred cases – at least as determined by prosecutors and the legal system – has indeed shown a shift over time. While annual data was not available prior to July 1998, monthly reports provided through the Department of Human Services ("Chapter 980" Reports) do contain cumulative "program-to-date" numbers, permitting comparison between the program's initial four years and the period between July 1998 and January 2002.

Table 23: Wisconsin Changes in Screening and Referral Practices

	June 1994-June 1998	**July 1998-Jan 2002**
Referrals	254	127
Prosecution Denied	18	4
Percent Denied Prosecution	7%	3%
Filings	246	123
Dismissals at Trial	50	3

The data in Table 23 clearly illustrates a relationship between the DOC's greater selectivity of cases and a decrease in the number of cases triaged out by prosecutors and the court system. Both prosecution denials and case dismissals have become relatively rare occurrences, each averaging one per year. As a result, the legal system has effectively proceeded with its cases primarily in accordance with the Department of Corrections' recommendations.

This phenomenon lends itself to varying interpretations. On one hand, it may be that the DOC has found a mechanism to effectively identify the "right" cases for civil commitment. Alternatively, it may also be that prosecutors and the rest of the legal system have relaxed the standards required for commitment. In either case, it is clear that the DOC's "gatekeeping" responsibility has become more central to the determination of who is ultimately committed under Chapter 980.

This development has corresponded to a shifting role of the DHS evaluators in the legal process. As discussed above, the DOC and the DHS essentially operate parallel evaluation systems, with the DOC conducting the pre-referral evaluation, and the DHS conducting statutory evaluations following probable cause. Considering that virtually all of DOC's referrals result in commitments, the data appears to indicate that the role of the DHS evaluation in the process has been rendered incidental at best.[89]

Population

Figure 21 depicts the total population held in DHS custody between July of 1998 and December 2004. Population figures for the Wisconsin program prior to July 1998 are not available for the purposes of this review. Since that time, however, the committed population has shown

---

[89] As a matter of practice, several prosecutors interviewed for this study have indicated that the DOC evaluation is typically more comprehensive, and therefore more useful in the prosecution of cases. This may be attributed to the fact that defense attorneys typically instruct their clients not to participate in clinical interviews with DHS evaluators, whereas the DOC often has the opportunity to conduct such an interview.

a gradual and fairly consistent pattern of increase at a rate of between 25 and 30 cases per year. Overall, the number of committed individuals, including those on supervised release, increased from 127 in July 1998 to an average of 243 in Fiscal 2004, an annualized average of approximately 21 cases per year (Wisconsin Legislative Fiscal Bureau, 2005). Based on the July 1998 baseline, the average number of annual commitments for the previous four years (June 1994-June 1998) was approximately 32 cases per year, indicating that commitment rates have declined slightly from previous levels.

Figure 21: Wisconsin Population Growth 1998-2004

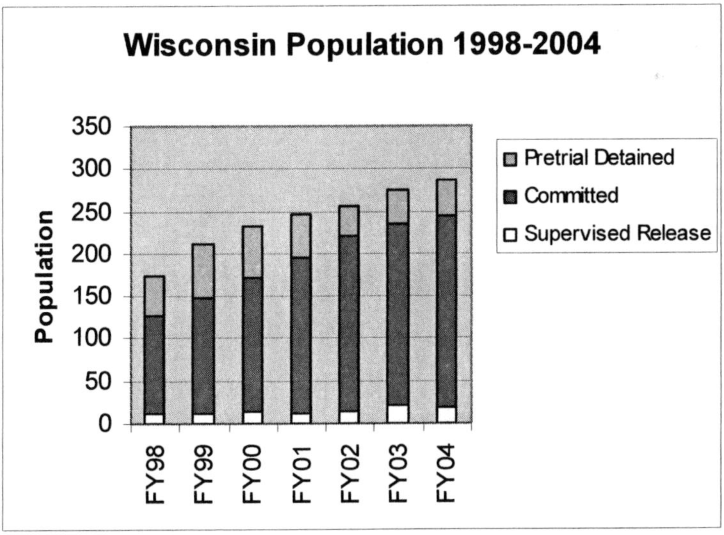

Treatment Participation

According to data provided by the DHS to the Legislative Fiscal Bureau in 1999, approximately 28% of the committed population actively refuses treatment, with the remaining 72% participating in treatment programming. About one third of this treatment group is involved in special programming for individuals with mental illness or cognitive impairments, with the balance involved in various phases of the standard treatment program. Of that group, just over half are engaged in the "core" program, with the balance in various stages of "pre-core" preparation.

Figure 22: Wisconsin Treatment Participation and Progress

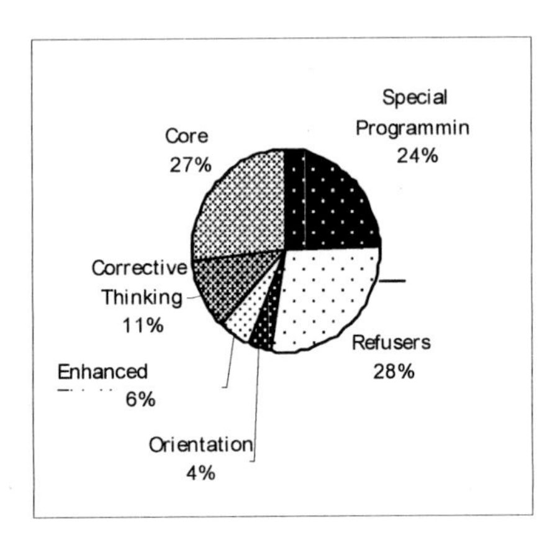

Wisconsin has one of more developed systems of supervised release of any of the states included in this study. While between 11 and 14 individuals remain on "supervised release" status, this number has remained relatively constant since 1998. Between 1995 and 2004, the program transitioned 44 cases into its supervised release program. Of this group, 20 cases, or 45%, had been revoked and returned to committed status, and another 16 cases, or 36% of the total, remained on supervised release status as of December 2004. 7 individuals, or 16%, had proceeded through supervised release as a gateway to eventual program discharge, and one case had died prior to discharge.90

[90] Case-level source data provided by DHFS, December 2004.

Kansas

Screening and Commitment

The Kansas system completed comparatively few commitments during the three years between the law's adoption and the decision in Kansas v. Hendricks. Between 1994 and 1997, the state released a total of 850 potentially eligible offenders, ordered psychological evaluations on 80 of those cases, and succeeded in committing 13 (Stovall, 1998). Beginning in 1998, however, the pace of commitments picked up dramatically, surging from fewer than five per year to over 20.

Figure 23: Kansas Screening and Commitment Activity

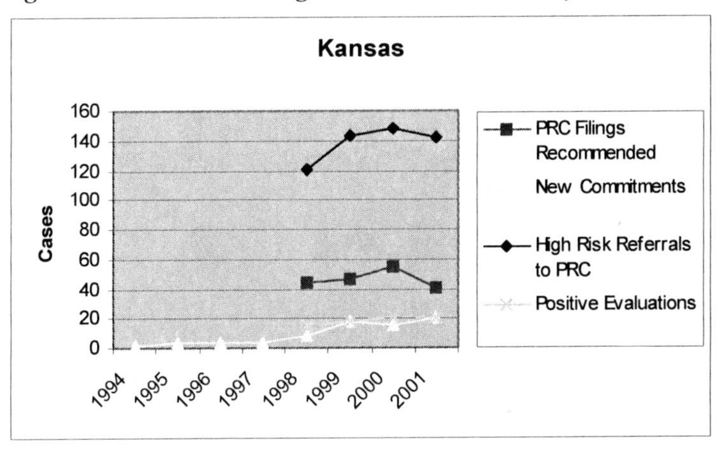

Figure 24 provides a closer look at some of the factors behind Kansas' commitment activities both pre-Hendricks and in the years following. The figure indicates that much of the variation has been not within the legal system, but rather in the process of screening and clinical evaluation. As a practical matter, Kansas courts have generally granted probable cause status in the vast majority of cases filed, leaving a significant portion of the pre-trial screening responsibility on DSRS evaluators. These results of these evaluations, however, have fluctuated substantially, beginning with a surge in the percentage of cases found to meet dangerousness criteria from approximately 20%

pre-Hendricks to 80% in the year after Hendricks, and continuing with a series of erratic shifts in evaluation outcomes. Also between 1998 and 2001, the percentage of cases deemed by the initial Department of Corrections assessment to be "high risk" essentially doubled.

Figure 24: Kansas Percent of Cases Clearing Key Decision Points

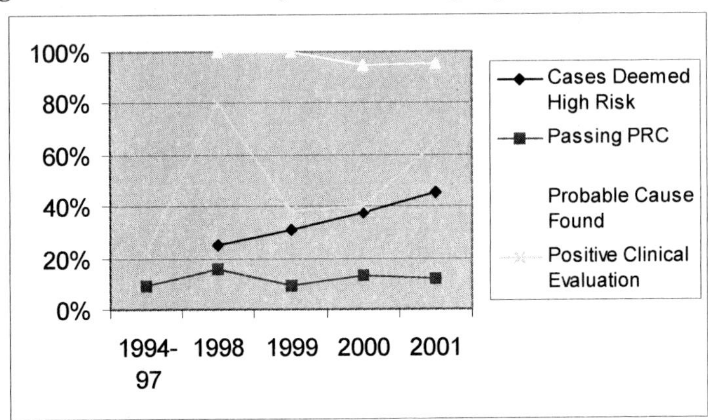

More recent data, however, appear to indicate a refinement of filing practices beginning in 2001. As noted in Table 24: Kansas Filings and Commitments, 2000-2004the state has seen a decline in the total number of petitions filed each year, yet an improvement in the percentage of cases filed that lead to commitment. These patterns suggest that the pre-commitment review process have become more effective in identifying prospective cases.

Table 24: Kansas Filings and Commitments, 2000-2004

Year	Cases Filed	Committed	Pending	% committed
2000	63	15		23.8%
2001	45	24		53.3%
2002	47	28		59.6%
2003	39	22		56.4%
2004	37	15	13	62.5%
Source: Kansas Attorney General's Office (% committed in 2004 is net of cases pending as of 12/31/04)				

Population

Consistent with the commitment trends noted above, the Kansas civil commitment program, after an initial period of tentative restraint, has grown significantly the years following the Hendricks ruling. Figure 25, depicting the program's population growth since the policy's inception, indicates a growth rate of fewer than 5 cases per year through 1997, and a current growth pattern in the vicinity of 20-30 cases per year. Adjusting for the size of the state and the potentially eligible population, this level of commitment activity ranks Kansas as a comparatively fast-growing civil commitment program.

Figure 25: Kansas Committed Population

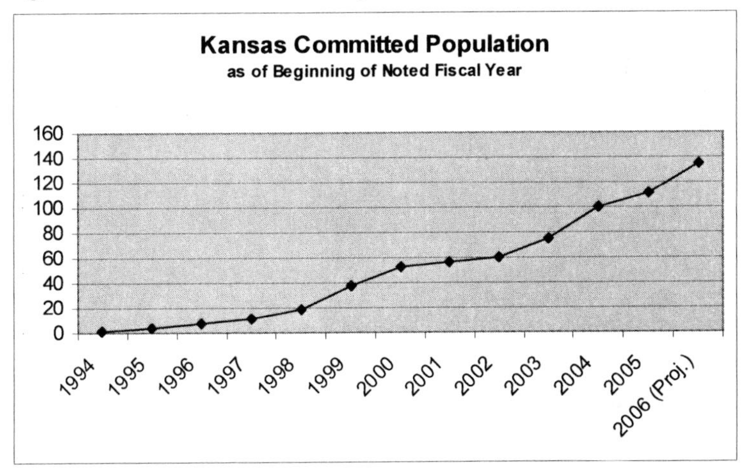

Treatment Progress

Table 25 indicates the treatment status of 112 individuals in DSRS custody as of July 1, 2004. Of this group, four individuals were grouped in the latter stages of the treatment program, involving transition back to the community, with the remaining 108 in the inpatient treatment Phases I-IV. Notably, however, this figure would more than double by March 2005, with 10 individuals in transitional phases by that date, and another four cases pending transfer to the transition phase of the program. These significant developments during the course of Fiscal 2005 denote a program very much at a transitional turning point in the management of its committed population.

Table 25: Kansas Treatment Program Status as of 7/1/04

Treatment Stage	**As of 7/1/04**	**Moved to transition between 7/04-3/05**	**Pending transitional status as of 3/05**
Phase I	5		
Phase II	63		
Phase III	34		
Phase IV	6		
Inpatient Treatment subtotal	**108**		
Phase V (transition)	1	5	4
Phase VI (supervised release)	1	1	
Phase VII (conditional release)	2		
Subtotal in Transition/Release	**4**	**10**	**14**

Source: Kansas Department of Social and Rehabilitation Services

California

The California SVP civil commitment program deals with a significantly higher number of cases than any of the states examined thus far. Figure 26 provides a broad overview of the screening, case filing, and commitment volume experienced since the program's inception in 1996. The data is drawn from information provided by the Department of Mental Health, which monitors cases from the point of DMH referral through commitment.

Figure 26: California Screening,Filing, and Commitment Patterns 1996-2004

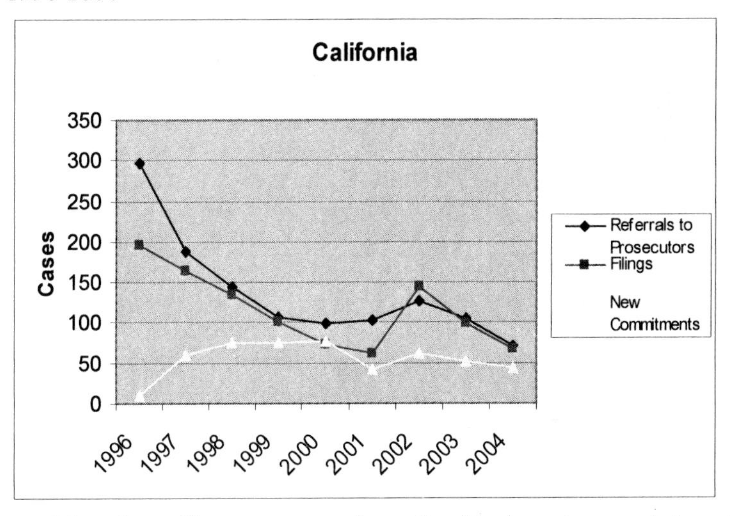

The chart illustrates a series of critical patterns relating to implementation practices both within and across systems. The referral patterns – specifically the volume of cases referred by the DMH to county prosecutors – show a peak level of 300 cases referred during the program's initial year, followed by three years of continual decline in case volume, and the settling of cases at approximately 100 per year. Cased filings by county prosecutors follow roughly the same pattern through 1999, but instead of showing a leveling pattern between 2000-

2002, have continued to decline. Commitments, clearly lagging behind filings by at least one year, appear to be following a similar pattern.

An alternative view of the system is presented in Figure 27, which reflects the allocation of "screening burden" across systems. The screening burden reflects the percentage of total potential cases (in this instance, sex offender discharges from the Department of Corrections) that each stage in the process eliminates from potential commitment.[91]

Figure 27: California Relative Distribution of Screening Burden

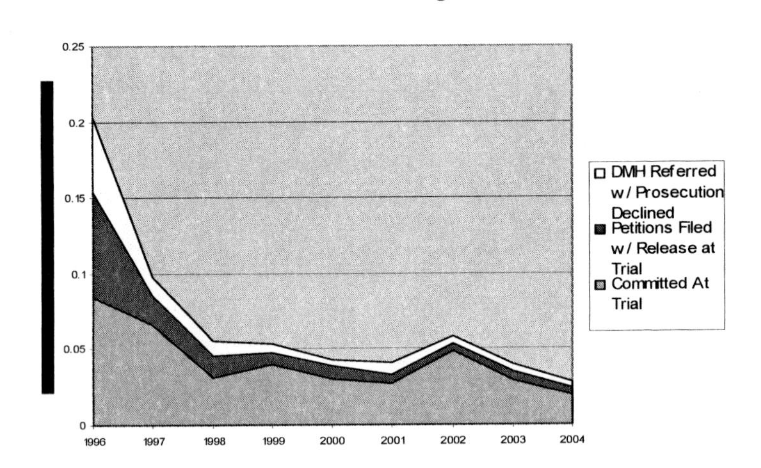

On a system-wide basis, the chart shows an initially high proportion of cases resulting in commitments, a pattern that becomes progressively moderated through 2001. It also ties this moderation to the increasingly prominent roles of the correctional system and initial DMH screening in reducing the number of cases sent on for further

[91] The screening burden calculation is not based on case-level data, but rather on aggregate dispositions at each stage of the process during a given year. Since many cases extend over two or more years as they proceed through the process, one should therefore not assume that the percentages may be applied to the total referrals in a given year.

review – a pattern indicating a measure of system maturity. Beginning in mid-2001 and continuing into 2002, however, the initial steps in the screening process have shown some "back-sliding", as the number of cases proceeding through the process has increased. This pattern may be at least partially attributed to the 2001 decision by the California Supreme Court (("People v. Torres," 2001), expanding the functional meaning of "qualifying offense," and therefore broadening the pool of potential commitments.

Population

Figure 28 depicts the growth in California's committed and detained populations from the program's inception in 1996 through mid-2002. While the initially high rate of growth began to show a moderating pattern (accompanied by a dip in the number of pre-trial detainees) in 1999, again we see a moderate surge occurring in the latter half of 2001 and into 2002. While this recent growth may easily be attributed to normal population fluctuations, at a minimum it indicates that the growing population has not diminished California's fundamental commitment to the policy.

Figure 28: California Committed and Detained Population

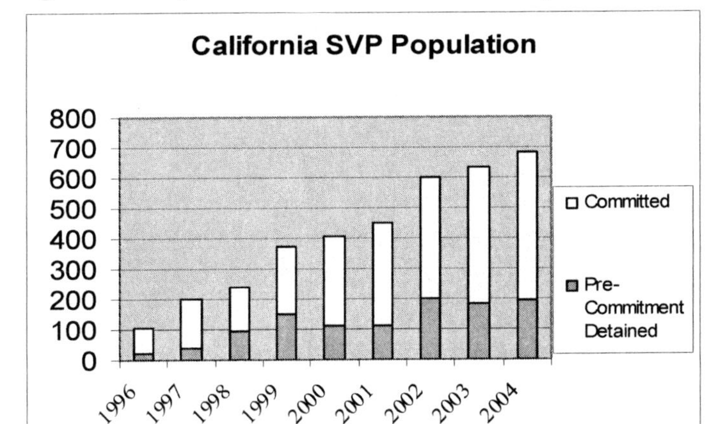

Treatment

As of May 2002, California's treatment program, based at Atascadero State Hospital, involved a total of 424 residents. The treatment status of that group, based on data provided by the Department of Mental Health, is indicated in Figure 29.

Figure 29: California Treatment Status of Committed Population

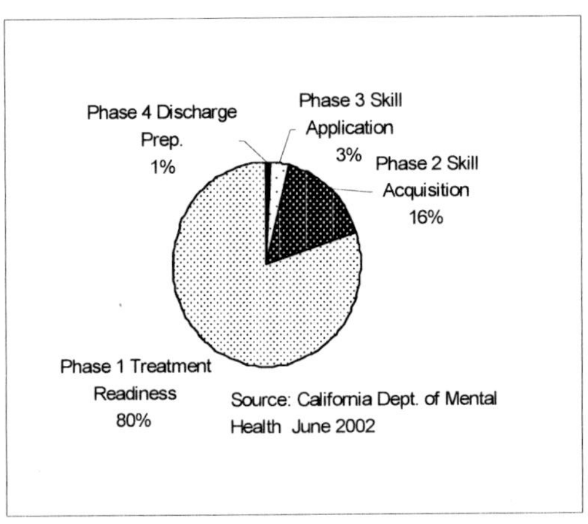

As previously described, California's treatment program is one of the most staff and resource-intensive in the current study, and has been in operation for six years. As the figure indicates, 80% of the population remains in "Phase 1", described by DMH as "for patients who have not committed themselves to actively working toward changing their sexual thoughts and behavior." (California Department of Mental Health, 2001). Of the remaining 20%, over ¾ are engaged in "Skill Acquisition", the most basic level of active treatment.

This level of participation and progress is far lower than any programs examined thus far, leading to essentially two possible interpretations – tougher cases, which indicate that the program is effectively screening the most recalcitrant sex offenders, or simply a less effective treatment program.

Florida

Like California, Florida's process of case screening, referral, and commitment is centrally monitored, producing a viable and relatively consistent source of data for analysis. In contrast with California, where the Department of Corrections and Board of Prison Terms screen out a significant portion of potential cases, Florida's Department of Children and Families receives virtually the entire universe of sex offenders released from incarceration in the state, permitting a substantially more comprehensive picture of the screening process. The data contained in this section is based on information provided by the DCF.

As with the preceding five states, we begin our review with a graph illustrating the patterns associated with case referrals, petition filings, and new commitments. Figure also includes information on trial activity in Florida's program.

Figure 30: Florida Screening, Referral, and Commitments 1999-2004

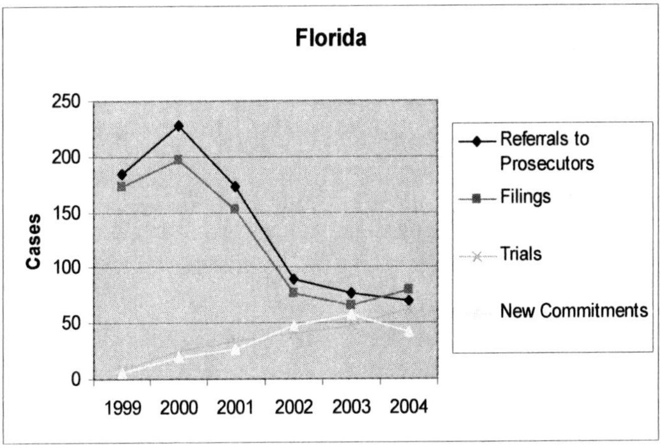

The graph illustrates several critical characteristics of Florida's implementation experience during the first five years of the policy. First, the start-up problems associated with the high initial volume of cases, discussed in the preceding narrative, is reflected in the comparatively high number of referrals during 1999 and 2000. Second, the graph illustrates the manner in which prosecutors have responded to the new law, filing petitions on the vast majority of referrals received from DCF. Third, we see a systemic and substantial gap between case filings and trials that has led, as will be demonstrated shortly, to a tremendous backlog within the legal system. Fourth and finally, we see a substantial decline in case referrals and associated case filings beginning in 2001 and continuing through 2004.

Figure 31 explores the shift in screening practices more closely, shedding light on some of the factors driving the comparatively high number of referrals during the program's first two years. During this period, the DCF's initial record review "screened in" between 18% and 20% of the cases it reviewed, leaving many of these cases to be screened out by the clinical review or the courts. Judges and juries responded, dismissing 19 cases during the first year prior to trial, and releasing another 3 at trial. During that same period, only 5 individuals were committed – approximately 18% of the case dispositions during the first year. In the ensuing periods, we see the initial record review process becoming significantly more selective, to the current point at which only about 6% of the cases proceed beyond that stage.

Figure 31: Florida Percent of Cases Clearing Key Decision Points

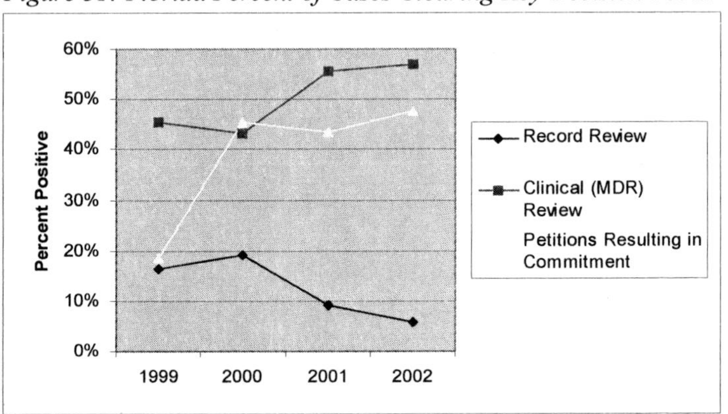

The figure also depicts an inverse relationship between record reviews and the clinical review process. On the surface, at least, this pattern seems to indicate that case screening system is effectively screening out cases of lower "clinical quality." It should be considered, however, that in contrast with the California system of independent review, Florida's recommendation following the clinical assessment comes from the Multi-Disciplinary Review Team, which contains, among others, the individuals responsible for the initial record review.

The third line indicated in Figure 31, labeled "Petitions Resulting in Commitment" is based on the percentage of petitions disposed during the course of each year that resulted in a commitment. A disposition can follow several forms – the individual can be released prior to trial due to case dismissal or a release order, can be released at trial, or can be committed at trial. Due to the extended period between case filing and trial, described in detail below, pre-trial dismissals and releases were fairly common, accounting for 76 of 149 case dispositions through April 2002.

Figure 32: Florida Time Between Petition and Trial

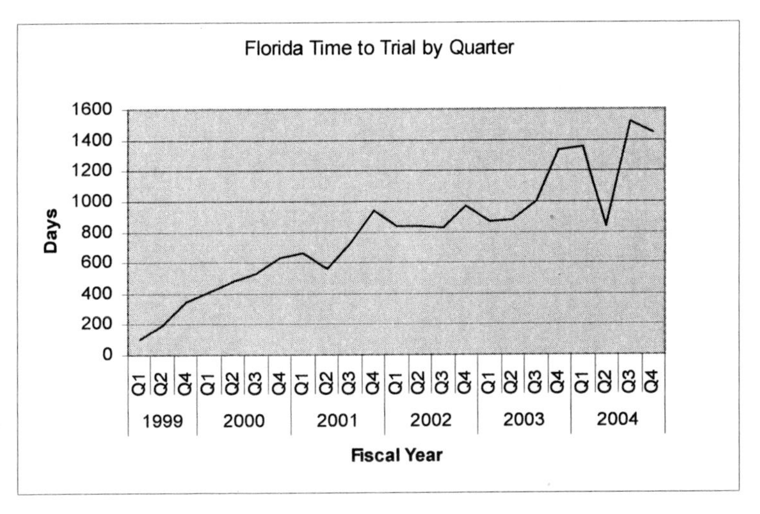

Note: No cases proceeded to trial in third quarter of 1999.

The output of the legal system has shown some growth over recent years, growing from 33 completed trials in 2001 to 63 in 2004. Yet through 2004, a total of 822 petitions had been filed since the program's inception, with only 218 completed trials. This has manifested itself in a steadily increasing length of time between the filing of the initial petition and trial, as indicated in Figure 32.

Population

The result of this backlog, in addition to resulting in increased likelihood of pre-trial dismissal, is reflected in a mounting proportion of pre-trial detainees held in DCF custody. The detained population, along with the committed population, is presented in Figure 33 below. While the illustrated proportion is likely to shift towards the committed group over time – especially given the recent decline in referrals – addressing this continuing imbalance remains one of the more significant implementation challenges facing the Florida program.

Figure 33: Florida Detained and Committed Populations

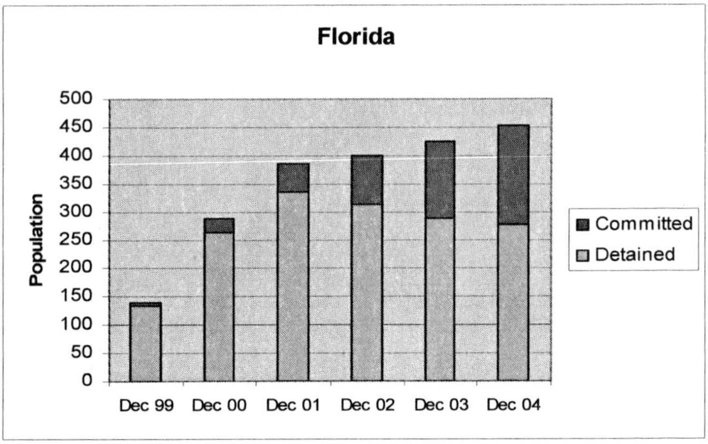

Treatment

Florida's treatment program, provided under contract with a private vendor, included 394 detained and committed individuals as of June 2002. Figure 34 represents levels of treatment participation as of that date, based on a monthly contract report provided to the DCF by its contracted vendor.

The figure indicates an overall treatment refusal rate of approximately 59%, although among committed individuals, the rate is closer to 50%. Of those participating in treatment, a good number have proceeded into latter stages. It should be noted, however, that Florida still has yet to establish a viable system for supervised release or a less restrictive alternative, effectively diminishing the practical significance of treatment progress.

Figure 34: Florida Treatment Participation

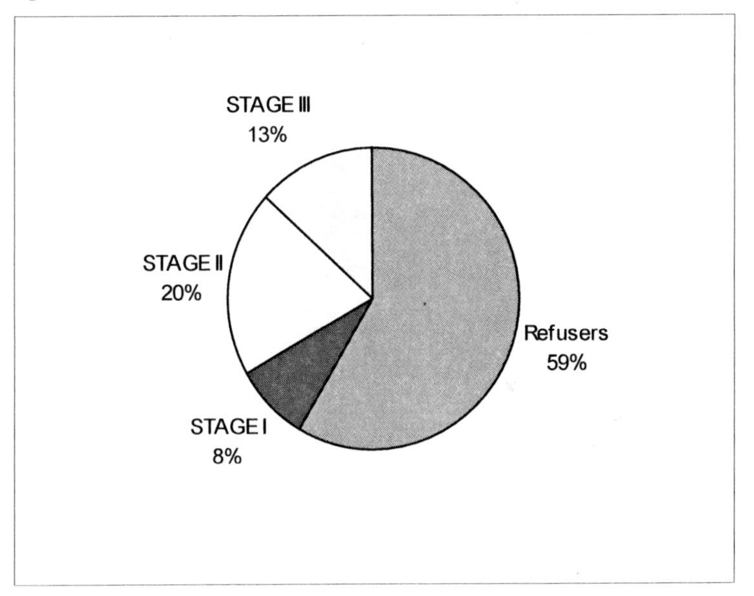

APPENDIX D: BUDGETARY ASSESSMENT

Washington

Virtually all of the state funding appropriated pursuant to the civil commitment provisions of Washington's Community Protection Act civil flows through the Department of Social and Health Services. Beyond funding for its directly operated programs, DSHS serves as a conduit for funds provided to the Attorney General and King County Prosecutors office, and for community mitigation and law enforcement funding connected to its LRA program (Washington Dept. of Social and Health Services).

Historical DSHS spending, based on Biennial Budget information provided through the Washington Office of Financial Management, is depicted in Figure 35. The figure shows a gradual increase, consistent with population growth, through the 1999-01 Biennium, and substantial increases in both the 2001-2003 and 2003-2005 Biennia.

Figure 35: Washington Spending and Population Trends

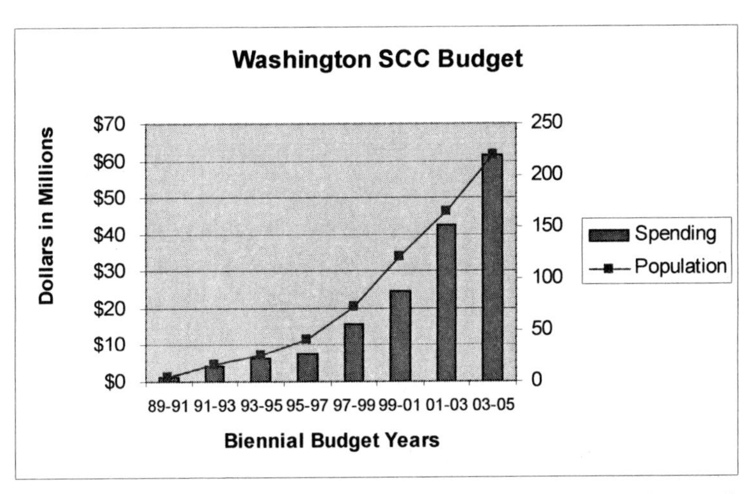

The DSHS budget for the Fiscal 2002-03 Biennium (from July 2001-June 2003), represented a 75 percent increase from prior funding levels, primarily due to a combination of population growth, court-ordered program enhancements, and the implementation of a major LRA initiative pursuant to court orders

DSHS 2003 program costs were approximately $105,000 for each committed male, and $250,000 for each committed female. Costs for supervised release are substantially higher, estimated at over $400,000 for each person on supervised release. The significant supervised release costs are associated with a range of legislative requirements, including the provision of LRA community mitigation funds, a 1:1 staffing ratio for individuals working and living in the community, and supplemental law enforcement requirements near the McNeil Island Facility. These per–person costs, according to DSHS, also include approximately $24-28,000 in allocated legal costs.

These figures are also notable for what they do not include. First, costs do not include the debt service on capital construction. According the state's 10 year capital plan, the SCC will have spent in excess of $90 million in facility construction and renovation by mid-2005. This includes approximately $16.5 million in prior years' projects and $73.5 million in current and planned projects, including approximately $53 million in FY02-03 (encompassing the first 268-bed phase of the new facility plus approximately $3.2 million for a 24-bed secure community transition facility), and an additional $20 million in FY04-05 for creation of additional SCC beds.[92]

The per-person costs cited by DSHS are also not inclusive of costs incurred by the Department of Corrections, which provides a range of transportation, food service, and perimeter security services for the SCC, costs associated with the End of Sentence Review Committee, costs incurred by the courts in the processing of SVP civil commitment cases, and costs associated with public defense of SVP cases.

---

[92] Debt service for all of these projects combined, assuming 7% interest over 30 years, amounts to approximately $7.3 million in annual costs. Depending on the population base that one chooses to spread these costs over, these projects add between $18-48K onto the annual cost per committed individual.

The significant increase to Washington's SVP program budget during the state's 2001 budget cycle is notable in at least two important respects. First, it demonstrates the powerful influence that the courts have exerted over the shape of Washington's civil commitment program – a demonstration that should be heeded by other states. Second, it provides a strong sense of the policy's "staying power" ten years after its original adoption. The legislature, in providing for this increase and for supplementing the increase with a significant infusion of capital construction funding, has effectively affirmed its ongoing commitment to the civil commitment policy.

This message has apparently not been lost on Governor Gary Locke, who in December 2001 submitted a Supplemental Budget aiming to close a $1.25 billion budget gap. Locke's proposal, which included $246 million in cuts to human services programs, included provisions to pass prosecution costs onto the counties (which in turn might have a moderate "chilling effect" on SVP filings), and scaled back community mitigation funds associated with the LRA program. Locke's proposal, though published in the Governor's proposed 2002 supplemental budget, was withdrawn before reaching committee.

Minnesota

The cost burden for Minnesota's program is essentially divided among five entities -- the Department of Human Services, which maintains responsibility for evaluation, treatment, and care and custody; the Department of Corrections, which is mandated to provide pre-petition screening services; the Attorney General, which provides legal representation for 81 of the state's 83 counties; the court system; and the counties, which are responsible for a range of costs including housing potential PP/SDP's awaiting trial and 10% of ongoing commitment costs.

Figure 36 indicates the approximate distribution of costs among these various entities, based on figures provided by the 1999 report of the Civil Commitment Study Group.

Figure 36: Minnesota Distribution of Costs

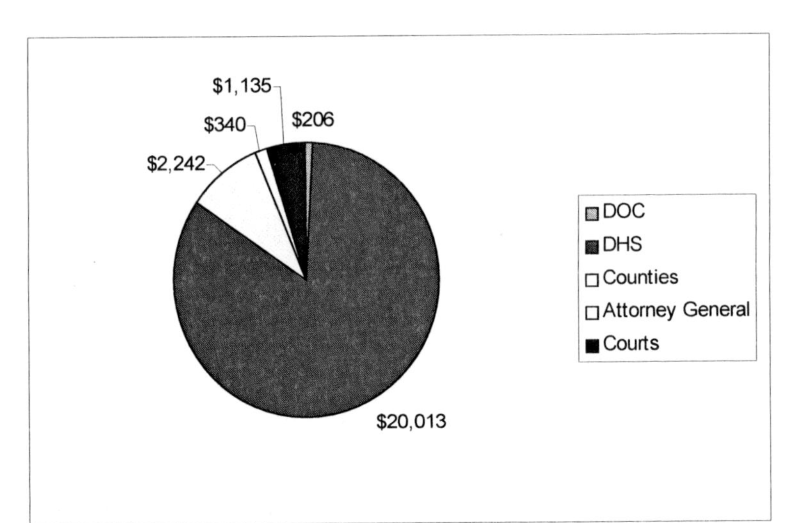

The majority of the program costs are those connected to the Department of Human Services for the implementation of the Minnesota Sex Offender Program. The MSOP, operating on the basis of state appropriations, calculates per diem rates including both direct and indirect operating expenses.[93] These rates, in turn, provide the basis for billing the counties for their required 10% share of housing and treatment costs.

The DHS has provided both direct budget and per diem rate information from Fiscal Year 1998 through the Fiscal Year 2002. On this basis, two "budgets" may be presented – one containing only direct operating costs as appropriated by the legislature, and the other containing both direct and indirect costs as derived from the approved per diem rates. The trends in these budgets, along with the average daily census for each year, are presented in Figure 37.

---

[93] Through Fiscal Year 2001, the Department operated with separate rates for its two MSOP facilities – beginning in FY02, the rate was consolidated at the lower of the two facility rates.

Figure 37: Minnesota Human Services Budget and Population

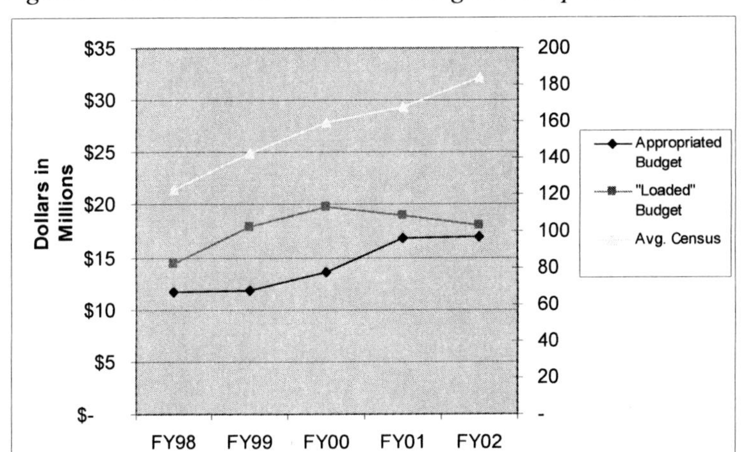

Regarding the relationship between the two budgets, the graph shows a narrowing gap, reflecting two programmatic and budgetary shifts – the FY01 transfer of population from the more expensive St. Peter site to the less expensive Moose Lake facility following the opening of a new 50-bed addition, and a budgetary policy decision to consolidate the daily rates at the lower Moose Lake level of $268 per patient/day. It is unclear whether this shift is connected to true budgetary savings within DHS or a shift in cost burden from the counties back to the state.

The graph highlights two other factors of note – a leveling of the general operating budget after several years of growth, and an associated divergence between population growth patterns and budgetary increases.

The Minnesota program has incurred periodic capital construction costs approximately every four years. The 1994 legislature authorized the construction of 150 beds – the 100-bed free-standing Moose Lake facility and a 50-bed addition to St. Peter, at a combined cost of approximately $28 million. Responding to the growing population in

1998, the state authorized a 50-bed Moose Lake addition, which was completed in 2001 at a cost of $5 million.

Until 2003, Minnesota's program had experienced a slowing rate of growth in program operating costs – a trend at least partially attributed to the decline in prosecutor referrals and the associated reduction in the rate of population expansion, as well as economies of scale resulting from capacity utilization. However, in response to events in late 2003, described elsewhere in this analysis, the state is looking at significant capital and operating costs to keep pace with recent surges in its population.

Moreover, the state has yet to fully grapple with the fundamental issue of the "back door." While the MSOP program has produced several indicators of treatment success, including comparatively high rates of treatment participation and a number of individuals progressing towards conditional release, the ability of the program to effectuate releases at any substantive level remains largely unknown. Not only may releases may be impeded by a variety of legal and political obstacles beyond the scope of the program, but the remedy to those obstacles – as we have observed in the case of Washington – may be prohibitive in its cost.

Wisconsin

Wisconsin's SVP program budget is allocated to several agencies. While the majority of state funds are allocated to the Department of Health and Family Services for evaluation, custody, treatment, and supervised release services, the state has also appropriated funding to the Department of Corrections Special Evaluation Unit (Wisconsin Legislative Fiscal Bureau, 1999b), prosecutor staffing resources both within the Department of Justice and in Brown and Milwaukee Counties (Wisconsin Legislative Fiscal Bureau, 1999a), and the state office of the public defender. Additional costs are borne by the counties for court expenses, prosecutor support, and pre-trial custody.

The DHFS budget consists of costs associated with provision of services at the Wisconsin Resource Center, the Sand Ridge Treatment Center, and within the Supervised Release Treatment Program. *Figure 38*, on the following page, illustrates the trend in evaluation, custody, and treatment costs, excluding supervised release, from Fiscal Year 1998 through the projected Fiscal 2003 budget. As a frame of reference, the graph also depicts the rate of population growth as indicated on the left hand axis.

While the graph illustrates a relatively steady rate of increase in population, it shows an accelerated growth in program costs beginning in FY01. This increase corresponds with the phase-in of the SRTC that commenced in mid-2001. The discrepancy in the two trend lines indicates a significant increase in the per-person cost, from approximately $48,000 per year in FY98 to $120,000 in FY02.

Figure 38: Wisconsin Program Budget and Population

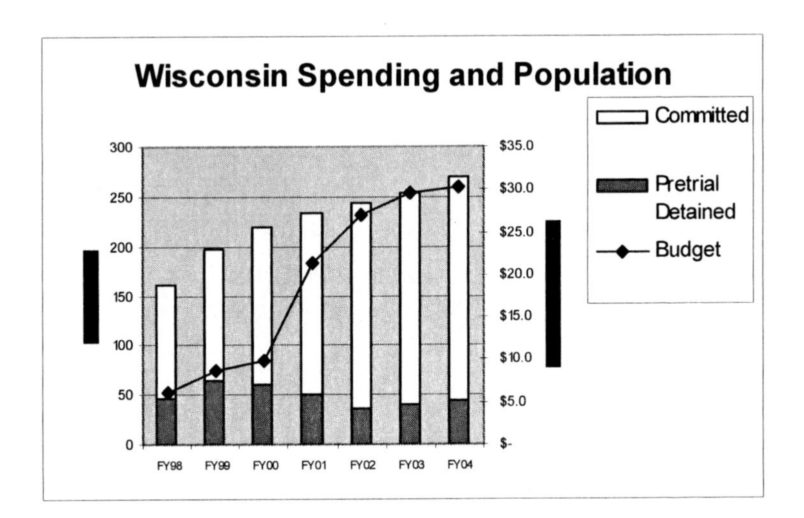

While the relationship between population and program costs has stabilized somewhat in recent years, the observed pattern is a powerful illustration of the relative costs involved in shifting to a "stand-alone" facility model of service delivery. In this case, the state was required to fund an additional $7 million in annual program operating costs, beyond core staffing costs, to cover the shift to Sand Ridge. There is strong evidence that other states preparing for program transition from "piggy-back" status to "stand-alone" status – notably Washington and California – are bracing for similar incremental cost increases.

A similar pattern, although on a lesser scale, may be observed for the Supervised Release Program. Supervised release costs are extremely variable, depending on the profile and requirements of the individual under release. A legislative fiscal bureau report notes that cost may range from $2,600 per month ($31K annually) to $10,800 per month ($130K annually). As the Washington experience has indicated, public safety concerns quite typically require extraordinary conditions of release that often exceed the costs of inpatient commitment.

For both the main treatment program and for supervised release, it must also be considered that the cited cost increases experienced in recent years do not account for debt service costs created by new facility construction. Sand Ridge was built at a cost of $39 million, resulting in likely annual debt payments of approximately $3 million (or $10K per bed), and increasing overall costs by about 10% over current levels. The supervised release facility, at a construction cost of $1.3 million, will likewise increase the functional operating costs of the supervised release program.

As indicated in the narrative, the Wisconsin Governor's exemption of the Sand Ridge program from the major across-the-board budget cuts levied upon human services and other state operations in the FY03 budget indicates that political and budgetary support for the SVP civil commitment policy remains alive and well. This development is rendered even more remarkable when viewed in the context of recent increases in the cost-commitment ratio.

Despite a decreasing number of referrals in recent years, the growth in the committed population remains relatively constant at between 25 and 30 per year, requiring yet another phase of capacity expansion.[94] Moreover, as described in our review of the previous two states, the great unknown remains the technical and political efficacy of the state's "back door" strategies—a key factor in determining the level of future resource requirements.

---

[94] During the Fiscal 2002 budget cycle, the Governor proposed a new 100-bed addition at the SRTC, at a budgeted cost of an additional $7 million (State of Wisconsin Building Commission, 2001).

Kansas

Concurrent with its increase in population, the Kansas program has witnessed a series of significant increases in its civil commitment program operating budgets over recent years. The figure below depicts the population growth trend between 1994 and 2006, and program budgets between Fiscal 2001 and 2006. Figures presented for 2005 and 2006 are based on projections set forth in the Governor's FY06 Executive Budget submission (Kansas Division of the Budget, 2005).

Figure 39: Kansas Budget and Population

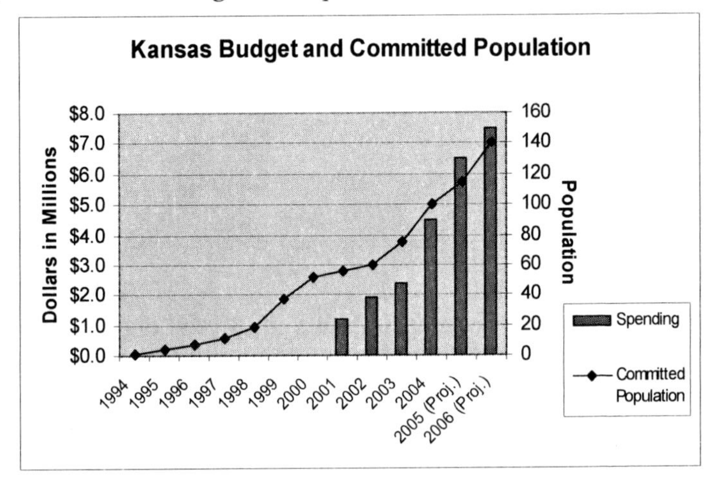

Notably, the program witnessed a near doubling of resources between 2003 and 2004, with double-digit percentage increases in subsequent years. With these increases, a program that was initially at the lower end of the spectrum in terms of cost-per-resident (approximately $22K per resident in 2001), has re-aligned with national standards in recent years (approximately $56K per resident in FY05).

In contrast with other programs examined here, Kansas has yet to incur significant facility construction and renovation costs. As observed in Wisconsin, however, the program's growth in recent years has created a sustained encroachment on capacity required for inmates in the Department of Corrections custody requiring inpatient psychiatric treatment and evaluation, leading policymakers to call for capacity expansion. In response, the state initiated a $16 million construction project in 2002, creating 250 new beds for DOC patients, and freeing the current facility for exclusive SVP use (Kansas Division of the Budget, 2003).

California

California's SVP program budget, aside from being significantly larger than any other in the current analysis, contains a range of provisions worthy of close examination.

The early history of the California SVP program budget, as described in the narrative, included a significant shifting of resources between agencies. In the program's first year, the Governor submitted a $33 million spending plan allocated as indicated in Figure 40 below.

Figure 40: California Initial Budget Plan

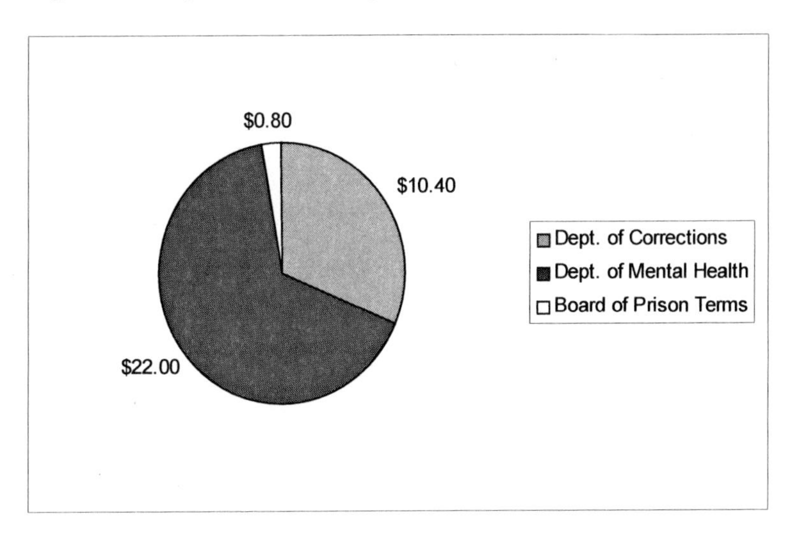

This initial program budget assumed that the Department of Correction, and not the Department of Mental Health, would provide for basic facility operations. As the program unfolded, however, the majority of program resources were shifted to DMH for housing and treating committed SVP's, primarily at Atascadero State Hospital.

Figure 41: California FY02 Budget Allocations

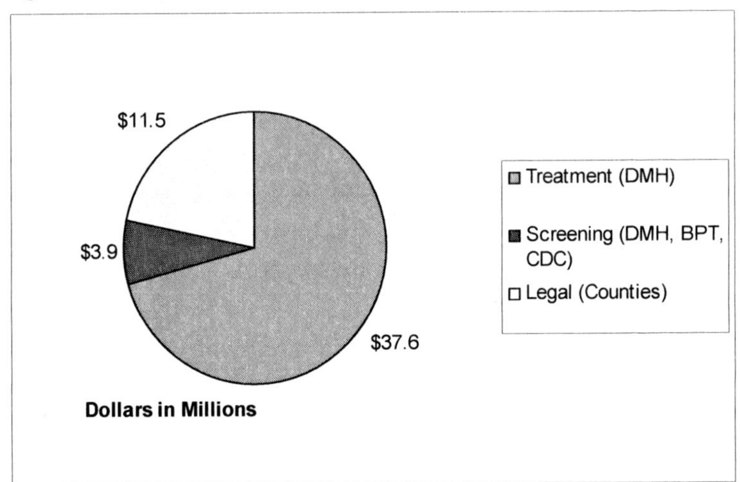

As a point of comparison, Figure 41 presents the FY02 SVP program budget from a functional perspective, isolating three separate parts of the process – the screening process, as performed by the California Department of Corrections, the Board of Prison Terms, and the Department of Mental Health; the legal process, including costs incurred by the counties connected to legal proceedings and detention of individuals pending trial; and the treatment process, involving inpatient care delivered by DMH at ASH and Patton State Hospital. We will consider each of these in turn.

Screening Costs

The California state budget provides resources to the CDC, BPT, and DMH to support the screening process. According to state budget schedules obtained from the California Department of Finance, the CDC is allocated $276K and the BPT is allocated approximately $426K for their dedicated SVP screening activities. The DMH incurred approximately $3.2 million in costs associated with professional evaluators in Fiscal Year 2002. This amount represented roughly a 15% increase from FY01 levels, and an approximate return to levels experienced during FY98 and FY99. While these evaluation costs likely represent the majority of DMH costs associated with case screening, they do not include costs associated with directly employed staff participating in the screening process.

All told, California's process for case identification and pre-referral screening is likely in excess of $4 million per year. While this figure may be contrasted with the systems of other states examined thus far, which conduct their screenings utilizing a less resource-intensive model, a question remaining for analysis regards the relative benefits and efficiencies that accrue from the state's alternative practices.

Legal Costs

Aside from the treatment services that will be described shortly, the most significant area of costs associated with SVP programs involves the costs incurred by the counties in the legal processing of SVP cases. The California legal system, including prosecutors, public defenders, and the district courts, is generally funded at the county level. In the case of the SVP program, however, the counties have successfully claimed the civil commitment of sexually violent predators as an unfunded state mandate, thereby permitting the counties to receive state reimbursement for any costs incurred, including both direct costs and a 10% indirect cost rate. Counties are also reimbursed for costs associated with housing pre-commitment detainees, who may be held at the county level or in DMH custody (Commission on State Mandates, 1998).

Since the first claim was filed in 1998, county reimbursements have shown significant variation, largely due to the fact that the date in which costs are claimed bears little relationship to the year in which costs were incurred. It is therefore somewhat difficult to attribute costs to specific years, and to accurately estimate current levels of spending. Though Fiscal Year 2001, an estimated $34.6 million was claimed by counties. Assuming a one-year lag in claims, this amount would generate an average of $8.7 million a year for the first four years of California's civil commitment program.

Looking forward, it is likely that the $8.7 million figure is a low estimate of future spending due to several factors. First, the incremental growth of the SVP population, coupled with the state's two-year limit on commitments, produces exponential increases in the required number of recommitment hearings that must be handled in a given year. Second, the system of state reimbursement essentially insulates counties from the costs of filing new petitions, and therefore contains limited fiscal restrictions on caseload growth. Third and finally, as discussed in our review of operational indicators, the state is experiencing a surge in cases that is likely to continue in the aftermath of the Torres ruling that operationally broadened the criteria for commitment.

Treatment Program Costs

As we have seen in the other four states that we have examined, by far the most significant cost associated with SVP programs involves the provision of custody and treatment services. As of March 2005, California's SOCP, with its roughly 500 current patients, accounts for approximately 45 percent of the currently occupied 1,100 beds at Atascadero State Hospital, with the proportion growing incrementally. By September 2005, this population is expected to have been shifted to the new 1,500-bed Coalinga State Hospital facility, specifically built for the SVP population.

The history of California's treatment program budget is presented along with the hospital's SVP population in Figure 42. The census figures shown reflect the population at the end of each fiscal year.

Figure 42: California DMH Treatment Budget and Population

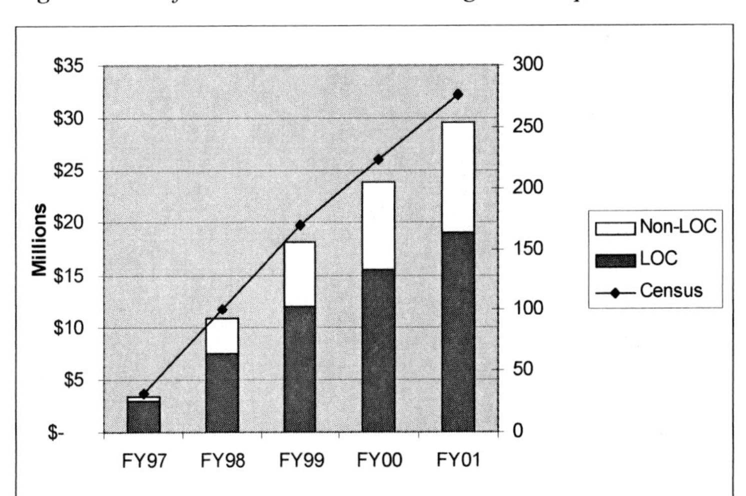

As indicated by the figure, the treatment program's budget has moved in lockstep with the growing population. This trend is not a matter of coincidence – rather, it reflects a funding methodology that indexes state appropriations to a weighted rate – currently $107,000 per patient – for each inpatient bed filled by the Department of Mental Health. The rate, according to the DMH and confirmed by the California Department of Finance and the Legislative Analysts' Office, represents a weighted statewide cost for DMH inpatients, including both SVP's and individuals with severe and persistent mental illness.

In applying the $107,000 rate, the Department of Mental Health distinguishes between "Level of Care" (LOC) expenses, and "non-LOC" expenses. The former reflects the incremental costs of each new patient, as derived by a specific series of per-patient staffing formulas developed for the SVP program. The "non-LOC" costs reflect, at least in principle, a portion of the indirect costs associated with facility operations, including shared infrastructure, managerial staffing, and other unallocated operations costs. This latter figure is essentially a "plug" number, derived by subtracting the budgeted LOC costs from the $107,000 times the budgeted population.

While non-LOC costs are not entirely fixed, they are presumably less likely to shift in response to modest fluctuations in the overall facility population. Assuming that the budget methodology is sound, one would therefore expect that LOC costs would increase at a faster rate that non-LOC costs, therefore taking on a progressively larger proportion of the overall budget. As the figure illustrates, however, this has not been the case – in fact, LOC costs have declined over time as a proportion of total costs, indicating that funds are accruing to the DMH budget in excess of the actual incremental costs of each newly committed SVP.

Moreover, a closer look at the "Level-of-Care" staffing ratios employed by the California program reflect a system more closely aligned with an inpatient psychiatric staffing model than with alternative models such as those employed by Minnesota. The program, for example, calls for 2.4 psychiatrists and 25.7 registered nurses – both relatively expensive forms of staff -- for every 100 patients. Although this staffing model assumes, moreover, that only 10 percent of the SVP population exhibits what is referred to in the community as "severe and persistent mental illness" (e.g. psychotic or other severely debilitating psychiatric conditions), these ratios are roughly comparable to those that one might find in an inpatient psychiatric setting in which 100% of the patients met such criteria.

By these appearances, the SVP program has proven to be somewhat of a budgetary windfall to the California Department of Mental Health. Yet while this analysis shows that the SVP population most likely brings more money into DMH's budget than it actually costs the system, this circumstance is likely to change upon the occupation of the Coalinga facility, scheduled to open in 2005.

One major area of cost typically not included in budget figures involves the cost of the facility itself. The $366 million facility, constructed at a cost of $244K per bed assuming full capacity, represents the largest SVP facility undertaken by any state. Its per-bed construction cost is moderately higher than Washington's $215 per bed cost, and significantly higher than the $186 per bed in Minnesota. Moreover, unlike these other states, it is unlikely based on current population trends that the facility will reach its capacity any time in the foreseeable future, functionally increasing the operational cost per bed. Amortizing this cost over a thirty year period at 7%, the facility construction contributes roughly $30 million to the annual program costs, translating into $50K in additional annual costs per patient, assuming the 2006 DMH estimate of 600 patients.

Looking Forward

Of the states examined thus far, California has reflected the most intense spending patterns on its SVP civil commitment policy. Through a generous caseload-driven funding system, it has provided the Department of Mental Health with a steady stream of revenue to support population growth. Through its system of county reimbursement, it has created a virtually open-ended entitlement program for county prosecutors wishing to pursue SVP cases. It has authorized construction of the nation's most expensive SVP facility – both on an absolute and a per-bed basis – and will likely see an increase in operating expenses from the first day of the facility's opening.

All of these factors point to a policy that appears quite robust as measured by policy makers' continued financial support, despite factors such as the tremendously low rate of treatment participation cited in the previous section. With a new 1,500-bed facility at its disposal, it appears likely that the state will continue to see substantial cost increases well into the coming decades.

Florida

As described in the program narrative, the budget for the Florida SVP program was a source of considerable debate during the initial committee consideration of the bill, and in the months immediately preceding and following the law's implementation in January 1999. During the spring of 1999, however, the Florida legislature appropriated funding across several state agencies for the purposes of implementing the SVP program, including the Department of Children and Family Services and several agencies involved in the legal system.

Legal System Funding

Before reviewing the DCF budget, which reflects the significant majority of resources connected to the program, initial consideration should be given to legal system funding. The Florida legal system is divided into 20 judicial circuits, with funding for prosecutor, public defender, and court services provided through state appropriations. This approach is in significant contrast to most other SVP states, in which such services are often supported through county revenues. Certain expenses associated with the courts are funneled and administered through an entity called the Justice Administration Commission (JAC).

Figure 43 indicates the approximate allocations for the legal system, including resources dedicated to prosecutors, public defenders and the Justice Administration Commission. The largest share of this pie -- $3 million for the current fiscal year – reflects case-related expenses such as expert witnesses and court reporter fees. This allocation was increased in FY03 from a level of approximately $1 million, following a series of highly publicized reports in late 2001 that SVP cases were being bottlenecked due to diminution of these funds.

Figure 43: Florida State Appropriated Legal Costs

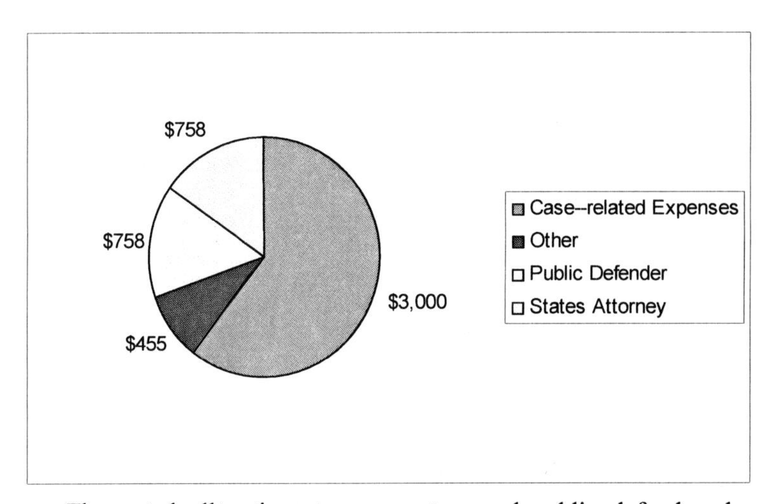

The noted allocations to prosecutors and public defenders has remained largely unchanged since the Fiscal 2000 budget, and in all likelihood reflect only a modest percentage of the staff resources associated with the legal management of civil commitment cases. As a point of comparison, Washington's program, which handles a significantly lower number of cases on a statewide basis, allocates $4.2 million per year in prosecution costs alone. It would therefore appear that states attorneys and public defenders must manage a considerable number of their caseloads through diversion of general resources, offering at least a partial explanation of some of the observed case backlogs within the legal system.

Evidence suggests that legal system backlogs experienced in Florida may be at least partially attributed to inadequate funding of the judiciary and other critical parts of the legal system. Beyond the cited limitations in dedicated prosecutor and public defense resources, it appears that the courts themselves have not been provided with any specific targeted appropriations to handle the workloads.

DCF Funding

The Fiscal 2002 funding levels for the Department of Children and Families are noted in Figure 44.

Figure 44: Florida DCF Program Costs

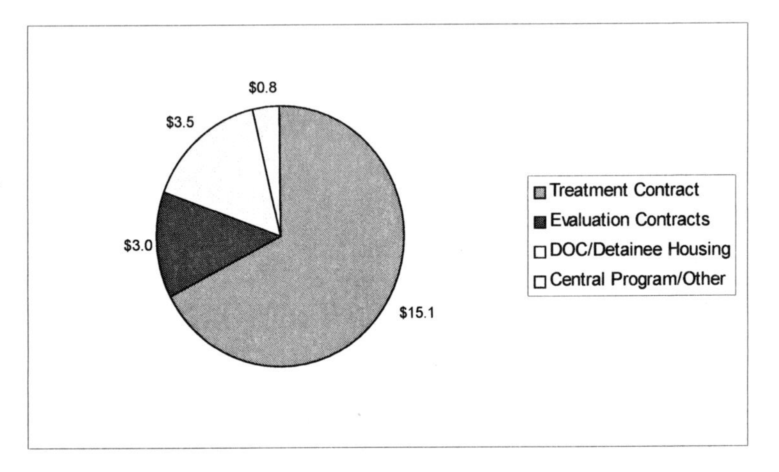

The funding is divided into four categories – evaluation costs, associated with psychology service contracts; treatment program costs, corresponding with the Liberty contract for provision of treatment and other services at the Florida Civil Commitment Center; DOC/Detainee costs, connected to security, transportation, and other services provided through the Department of Corrections or private correctional providers; and central office costs, associated with funding for direct program staff and support service contracts.

The noted contract costs of approximately $15 million are based on actual Fiscal 2002 invoices submitted by Liberty and paid through DCF. As previously described, it remains unclear how the DCF will accommodate growth in treatment costs associated with population increases and with the new contract that the agency must negotiate with its private vendor.

Figure 45, noting the trends in program costs and the associated population, indicates the challenge facing the DCF. In December 2001, the agency proposed an increase of $8.9 million to cover these increased costs – a request that was not included in the Governor's FY03 budget. Since that time, the program budget has essentially remained funded at FY 2002 levels for FY 2003, FY 2004, and FY 2005. At the time of this writing, the Governor's FY 2006 budget submission to the Florida legislature proposes level-funding the program for a fifth straight year, despite a population increase of over 25% during this period, and despite the legal challenges and program difficulties described in Appendix A. Indeed, the state's alleged move to ration treatment, as set forth in the Canupp v. Liberty complaint – may have been an agency response to manage a growing population in the face of level funding.

Figure 45: Florida DCF Budget and Population

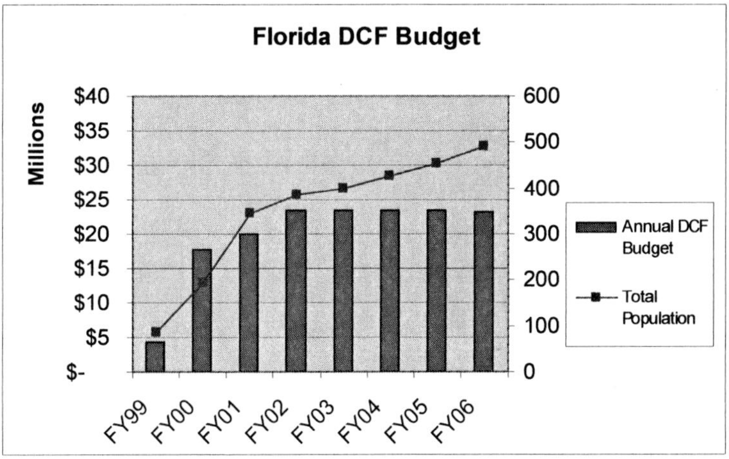

Florida DCF Budget

Millions

$40
$35
$30
$25
$20
$15
$10
$5
$-

600
500
400
300
200
100
0

FY99 FY00 FY01 FY02 FY03 FY04 FY05 FY06

Annual DCF Budget
Total Population

Looking Forward

Where California has opted to maintain its SVP program through virtually open-ended sources of funding, Florida has chosen the opposite tact, with both the Governor and the legislature choosing to level-fund the program during a period of formative growth. Yet with litigation challenging the state's treatment program pending, and the current $16 million vendor contract set to expire in June 2005, the adequacy of state funding for custody and treatment remains an open question. In light of these circumstances, the state may need to make difficult choices regarding the path it wishes to take with regard to its civil commitment program. Indeed, there are some indications that these choices are already being made – the significant decline in the number of cases referred by DCF for potential prosecution may be at least partially influenced by agency's consideration of its resource limitations.

Further, Florida remains the only state in this study that has neither legislative provisions nor funding available for supervised or transitional release. As noted throughout the other state case studies, this leaves a fundamental cost element largely unresolved.

References

Allen v. Illinois,, 478 364 (478 1986).

American Psychiatric Association. (1996). Amicus curiae brief submitted to U.S. Supreme Court in support of respondent in Kansas v. Hendricks.

American Psychiatric Association. (2001). Amicus curiae brief submitted to U.S. Supreme Court in support of respondent in Crane v. Kansas.

Appelbaum, P. (1997). Law and Psychiatry: Confining Sex Offenders. *Psychiatric Services, 48*(10), 1265.

ARCW Chapter 71.09, (2001).

Associated Press. (1992, October 14, 1992). Girl's Murderer Freed From Prison. *Wisconsin State Journal,* pp. 5C.

Associated Press. (1993, November 4, 1993). Bills to Focus On Sex Offenders Slaying of Student is Impetus for Move. *Wichita Eagle,* pp. 3D.

Associated Press. (1994, May 5, 1994). Governor Disputes Billing for Murderer. *Wisconsin State Journal,* pp. 2B.

Associated Press. (2003, March 15, 2003). State to Pay $1 Million for Sex Predator Oversight.

Associated Press. (2004, June 16, 2004). Morford's Oak Creek Move OK'd. *Milwaukee Journal Sentinel,* pp. 1A.

Association for the Treatment of Sexual Abusers. (2001a). Amicus curiae brief submitted to U.S. Supreme Court in support of respondent in Crane v. Kansas.

Association for the Treatment of Sexual Abusers. (2001b). *Practice Standards and Guidelines for Members of the Association for the Treatment of Sexual Abusers*. Beaverton, OR.

Austin, J., Hardyman, P., Henry, A., & Clark, J. (1999). *Three Strikes and You're Out: The Implementation and Impact of Strike Laws*. Washington DC: National Institute of Justice.

Bardach, E. (1977). *The Implementation Game*. Cambridge, MA: MIT Press.

Blacher, R. (1995). Comment: Historical Perspective of the 'sexual psychopath' statute from the revolutionary era to the present federal crime bill" Mercer Law Review. *Mercer Law Review, 46*(Winter 1995).

Boerner, D. (1992). Confronting Violence: In the Act and in the Word. *University of Puget Sound Law Review, 15*(3), 525-577.

Brakel, S. J., & Cavanaugh, J. L. (2000). Of Psychopaths and Pendulums: Legal and Psychiatric Treatment of Sex Offenders in the United States. *New Mexico Law Review, 30 (69)*(Winter 2000).

California Department of Mental Health. (2001). *Phases of the Treatment Program*. Retrieved, from the World Wide Web: www.dmh.cahwnet.gov/SOCP/faqs.htm

California Legislative Analyst's Office. (1996). *LAO Analysis of the 1996-97 Budget Bill*. Sacramento.

California Legislative Analyst's Office. (1997). *LAO Analysis of the 1997-98 Budget Bill: Health and Social Services Crosscutting Issues*. Sacramento.
California Legislative Analyst's Office. (2001). *Analysis of 2001-02 Budget Bill: Capital Outlay, Department of Mental Health*. Sacramento: California Legislature.
California Office of the Governor. (2002, April 25, 2002). Governor Davis Releases Statement on Supreme Court Ruling On Sexual Predator. *Press Release*.
California State Assembly. (1995). *Bill History: Assembly Bill 888 (Rogan) Sexually Violent Predators*. Retrieved, from the World Wide Web: www.assembly.ca.gov
California State Senate. (1994). *Bill History: Senate Bill 41 (1st Ex. Sess)*.
Callender, D. (1992, October 17, 1992). Kasten Cites Killer in Rapping Feingold. *Capital Times*, pp. 3A.
Campbell, P. (2001). *The Rape Revisionist*. theStranger.com. Retrieved, from the World Wide Web: http:\\www.thestranger.com/2001-02-01/feature.html
Campbell, T. W. (2000). Sexual Predator Evaluations and Phrenology: Considering Issues of Evidentiary Reliability. *Behavioral sciences & the law, 18 Part 1*, 111-130.
Canupp v. Liberty Behavioral Health 2004).
Capital Times. (1994, May 27, 1994). Thompson Signs Sex Crime Bill. *Capital Times*.
Center for Sex Offender Management. (2000). *Community Supervision of the Sex Offender: An Overview of Current and Promising Practices*. Silver Spring. MD: Center for Sex Offender Management.
Chabria, A. (2002, April 14, 2002). The Bureaucrat and the Bogeyman. *Los Angeles Times Magazine*, 21.
Commission on State Mandates. (1998). *Parameters and Guidelines: Sexually Violent Predators (CSM File# 4509)*. Sacramento: California Commission on State Mandates.
Correctional Privatization Commission. (2000). *Request for Proposals for Designing, Financing, Acquiring, Leasing, Constructing, and Operating of One 600-Bed, Secure Civil Confinement and Treatment Facility for Sexually Violent Predators*. Tallahassee: State of Florida.
Cunningham, M., & Reidy, T. (1998). Antisocial Personality Disorder and Psychopathy. *Behavioral Sciences & the Law, 16*, 333-340.
Daubert v. Merrell Dow Pharmaceuticals, 509 579 1993).
Decker, C. (1995, Octpber 11, 1995). Tougher Sex Offender Law Signed; Legislation: Applauded by activists at Covina ceremony, governor approves prolonged confinement of felons if they are found mentally defective when their prison;. *The Los Angeles Times*.
Denno, D. (1998). Symposium: Life Before Modern Sex Offender Statutes. *Northwestern University Law Review, 92*(Summer 1998), 1317.

DesLauriers, A., & Gardner, J. (1999). The Sexual Offender Treatment Program of Kansas, *Schlank, Anita (Ed); Cohen, Fred (Ed). (1999). The sexual predator: Law, policy, evaluation and treatment.* (pp. 11-11-11-26). Kingston, NJ, US: Civic Research Institute.

Douglas, M. (1992). *Risk and Blame* (Paperback ed.). New York, London: Routledge.

Duran, S. (2001, November 26, 2001). Special Master: State Making Progress on Treatment for Sexual Predators. *News Tribune,* pp. www.tribnet.com.

Ennis, B., & Litwack, T. (1975). Psychiatry and the Presumption of Expertise: Flipping Coins in the Courtroom. *Cal L Rev., 62,* 693-723.

Fisher, M. (1993, September 10, 1993). 'America's Most Wanted' Prompts Fugitive's Surrender. *AP Newswire,* pp. PM Cycle.

Fitch, W. L., Hammen, D. (2001). *Sex Offender Commitment in the United States.* Paper presented at the National Association of Mental Health Program Directors - Forensic Division, Cincinnati, Ohio.

Florida Department of Children and Families. (2002). *Request for Proposals.* Tallahassee.

Florida Department of Children and Families. (2003). *Status of Adults Referred for Commitment to SVPP.* Monthly charts provided by program on-file with author.

Florida Department of Children and Families. (2004). *Monthly Caseflow Report, September 2004.* Tallahassee, FL.

Florida House of Representatives Committee on Family Law and Children. (1998). *Bill Research and Economic Impact Statement: Relating to Bill # HB3327.* (March 14, 1998) Tallahasee.

Florida House of Representatives Committee on Health and Human Services Appropriations. (1998). *Bill Research and Economic Impact Statement, Bill # HB3327 (Revised by Committee).* (March 26, 1998) Tallahassee.

Florida Legislature. (1998). *Bill Summary and History: H 3327 Relating to Sexually Violent Predator Treatment.* Retrieved, from the World Wide Web: http://www.leg.state.fl.us/Session/index.cfm?Mode=Bills&SubMenu=1&BI_Mode=ViewBillInfo&BillNum=3327

Florida Legislature. (1999). *General Appropriations Act and Summary Statement of Intent for Fiscal Year 1999 - 2000.* Tallahassee.

Florida Office of Inspector General. (2004). *Report Summary, Case #2004-0043-WB.* Tallahassee, FL: Department of Children and Families.

Florida Office of Inspector General. (2005). *Report Summary, Case #2004-0083.* Tallahassee, FL: Department of Children and Families.

Florida Office of Program Policy Analysis and Governmental Accountability. (2000a). *The Sexually Violent Predator Program's Assessment Process Continues to Evolve, Report No. 99-36.*

Florida Office of Program Policy Analysis and Governmental Accountability. (2000b). *Special Review: The Escape from Martin Treatment Center for Sexually Violent Predators, Report No. 99-58*. Tallahassee.

Florida Office of the Governor. (1999). *Executive Order #99-257*. Tallahassee.

Frye v. United States, 293 1013 (DC Cir. 1923).

General Accounting Office. (1989). *The Prospective Evaluation Synthesis*. Washington DC: United States General Accounting Office.

Goggin, M. L. (1990). *Implementation theory and practice : toward a third generation*. New York, N.Y.: HarperCollins Publishers.

Governor's Commission on Sex Offender Policy. (2005). *Final Report*. St. Paul: Minnesota Office of the Governor.

Grisso, T. (March 6, 2000). *Ethical Issues in Evaluations for Sex Offender Re-Offending*. Paper presented at the Sinclair Seminars, Madison, WI.

Grossman, L. S., Martis, B., & Fichtner, C. G. (1999). Are Sex Offenders Treatable? A Research Overview. *Psychiatric Services, 50*(March 1999), 349-361.

Group for the Advancement of Psychiatry. (1977). *Psychiatry and Sex Psychopath Legislation: The 30s to the 80s*. New York: Mental Health Materials Center.

Gustafson, P. (1994, September 3, 1994). Petition Filed Under New Law to Commit Linehan. *Star Tribune,* pp. 1B.

Hall, G. C. (1995). Sexual Offender Recidivism Revisited: A Meta-analysis of Recent Treatment Studies. *Journal of Consulting and Clinical Psychology, 63*, 802-809.

Halvorsen, D. (1994, September 1, 1994). Sexual Predator Bill OK'd, Signed. *Minneapolis Star Tribune,* pp. 1A.

Hamilton, G. (2002). CASENOTE: THE BLURRY LINE BETWEEN "MAD" AND "BAD": IS "LACK-OF-CONTROL" A WORKABLE STANDARD FOR SEXUALLY VIOLENT PREDATORS? *University of Richmond Law Review, 36*(May 2002), 481.

Hanson, R. A. (1998). What Do We Know About Sex Offender Risk Assessment? *Psychology, Public Policy, and Law,, 4*, 50-72.

Hanson, R. K., & Harris, A. J. R. A. D. o. t. S. G. o. C. (2000). Where Should We Intervene? Dynamic Predictors of Sexual Offense Recidivism. *Criminal Justice and Behavior 27, no, 1,* 6-35.

Hargett et. al. v. Baker et. al. 2002).

Hargrove, E. (1975). *The Missing Link*. Washington DC: Urban Institute.

Hart, S. D. (2000, September 24-26, 2000). *Using Actuarial Tests to Assess Risk of Sexual Violence for Sentencing and Commitment*. Paper presented at the Sex Offender Committment Defender Association, Chicago, Illinois.

Hiaasen, S., & Stapleton, C. (1999, January 31, 1999). Problems Beset Start-Up of Ryce Sex Offender Act. *Palm Beach Post,* pp. 1A.

In Re Hendricks, 259 246 (Kansas 1996).

In Re Linehan, 518 609 (Minn. 1994).

In Re Rickmyer, 519 188 (Minn. 1994).

In Re Young, 857 989 1993).
Janus, E., & Meehl, P. (1997). Assessing the Legal Standard for Prediction of Dangerousness in Sex Offender Commitment Proceedings. *Psychology, Public Policy, and the Law, 3*(March 1997), 33.
Janus, E. S., & Walbek, N. H. (2000). Sex Offender Commitments in Minnesota: A Descriptive Study of Second Generation Commitments. *Behavioral Sciences & the Law, 18*, 343-374.
Jimmy Ryce Act Enforcement Task Force. (2000). *Final Report, February 2000*. Tallahassee.
Kansas Department of Social and Rehabilitation Services. (2005). *2005 Finger Tip Facts*. Topeka, KS: Kansas Department of Social and Rehabilitation Services.
Kansas Division of the Budget. (2002). *FY 2003 Governor's Budget Report*. Topeka.
Kansas Division of the Budget. (2003). *FY 2004 Governor's Budget Report*. Topeka.
Kansas Division of the Budget. (2005). *FY 2006 Governor's Budget Report*. Topeka.
Kansas v. Crane, 534 407 2002).
Kansas v. Hendricks, 521 346 1997).
Konrad, R. (2003, March 3, 2003). Child Molester to Remain in Hospital Until Supervisor Hired. *Associated Press*.
La Fond, J. Q. (1992). Washington's Sexually Violent Predator: A Deliberate Misuse of the Therapeutic State for Social Control. *University of Puget Sound Law Review, 15*(3), 655-703.
La Fond, J. Q. (1998). The costs of enacting a sexual predator law. *Psychology, Public Policy, & Law, 4*(Mar-Jun 1998).
La Fond, J. Q. (2003). The Costs Of Enacting A Sexual Predator Law And Recommendations For Keeping Them From Skyrocketing. In B. J. Winick (Ed.), *Protecting society from sexually dangerous offenders: law, justice, and therapy*. Washington DC: American Psychological Association.
Lewis, P. (1990, July 26, 1990). Screening for Sexual Predators Tossed Out. *Seattle Times*, pp. B7.
Lieb, R. (1996). *Washington State Sexually Violent Predators: Profile of Special Commitment Center Residents*. Olympia, WA: Washington State Institute for Public Policy.
Lieb, R., & Matson, S. (1998). *Sexual predator commitment laws in the United States : 1998 update*. Olympia: Washington State Institute for Public Policy.
Lieb, R., & Nelson, C. (2001). Treatment Programs for Sexually Violent Predators -- A Review of the States. In A. Schlank (Ed.), *The Sexual Predator*. Kingston, NJ: Civic Research Institute.

Marques, J. K. (2001). Professional Standards for Civil Commitment Programs. In A. Schlank (Ed.), *The Sexual Predator*. Kingston, NJ: Civic Research Institute.

Mayers, J. (1994, March 21, 1994). Doyle Lashes Back at GOP. *Wisconsin State Journal,* pp. 3B.

Mazmanian, D. A., & Sabatier, P. A. (1983). *Implementation and public policy*. Glenview, Ill.: Scott Foresman.

Mazmanian, D. A., & Sabatier, P. A. (1989). *Implementation and public policy; with a new postscript*. Lanham, MD: University Press of America.

McCaffrey, K. (1994). Comment: The Civil Commitment of Sexually Violent Predators in Kansas: A Modern Law for Modern Times. *Kansas Law Review, 42*(Summer 1994), 887.

McDonald, D., Fournier, E., Russell-Einhourn, M., & Crawford, S. (1998). *Private Prisons in the United States*. Cambridge, MA: Abt Associates.

McGill, N. (1998, November 15, 1998). Son's Death Led Parents to Activism. *Florida Times-Union,* pp. A-2.

McKee, M. (2002, April 26, 2002). Court Offers Guidelines in Ghilotti Case. *The Recorder,* pp. 1.

Miami Herald. (1998, April 7, 1998). Against Sex Predators. *Miami Herald.*

Minnesota Attorney General. (1989). *Attorney General's Task Force on the Prevention of Violence Against Women*. St. Paul, February 15, 1989.

Minnesota Dept. of Corrections. (1998). *Report of the Civil Commitment Study Group*. St. Paul.

Minnesota Dept. of Corrections. (2000). *Sex Offender Policy and Management Board Study*. St. Paul, MN.

Minnesota Legislative Auditor. (1994). *Psychopathic Personality Commitment Law*. St. Paul, MN: Program Evaluation Division, Office of Legislative Auditor.

Minnesota Sentencing Guidelines Commission. (2005). *Report to The Legislature*. St. Paul: Minnesota Sentencing Guidelines Commission.

Nakamura, R. T., & Smallwood, F. (1980). *The politics of policy implementation*. New York: St. Martin's Press.

National Association of State Mental Health Program Directors. (1997). *Position Statement on Laws Providing for the Civil Commitment of Sexually Violent Criminal Offenders*. Retrieved, from the World Wide Web: www.nasmhpd.org/sexpred.htm

National Mental Health Association. (1998). *Detaining 'Sexual Predators' in the Mental Health System*. Retrieved, from the World Wide Web: www.nmha.org/position/ps33.cfm

O'Neill, L. (1994, Nov 18, 1994). Parole of Rapist to Covina Draws Outrage From Officials Crime: Reginald Donald Muldrew is suspected of more than 200 sexual attacks during the 1970s. A protest rally in Civic Center Park is planned;. *The Los Angeles Times*.

O'Toole Jr, L. J. (2000). Research on Policy Implementation: Assessment and Prospects. *Journal of Public Administration Research & Theory, 10*(Issue 2), 263.

Otto, R. (1994). On the Ability of Mental Health Professionals to "Predict Dangerousness": A Commentary on Interpretations of the "Dangerousness" Literature. *Law and Psychology Review, 18*(43).

People v. Poe, 74 826 (Cal. Ct. App. 1999).

People v. Superior Court of Marin County (Patrick Ghilotti), 27 888 (Supreme Court of California 2002).

People v. Torres, 2001 3104 (Supreme Court of California 2001).

Petrila, J., & Otto, R. (2001). Admissability of Expert testimony in Sexually Violent Predator Proceedings. In A. Schlank (Ed.), *The Sexual Predator*. Kingston, NJ: Civic Research Institute.

Pommer, M. (1994, March 24, 1994). Thompson Version of Willy Horton? Politics Enter Parolee Flap. *Capital Times*.

PR Newswire. (2001, May 3, 2001). Wackenhut Corrections Subsidiary Selected for Contract Award With Florida Dept. of Children and Families to Build and Manage a 600-bed Secure Civil Confinement and Treatment Facility.

Pressman, J. L., & Wildavsky, A. B. (1973). *Implementation: How great expectations in Washington are dashed in Oakland; or, Why it's amazing that Federal programs work at all, this being a saga of the Economic Development Administration as told by two sympathetic observers who seek to build morals on a foundation of ruined hopes*. Berkeley: University of California Press.

Protecting Society From Sexual Predators. (1990, October 26, 1990). *Seattle Post-Intelligencer*, pp. A14.

Quinsey, V. L., Harris, G. T., Rice, M. E., & Cormier, C. (1998). *Violent Offenders: Appraising and Managing Risk.* Washington, D.C: American Psychological Association.

Rainey, J. (2000, August 3, 2000). Coalinga Gets its Wish. *Los Angeles Times*, pp. A3.

Reardon, J. (1992). Sexual Predators: Mental Illness or Abnormality? A Psychiatrist's Perspective. *University of Puget Sound Law Review, 15*(3), 849-853.

Rein, M., & Rabinovitz, F. (1978). Implementation: A Theoretical Perspective. In M. W. Weinberg (Ed.), *American Politics and Public Policy*. Cambridge, MA: MIT Press.

Samolinski, C. (1999a, January 1, 1999). New Predator Law Brings Both Promises and Problems. *Tampa Tribune*, pp. 1.

Samolinski, C. (1999b, February 16, 1999). Sexual Predator Treatment Examined. *Tampa Tribune*, pp. 1.

Sarbaugh-Thompson, M., & Zald, M. N. (1995). Child labor laws. *Administration & Society, 27*(Issue 1), 25.

Schlank, A. (1999). The Minnesota Sex Offender Program. In F. Cohen (Ed.), *The Sexual Predator*. Kingston, NJ: Civic Research Institute.

Schneider, P. (1994, March 14, 1994). Some See No Justice in Lawmakers' Plans; Is it Just "Sound Bite Legislation"? *Capital Times,* pp. 1A.

Schwartz. (1999). The Case Against Involuntary Civil Commitment. In F. Cohen (Ed.), *The Sexual Predator*. Kingston, NJ: Civic Research Institute.

Seling v. Young, 531 250 2000).

Siegel, B. (1990, May 10, 1990). Locking Up Sexual Predators. *Los Angeles Times,* pp. A1.

Specht v Patterson, 386 605 1967).

St. Petersburg Times Editorial. (1999, January 4, 1999). 'Treating' Sex Offenders. *St. Petersburg Times*.

State of Wisconsin Building Commission. (2001). *2001-2003 Capital Budget Recommendations*: Wisconsin Dept. of Administration.

State v. Kienitz, 585 609 1999).

Stovall, C. (1998). The State's Response to Sexual Offenders. *Kansas Journal of Law and Public Policy*(Spring 1998).

Sutherland, E. H. (1950). The diffusion of sexual psychopath laws. *American Journal of Sociology, 56*, 142-148.

Taylor, P. (2001). I Am A Child Molester. *Milwaukee Magazine*.

Turay v. Seling 1991).

Turay v. Weston 1994).

U.S. General Accounting Office. (1996). *Sex Offender Treatment: research inconclusive about what works to reduce recidivism*. Washington DC.

UPI. (1990, February 12, 1990). Man Gets 50-Year Sentence in Rape of Pierce County Woman. *Seattle Post-Intelligencer,* pp. B1.

Van Meter, D., & Van Horn, C. (1975). The Policy Implementation Process: A conceptual framework. *Administration and Society, 6*(4), 449.

Wallace, A. (1994, April 6, 1994). Wilson TV Ads Attack Brown on Issues of Rapist's Release. *Los Angeles Times,* pp. A3.

Washington Dept. of Social and Health Services.*Overview of SCC Budget*. Retrieved, from the World Wide Web: http://www1.dshs.wa.gov/budget/pdf/SCCBudSum.pdf

Washington Dept. of Social and Health Services. (2000). *Special Commitment Center: Secure Community Housing Criteria and Site Selection Process*. Olympia.

Washington Dept. of Social and Health Services. (2001). *Report to the Legislature: Efficiency of Staffing Patterns at the New Special Commitment Center on McNeil Island*. Olympia.

Washington Dept. of Social and Health Services. (2002). *Allocation of Additional Secure Transition Facility Beds Per RCW 71.09.250 (6) and ESSB 6594*. Olympia.

Washington Dept. of Social and Health Services. (2003, April 4, 2003). Press Release: DSHS Adds A Forest Area Location as a Potential Sex Offender Housing Site.

Washington Office of the Governor. (1989). *Executive Order #89-04*: Wash. St. Reg. 89-13-055.
Washington State Office of Financial Management. (2001). *Ten Year Capital Plan, 2001-2003 Biennial Budget*. Olympia.
Wettstein, R. (1992). A Psychiatric Perspective on Washington's Sexually Violent Predator Statute. *University of Puget Sound Law Review, 15*(3), 597-633.
Whereatt, R. (1994a, August 12, 1994). Laws Proposed to Keep Predators off Streets. *Star Tribune,* pp. 1A.
Whereatt, R. (1994b, July 7, 1994). Specter of Freed Sex Predators Worries Officials. *Star Tribune,* pp. 1B.
William M. Mercer Inc. (1999). *Study of the Programmatic and Facility Needs of the Florida Sexually Violent Predator Program.*
Wisconsin Department of Health and Family Services. (2004). *Report to the Advisory Committee on the Siting of an SVP Transitional Facility in Milwaukee County*. Sand Ridge, WI.
Wisconsin Legislative Fiscal Bureau. (1999a). *Prosecutors for Sexually Violent Person Commitment Cases (Paper 376)*. Madison.
Wisconsin Legislative Fiscal Bureau. (1999b). *Sexually Violent Person Evaluation Unit (Paper 335)*. Madison.
Wisconsin Legislative Fiscal Bureau. (1999c). *Staffing of Brewer Creek Facility for Sexually Violent Persons (Paper 520)*. Madison.
Wisconsin Legislative Fiscal Bureau. (1999d). *Supervised Release of Sexually Violent Persons*. Madison.
Wisconsin Legislative Fiscal Bureau. (2001). *Supervised and Conditional Release (Paper 502)*. Madison.
Wisconsin Legislative Fiscal Bureau. (2002). *Across-the-Board GPR Budget Reductions (LFB Paper #1120)*. Madison.
Wisconsin Legislative Fiscal Bureau. (2005). *Civil Commitment of Sexually Violent Persons (Informational Paper #52)*. Madison.
Wisconsin Office of the Governor. (2002). *2002-2003 Budget Reform Bill Summary*. Madison.
Wood, F. (1991). *Risk Assessment and Release Procedures for Violent Offenders/Sexual Psychopaths, Final Report*: Minnesota Department of Corrections.
Zonana, H. (1997). The Civil Commitment of Sex Offenders. *Science, 278,* 1248.

Index